WATER AND SPIRIT PROGRAM

Be Born Again

An RCIA Catechesis for High School and Adult Confirmation

TEACHER'S ANNOTATED EDITION

Joanne Parnell Mongeon, Ph.D.

Benziger Publishing Company
Mission Hills, California

Cover Art: Woodcut by Byron Gin

Photographers: The Crosiers/Gene Plaisted 11, 15, 36, 41, 49, 51, 54, 77, 83, 85, 88, 91, 99, 102, 106, 127, 128, 144, 147, 148, 150, 153, 154, 157, 164, 167, 168, 171, 174, 179, 181; Mary Kate Denny/PhotoEdit 26; Editorial Development Associates 74; Tony Freeman/PhotoEdit 4; Robert Lentz/Bridge Building Icons (Burlington, VT) 96; Phil McCarten/PhotoEdit 21; N C Photo, National Catholic News Service 94; Alan Oddie/PhotoEdit 35, 86; James L. Shaffer 23, 28, 33, 42, 46, 52, 57, 62, 70, 78, 80, 105, 110, 118; Steve & Mary Skjold Photographs 8, 138; David S. Strickler/Strix Pix 6, 16, 19, 25, 30, 39, 44, 122, 136, 162, 172, 176; Bill Thomas/ PhotoEdit 60; James G. White 73.

Dedication
For my parents, Francis W. Parnell and Dorothy Lalor Parnell

Nihil Obstat:
Rev. Robert J. McManus, M.A., S.T.D.
Censor Deputatus

Imprimatur:
†Louis E. Gelineau, D.D.
June 29, 1989

Send all inquiries to:
Benziger Publishing Company
15319 Chatsworth Street
Mission Hills, California 91395

Printed in the United States

ISBN 0-02-655921-8 (Student Edition)
ISBN 0-02-655922-6 (Teacher's Annotated Edition)

2 3 4 5 6 7 8 9   93 92 91 90

⌐ CONTENTS

Be Born Again

I ask:
What does it mean to be born again, Lord?
How can I return to the womb from which I came?

And Jesus answers:
Unless you are born again of the Spirit,
you cannot enter my kingdom.
Be born again
in beginning to become
a person of love, and courage, and hope.
As you grow in faith,
I walk with you, and guide you on your journey.
Be born again
so you can live
without fear or anxiety,
about the present or the future.
As we walk together through your life, be healed:
Be healed of hurts and injuries,
and know that you are loved.

As Spirit-fire descends,
Be born again
To Love.

My prayer is that you will come to know Jesus, who loves you so very much, and that you will accept him and his Church. As you read the letter in each chapter, which I have written as being from your sisters and brothers in the Christian community, know that we all travel with you. May you be filled, melted, and molded by the Holy Spirit to spread the Good News: Jesus is definitely *alive*, and *well*, and living in your heart and mine.

Your sister in Christ,

Joanne Mongeon, Ph.D.

Dr. Joanne Mongeon

INTRODUCTION

Each new experience you have becomes a part of you—part of your own faith journey through life. Nobody becomes a follower of Jesus Christ all by him or herself. Your faith story began before you were born, with parents and grandparents who followed Jesus and belonged to his Church. When you were born, you may have been baptized into the Faith and become a member of the Catholic community. But even then, becoming a Catholic is a process that is still going on for you.

Now the time has come for you to take the final step in your initiation as a Catholic Christian. You are about to prepare for the celebration of the sacrament of Confirmation. This book is a tool for you to use in the process of preparation. Only you can go through the steps of this process. Neither a book, nor a class, nor the advice of family and friends can do your preparing for you. However, the process outlined in this book can be of great help to you.

The process used in this book is based on the way adults become members of the Catholic Church. In 1972, the Holy Father and the bishops restored an ancient custom called the *catechumenate*. This word is taken from the Greek and means "a time of instruction." During the time of instruction, adult converts go through a series of stages and steps to become fully initiated members of the Catholic Church. They follow some of the same steps men and women followed in the earliest days of the Church. The new catechumenate is called the *Rite of Christian Initiation of Adults*. During this process, candidates study, pray, and receive the sacraments of Baptism, Confirmation, and First Eucharist.

Even though you have already been baptized and have already received Eucharist, your bishop would like you to go through a similar period of instruction before you receive the final sacrament of initiation. You will take many of the same steps adult converts do. The following chart will help you see the stages you will be going through, how they compare to the stages in the Rite of Christian Initiation of Adults, and the meaning of each stage.

Your process will follow the rhythm of the liturgical year. As you pass through Ordinary Time, Advent, Christmas, Lent, and Easter, your prayer and sharing will reflect the meaning of each season. In addition, you will be reading stories and doing exercises which will help you explore and understand your own faith, especially as you live it out in your everyday life. You will also spend a lot of time sharing the Scriptures and the words of the Holy Father. These words will serve to remind you that your gift of faith comes from God through his Son, Jesus Christ. Your faith is kept alive in the community of the Church through the teachings of the Holy Father and the bishops.

As you go through your "catechumenate," your time of instruction, there is only one quality which is demanded of you. That quality is *openness*. Try your best to be open to the demands made on you during your preparation. Be open to one another in this group of candidates. Be open to your leader, teacher, or facilitator. But most of all, be open to the working of the Holy Spirit in your heart. This time of preparation can be some of the most important hours of your life. During this preparation, you are learning what it means to be a fully initiated, adult member of the Body of Jesus Christ on earth—the Church.

YOUR STAGE	CHRISTIAN INITIATION	MEANING
1. Getting Ready	The *precatechumenate*	A time of beginning and a time of questioning.
2. The Journey	The *catechumenate*	A fairly long time for learning or reviewing the basics of the Catholic Faith. A time to start thinking and acting like a fully initiated member of the Church.
3. Seeing the Light	*Illumination*, or *election*: the candidate receives the sacraments of initiation.	A time to become a fully initiated member. A time of celebration and for being proud and happy to belong to the Body of Christ.
4. Alleluia	*Mystagogia*: after-initiation instructions. The word means "sharing the mysteries."	A time for the new member to make sure that he or she can truly think and act like a member of the Body.

Be Born Again

STAGE 1

Getting Ready

Inertia is a very important law of nature. Simply stated, the law of inertia means that whatever is at rest tends to remain at rest and whatever is in motion tends to remain in motion. This law not only applies to rocks nestled on hillsides or cars careening down interstate highways, it also applies to what goes on inside a person.

In the process of Christian initiation, the Church has provided a stage for "getting the ball rolling"—for overcoming inertia. This stage is called the time of inquiry, or the precatechumenate. As far as your preparation for Confirmation is concerned, this stage is called "Getting Ready." For the next six sessions, you will put the preparation process in motion. You will review your life story. You will share your story with the group. You will also review what is required of you as you begin your preparation to become a fully initiated member of the Family of God.

You Have a Story

AIM

To introduce the candidates to the Confirmation process.

The candidates' faith journey begins at the focus on life stories—their own life stories and the life story of Jesus. Jesus used stories to reveal the Word of God. And so, as you work with the candidates, you will be following in Jesus' footsteps, encouraging the candidates to share stories about themselves with others in the class, in order to expand their self-knowledge and develop their self-esteem. By directing the candidates to focus on their own life patterns and those of others in the group, you will help them recognize that similar themes recur in everyone's story, and that the recurring theme in Jesus' life is God's love for all his people.

Introduce yourself and describe the format for each week's class. Inform the candidates that, if possible, they should bring a Bible to each group meeting. The candidates should feel free to fill in the answers to questions and reflections in the text itself and use it as a journal. Some may wish to use a journal-notebook to supplement their Confirmation text or to work out specific exercises on a separate sheet of paper.

Resources

You may find the following discussions in this manual to be especially useful reading before beginning the process:
- Candidate Text, TM page 14
- Suggestions for Teaching, TM pages 16–17
- Helpful Attitudes, TM pages 17–18
- Forms of Questioning to Use with the Candidates, TM page 18
- Characteristics of Adolescents, TM pages 21–22
- Respecting Individual Differences, TM pages 22–23

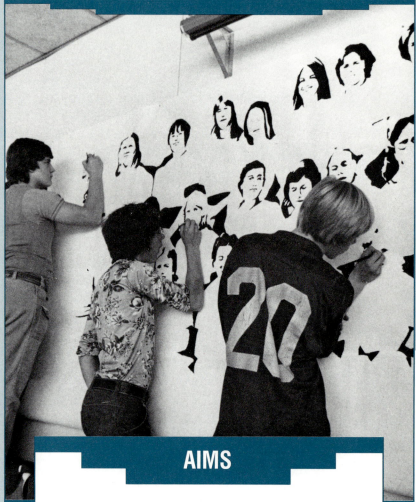

AIMS

This step will help you discover that each member of God's Family has a story to tell as he or she follows the path of Jesus to the Father.

- By sharing your story with others, you can grow in self-knowledge—the first step in learning to love yourself and others.

- Other people's love and concern influence how you perceive yourself and the world around you.

- The story of Jesus' life has a recurring theme— God loves you.

The Word of God

After John's arrest, Jesus appeared in Galilee proclaiming the Good News of God: "This is the time of fulfillment. The reign of God is at hand! Reform your lives and believe in the Gospel!"

As he made his way along the Sea of Galilee, he observed Simon and his brother Andrew casting their nets into the sea; they were fishermen. Jesus said to them, "Come after me, and in the future, you will catch people in your nets." They immediately abandoned their nets and became his followers. Proceeding a little farther along, he caught sight of James, Zebedee's son, and his brother John. They too were in their boat putting their nets in order. He summoned them on the spot. They abandoned their father Zebedee, who was in the boat with the hired men, and went off in his company. Shortly afterward, they came to Capernaum, and on the Sabbath he entered the synagogue and began to teach. The people were spellbound by his teaching because he taught with authority, and not like the scribes *(Mark 1:14–22)*.

This Scripture passage may be used as an opening prayer, or later as part of the *Reflect* activities on pages 13–14.

Group Reunion

At the beginning of each session, you are invited to share your faith with the other members in your Confirmation group. Although there are no strict guidelines for this kind of sharing, it will generally involve the following areas:

—*Prayer.* What thoughts or moments have you shared with God? How have you become more attuned to God's message to you?

—*Study.* What insights into your faith journey have you gained through study? Scripture? a religious book? a film? a song?

—*Action.* What have you done to show that you are a member of God's Family? How have you helped to bring Christ into your world?

To begin your sharing this session, take a few moments to introduce yourself to the other members of the group.

GROUP REUNION

The sharing which takes place during Group Reunion is important for the success of the *Water and Spirit* process. The Group Reunion will become routine and familiar to the candidates and will provide a way for them to share and to assess their spiritual growth as shown by their weekly prayer, studies, and actions. As the candidates continue to meet and share stories from their lives, they will become aware that the Confirmation preparation process has to be a part of their daily lives. There is an expanded discussion of the Group Reunion on page 15 of the Teacher's Manual at the back of this book.

Read aloud the description of the group sharing process. Explain that during each Group Reunion, there will be time for sharing details about their prayer lives, the studying and reading they have done, and the events that have taken place during the week which relate to the Confirmation preparation process. Share some details about your own family, interests, or friends, and then indicate what you like best about yourself. Next, ask each candidate in turn to follow your example and to share some details about his or her life.

the group or
that they un-
eir lives are sto-
ed, even though
easy. Emphasize
gh it may be fright-
gs about oneself to
others, int to take the risk that
sharing entail. Ask a few volunteers to
describe their feelings about taking risks
and becoming vulnerable by sharing life
stories.

In their school assignments, some of
the candidates may have read biogra-
phies of famous people. Ask volunteers
to discuss how a biography reveals patterns or themes in a person's life. Has
anyone in the group ever read a biography in which there was absolutely no
main theme or pattern in the subject's life?

What Is the Story?

In Geoffrey Chaucer's *Canterbury Tales*, a collection of stories written in the fourteenth century, the narrator of the stories sets the action in motion by describing the twenty-nine other pilgrims who meet on their journey to Canterbury. As one learns the pilgrims' stories, each character becomes an individual. For example, the Parson, introducing his tale, reveals himself to be simple and genuine. As his story unfolds, the effects of one person's story on the lives of other people are explored.

Your own life is a story, and like all stories, it can be shared with others. When you look more closely at your life, you begin to discover patterns and directions that you might not have seen before. Certain high points and low points take on new meaning when seen in the context of other events in your life. And by going through the process of actually telling someone your life story, the meaning behind events in your life becomes clearer to you as well as to the listener.

Sharing your story can sometimes be difficult because you need to trust those with whom you share. Also, in sharing your story, you risk being different or laughed at. But if you want to grow in self-knowledge, you have to drop the masks you wear. You have to be courageous and share who and what you are with those who share your life.

Habits and Interests

A good way to begin to look more closely at your life is to take inventory about your hobbies and interests. Look at the following questions and try to answer them for yourself. You might be surprised at how much your answers tell about the kind of person you are!

1. What kind of reading do you enjoy most?

_____

_____

2. If you don't like to read, why do you think you dislike reading?

_____

_____

3. What school work do you enjoy most? Least?

_____

_____

4. What are your hobbies and outside interests?

_____

_____

5. Do you regularly watch any television programs? What are your favorite TV programs?

_____

_____

6. How often do you go to the movies? Name three movies you liked very much.

_____

_____

7. Name the hero and heroine you like most in the movies (you know, movie stars!).

_____

_____

8. What magazines do you read most? Why?

_____

_____

9. List about five books you have read within the past year or
   so. Underline the one you liked the best.

_____

_____

10. Who is your favorite singer and musical group? What's your
    favorite album?

_____

_____

   Often, the way others see us isn't at all like we see ourselves.
How does the way you see yourself differ from the way others
see you?

	OTHERS SEE ME	I SEE MYSELF
Looks or Appearance		
Actions in Crisis		
Speech		

Thoughts on:
  Myself
  Friends
  School
  Music
  God		

One-on-one

On the lines below or on a separate sheet of paper, answer the following questions. Then, share what you have written with your fellow candidates.

The candidates may enjoy working on this activity in small groups of three or four as they discuss the questions and share their stories with one another.

1. As a child, whom did you trust the most? What was one experience which showed why you felt loved by that person?

_____

_____

_____

2. Which friend, teacher, or adult has had the biggest influence on your life? Can you think of one incident which proved to you that this person really cared? Tell the story.

_____

_____

_____

STUDY

Read this section aloud to the candidates. When you reach the part instructing them to "stay in that moment," pause for a few minutes to allow them to re-experience the feeling of being loved. Then, continue reading the section aloud. After this section is completed, spend a brief time with them discussing their feelings about the sacrament of Confirmation.

Although the candidates come from different religious education backgrounds and family practices, in a sense they all start out as equals in beginning the preparation for Confirmation. As a group, they are beginning something new together.

Direct the candidates to read the text section themselves. Then, present them with the statement, "We have begun the journey." Ask volunteers to tell what they think this statement means. Spend a few moments discussing the candidates' ideas about beginning the journey to Confirmation.

Jesus' most profound teachings were not presented in dry, academic discourses or abstract sermons. Instead, he used stories and parables to explain the mystery of the kingdom of God. The Gospels capture this method of teaching and present these stories to anyone who will listen.

Direct the candidates to read this section. Be sure there are a few Bibles avail-

▌STUDY

God's Story Is Love

Jesus shared his love and his life with his friends. He told stories about his Father and himself in the parables for the crowds. Together, he and his friends prayed, shared, ate, laughed, and cried. Some of his friends and some of their friends have handed down to the Church the stories of Jesus they shared. These are collected in the New Testament. And they are a way to know Jesus and his Father.

In your imagination, go back in time. Recall a person who loved you and the experience of being loved. Stay in that moment for a few minutes. Now realize that as much as that person loved you, the love God has for you is even greater than all the human love imaginable.

Your story began before you were born, in the story of your family, as one generation after another handed down the Catholic Christian tradition. When you were born, the Church welcomed you into the Family of God through Baptism, and you began the journey to full Christian living. As a child, you received the Holy Eucharist as food for your journey, and now you prepare to receive the third sacrament of initiation—Confirmation.

Initiation

Initiation is a beginning, a setting out, a going forth. Your initials are the beginning letters of your name. If you initiate a project at school, you are the one who begins that project.

Like many native American tribes, the Navaho participate in rites of initiation which allow young people to become members of "the People," as the Navaho call themselves. Through the initiation ceremony, the young men and women may fully enter into the ceremonial life of the tribe.

In the early life of Christianity, becoming a Christian meant experiencing the Way of Jesus and living it out before making a final and full commitment to Jesus and the Christian community. You, too, are being asked to accept the call of Jesus to a new way of living and to bring him more fully into your life story. But first, you must understand what that call means. Only then will Confirmation be what it is meant to be for you—the beginning of a journey which leads you more and more into the mystery of Jesus' Way.

You are a member of a Church, with a story all its own—a story written with lives given over to the Lord Jesus. Jesus' public life is a story, too—a story that ended and began in his death and resurrection.

Jesus also told stories . . .
about a farmer planting seeds in all kinds of ground,
about a father prodigal enough to love a foolish son,
about a merchant who sold all he had to buy one really valuable pearl,
about a woman rejoicing at finding a tiny coin,
and about a God who cares about fallen birds and hairs on the head—
a Father who cares about you.

Take a few moments to jot down some thoughts on your favorite New Testament story. Explain why it is your favorite and in what way it has affected your life. Be prepared to share your response.

able for those who do not have their own Bibles in class. After they have jotted down notes about their favorite New Testament stories, ask volunteers to indicate why they made their particular choices.

⌐ REFLECT

From the Holy Father

I want to remind you of the encounters that Jesus himself had with the youth of his day. The Gospels preserve for us a striking account of a conversation Jesus had with a young man. We read there that the young man put to Christ one of the fundamental questions that youth everywhere ask: "What must I do?" and he received a precise and penetrating answer. Jesus looked at him with love and said to him, "Come and follow me." But see what happens: the young man, who had shown such interest in the fundamental question, "went away sad, for he had many possessions" *(Mark 10:22)*. Yes, he went away, and—as deduced from the context—he refused to accept the call of Christ (Pope John Paul II, Boston, Massachusetts, October 1, 1979).

REFLECT

Note: These sections may be done in class or as "at home" assignments.

The Word of God: Point out to the candidates that the Apostles were very young when they first encountered Jesus—probably in their late teens or early twenties. Ask them to close their eyes and try to imagine the scene of Jesus calling the Apostles as you read the passage on page 7 slowly, meditatively.

From the Holy Father: Allow a few moments for the candidates to read the message of Pope John Paul II. Note the question of the rich young man, "What must I do?" Ask: What do you think the young man was looking for? Invite individual responses.

Dear Candidate

Dear Candidate: Ask a volunteer to read the letter to the candidate. Then use the opportunity for the candidates to raise any questions they have about the Confirmation process.

Y ou can probably remember waiting and waiting for a special event to take place. It may have seemed that the waiting time would last forever. This feeling of anticipation, however, also made the event when it finally came even more exciting.

The getting-ready phase of becoming a fully initiated Christian can also be an exciting time. In many ways, you have been getting ready for Confirmation all your life. But now, the preparation time is more intense. Use these final moments well. Learn more and more about yourself, share your faith journey with others, trust those who care about you, and most of all, take time to talk to your friend, Jesus. The process you are beginning will end when you answer Jesus' call to follow him and are confirmed, but your answer will continue forever.

Your Family in Christ

RESPOND

RESPOND

These questions help the candidates to probe further the content of each step and to make a personal response to the material. Direct the candidates to write out their answers to the questions in the space provided before the next group meeting. If there is time, you may wish to use question 2 for discussion during the present session.

1. Think of yourself as beginning a new chapter in your life story. How would you like this new chapter to be different from the previous ones?

2. How do you prepare for a new event in your life, such as beginning a new school year or moving to a new house or apartment? Do you pull back and just let it happen? Do you jump in and get involved? What is your attitude toward preparing for Confirmation?

Getting Ready

Lord, I want to learn more about myself and about other people.
I want to learn more about you.
But getting ready means getting rid of anything that might hold
   me down or trip me up.
I want to get rid of that part of me that acts foolish when I need
   to be serious.
I need to get free of the burden of not caring and the baggage of
   caring about the wrong things.
Help me, Lord, to take the focus off myself and my problems.
Help me to focus my vision more and more on your life and your
   Way.
Lord, I have lots of questions—
   questions about who I am
   and why I am here
   and how to make my life better.
I have stories to tell and questions to ask.
And, Lord, I want to hear your story, too.
Help me, Lord.
Help me get started.

REACH OUT

This section is found only in the lesson plan. It offers suggestions for ways in which you can personally encourage the candidates to carry out each particular step during the week. *Reach Out* should be presented toward the end of each session.

For this week, simply ask the candidates to make a point of discussing their reactions to the first session with a close friend or family member and to have that person, in turn, restate to the candidate what he or she thought the candidate was expressing. The candidates can jot down the results of this exercise in their journal-notebooks.

PRAYER

Use this prayer to conclude the session. You may wish to ask volunteers to read individual verses and then end the prayer with a moment of silence.

Follow Me

AIM

To help the candidates reflect on their life stories and experience the call to follow Christ.

Most young people have a certain degree of preoccupation with the signs and symbols that indicate their maturity and their entrance into the adult world. Wearing certain styles of clothing, getting a driver's license, owning a car, having a part-time job—all have symbolic meaning to young people. They are very concerned with being recognized and affirmed as young adults by society. The sacrament of Confirmation will confer on the candidates the recognition and acceptance of their full membership in the Catholic Church.

This step uses autobiography as a tool to help the candidates expand their self-knowledge and focus on their life stories. By developing their awareness of the patterns and directions in their own life stories, the candidates will be better able to establish goals as followers of Christ and to maintain a plan of action to attain their goals. By working and sharing together, the candidates will grow in their relationship with one another and with Jesus.

Resource

You may find the following helpful in preparing the lesson for this step:
- Form 23, Suggested Method for Scripture Sharing

AIMS

This step will help you to examine the direction in which your life is going and to reflect on what it means to follow Christ.

- As a follower of Jesus, you are asked to accept the challenge to love and to serve.

- Reflecting on your life story helps you to set your goals as a follower of Jesus and to work out a plan of action to attain these goals.

- God is always with you on your journey of faith, helping you and comforting you.

- Through the sacraments, you and the other members of Christ's Body live and grow in your relationship with Jesus and one another.

The Word of God

The word of the Lord came to me thus: Before I formed you in the womb I knew you, before you were born I dedicated you, a prophet to the nations I appointed you. "Ah, Lord God!" I said, "I know not how to speak; I am too young." But the Lord answered me, Say not, "I am too young." To whomever I send you, you shall go; whatever I command you, you shall speak. Have no fear before them, because I am with you to deliver you, says the Lord. Then the Lord extended his hand and touched my mouth, saying, See, I place my words in your mouth! This day I set you over nations and over kingdoms, to root up and to tear down, to destroy and to demolish, to build and to plant (*Jeremiah 1:4–10*).

Group Reunion

Last session, you tried to get to know the other members of your group a little better. This simple exercise will keep that process going.

1. Take a few moments to think of a way to describe yourself in one sentence.
2. Share that description with the group.
3. Compare notes on how it felt to talk about yourself.
4. Discuss what can be done to make it easier for the members of your group to get the most out of each Group Reunion.

This Scripture passage may be used as an opening prayer, or later as part of the *Reflect* activities on pages 23–24.

GROUP REUNION

Allow a few moments for the candidates to think of a way to describe themselves in one sentence. Have them take turns sharing their descriptions with others in the group. (If the class is large, divide the candidates into groups of three or four.)

After everyone has shared, give the group a few moments to compare notes on how it felt to talk about themselves. Ask if there are any suggestions of ways to help everyone get the most out of Group Reunion.

PREPARE

This section explores the nature of discipleship and the kinds of demands Jesus asks of his followers. The passage from Saint John's Gospel shows how it took the Apostles time to understand the demands that Jesus was placing on them. It was only after the resurrection that they understood that discipleship meant loving Jesus to the point where his life became part of their own.

Read the opening paragraph aloud, and then ask volunteers to take turns reading the three paragraphs of John 21:15–19. Spend a few moments discussing the following question: "What do you think it means to be a follower of Christ?"

▌ PREPARE

Discipleship

You are familiar with the terms *leader* and *follower*. Most leaders demand loyalty, respect, dedication, and personal sacrifice. Following Jesus certainly involves all of these qualities, but first and foremost it means loving him in such a way that his life becomes part of your own life story.

> When they had eaten their meal, Jesus said to Simon Peter, "Simon, son of John, do you love me more than these?" "Yes, Lord," he said, "you know that I love you." At which Jesus said, "Feed my lambs."
>
> A second time Jesus put his question, "Simon, son of John, do you love me?" "Yes, Lord," Peter said, "you know that I love you." Jesus replied, "Tend my sheep."
>
> A third time Jesus asked him, "Simon, son of John, do you love me?" Peter was hurt because he asked a third time, "Do you love me?" So he said to him: "Lord, you know everything. You know well that I love you." Jesus said to him, "Feed my sheep. I tell you solemnly: as a young man, you fastened your belt and went about as you pleased; but when you are older, you will stretch out your hands, and another will tie you fast and carry you off against your will."
>
> (What he said indicated the sort of death by which Peter was to glorify God.) When Jesus had finished speaking, he said to Peter, "Follow me."
>
> (John 21:15–19)

I've heard all the stories about Peter and the men dropping their nets, leaving everything, and following Jesus, and I'm amazed.

Oh—I'm sure He was a really magnetic person and all that—but to leave everything you have, everything you've worked for, to just leave it all and not look back?

I don't know if I could do that.

Well, maybe I could do it for a little while, but then I'm afraid I'd get bored or something. I'm afraid that once the newness wore off, I'd find myself saying, "Is that all there is to this Christian life?"

And I'm afraid: afraid that if I left everything to follow Him I'd be stuck with nothing of my own—and I'd be lost.

Oh, I know: He will always be there and He will provide everything I need. That's what they always say. But you can't believe everything you hear.

Besides, my guidance counselor says I have to have a clear, definite idea of where I'm going and how I'm going to get there. And my parents say idealism and religion and stuff are all right—but you can't pay bills with ideals and religion.

So I have to take care of myself, don't I? Well, don't I?

Lord—what do you think?

One-on-one

Write your answers to the following questions, and if you wish, you may share your answers with your fellow candidates.

1. What would Jesus ask you to do if he were here right now? How would you answer? Is there anything you would refuse to do?

Direct the candidates to work privately while answering each of the questions. Suggest that they think about their answers before writing. When they have finished, involve them in a discussion of their responses. As you participate in the discussion, guide the candidates to the understanding that the followers of Christ are on a journey of faith that requires an *active* commitment—words are not enough.

2. Which of the causes listed below would be important enough to dedicate your whole life to? You are not limited to one choice. Give reasons for your choices.
   a. Working for gun-control legislation
   b. Joining a religious community
   c. Establishing a successful corporation
   d. Building a world of justice and peace
   e. Becoming a famous athletic champion
   f. Wiping out political corruption and organized crime
   g. Other

3. Read the following statements and indicate which one you agree with most strongly. State the reasons for your choice.

   a. Most people I know want to join a great cause that will benefit the world. They will make the necessary sacrifices, even without support from others.

   b. Most people I know want to join a great cause. They will make the necessary sacrifices but need to be inspired by other dedicated people first.

   c. Most people I know want to join a great cause, but they hesitate to make the sacrifices and so back out of any commitment.

   d. Most people I know want to live their private lives comfortably and not be disturbed by great causes or sacrifices.

4. Describe one way in which the Church is now challenging you to follow Christ in your life.

Your Life Story

One reason for looking at your life as a story is to help you see the direction your life is taking: where you are now, where you have been, and where you are going. Sketching out your autobiography is a way of stepping back and evaluating the direction.

Write an outline in which you explore who you are. List the influences that have helped to make you what you are: your family, your neighborhood, your friendships. Next, outline the ways in which various teachers and courses in school have helped you to form your ideas.

Then, list your interests, hobbies, work, and any travel. State your goals for work or college. Explain how, if at all, these work or study goals are influencing your life today. How might these goals affect your life in five or ten years?

Finally, describe the role God plays in your life and the role you want him to play in the future.

STUDY

Direct the candidates to read the text material themselves and to begin work on their autobiographical sketches. The text suggests some of the areas to be included. It would be a good idea for you to draw up your own autobiographical outline and make it available to the candidates.

After the outlines are completed, spend some time discussing the candidates' goals and how they influence their lives today. End this section by asking the candidates to round out their autobiographies (by making additions or changes) during the week. Explain that they will be collected during the next session, placed in a folder, and made available to the group in order to become acquainted with the details of the other candidates' lives.

Before the candidates go on to "Highlights on the Journey of Faith," point out that Baptism, Eucharist, and Reconciliation are special highlights in the life of the Christian. The candidates should be familiar with the circumstances surrounding these important events in their faith lives. Direct the candidates to read through the questions in this section and answer any that they can now. Ask them to complete the questionnaire after they have found the remaining information they need.

Highlights on the Journey of Faith

As you begin to prepare for Confirmation, review some of the highlights of your faith story. Use the questions below as a guide to reflect on your baptism, reception of Eucharist, and celebration of Reconciliation. You may wish to consult your parents for some of the answers.

1. Who is the priest who baptized you?

2. Who are your godparents?

3. What do your parents or godparents remember about your baptism?

4. How old were you when you received Holy Communion for the first time?

5. What does the sacrament of Holy Eucharist mean to you now?

6. How often do you receive the Eucharist?

7. How old were you when you received the sacrament of Reconciliation for the first time?

8. How often do you receive the sacrament now? Why?

▌REFLECT

From the Holy Father

Listening to what you are telling me by your presence and through your representatives, I know that you are very much conscious of having a special mission in this world, of being partners in the mission of the Church.

I also know that in fulfilling your mission you are willing to give, you are willing to share, and you are willing to serve. And you are willing to do all this together, not alone! In this you are like Jesus: Jesus gave and he served and he was never alone. He tells us: "The one who sent me is with me. He has not left me alone" (*John 8:29*).

Yes, dear young people, I too want to speak about your mission, the reason for your life on earth, the truth of your lives. It is extremely vital for you to have a clear idea of your mission, in order to avoid being confused or deceived. In speaking to the Christians of his time, St. Paul explicitly urged them: "Let no one deceive you in any way" (*2 Thessalonians 2:3*). And today I say the same to you, young people of America: "Let no one deceive you in any way"—about your mission, about the truth, about where you are going. Let no one deceive you about the truth, about where you are going. Let no one deceive you about the truth of your lives (Pope John Paul II, New Orleans, Louisiana, September 12, 1987).

REFLECT

Note: These sections may be done in class or as "at home" assignments.

The Word of God: Read the passage from Jeremiah on page 17 to the group. Note that Jeremiah felt he was too young and unprepared to answer God's call to be a prophet. Discuss what it means to be prepared to answer God's call.

From the Holy Father: Have the candidates read this excerpt from John Paul II and ask them to discuss what kinds of important questions young people are asking today. Where do young people look for the truth?

Dear Candidate: Read or summarize this letter to candidates and begin a brief discussion on the question of openness. Is it easy to be open with others? with God? What is the connection between being open and becoming aware of the direction in your life? How do others help you see the direction in your own life?

Dear Candidate

The story of the call of Jeremiah is a little like your call to be confirmed. He was afraid of the consequences of becoming a prophet. You, too, might be a bit worried about what will be expected of you when you are a fully initiated follower of Jesus. You will be making Jesus' story your own. But that doesn't mean that your story is less important. Christ is calling you to a great challenge: to follow him more closely. There are ways in which you can begin preparing for this great challenge. Begin by looking at your own life story. Notice the direction in which your journey is taking you. Are you moving closer to Christ? Do you need some mid-course corrections?

Be open to truth, to goodness, and to beauty. Be open to the promptings of the Spirit when you pray. This openness will help you hear the call of Jesus more clearly. Remember God's promise to Jeremiah and be willing to share part of your story from time to time with other members of the Christian community. You are not alone on the journey. As a Pilgrim People journeying together, we keep our faith alive and strong by sharing our faith stories with one another. It is in this way that we reveal our joys and sorrows, our fears and successes. Remember, your brothers and sisters in the community travel with you and support you in your efforts to set God's word in your mouth, to build, or to plant.

Your Family in Christ

RESPOND

Direct the candidates to write their answers to the questions in the space provided before the next meeting. If there is time, you may wish to use question 1 for group discussion during this session.

▌RESPOND

1. How do you think the Lord wants you to change direction and move closer to him?

2. How can the realization that others in the Christian community have problems and struggles as well as joy and happiness help you?

The Disciple

Jesus, being your follower is not always easy or popular.
Sometimes, when I try so hard to help, to be of service, no one
even notices.
But then, you never promised that following you would be glam-
orous.
Is washing the family car or cooking a meal for my little brother
really part of being your disciple?
These little things certainly won't make the news.
Teaching CCD or serving on the liturgical committee would seem
to be more challenging.
And yet, you tell me that all these things are different suits cut
from the cloth of discipleship
Lord, I don't know how to follow you.
But you know where I can be most useful, most effective.
I want to be there for you, Jesus,
no matter what it costs.
And when I feel like quitting,
help me to keep going,
to keep loving.
For in the end,
it will be my love for others
which will make the difference to you.
Help me, Jesus.
Teach me to follow well.

REACH OUT

On the board, newsprint, or a transparency, write down the following directions:
"Ask a family member, a neighbor, or a
friend to share one important event in his
or her life story. Record the details of the
story in your journal-notebook for discussion during the next Group Reunion."
Urge the candidates to spend a little time
with the other person talking about how it
feels to open himself or herself to someone else.

PRAYER

You may wish to close the session with
this prayer. Ask one candidate to read the
first six verses and a second to read the
remaining verses. At the end of the
prayer, have the group join hands and respond, "Jesus, we are your disciples."

Ministry

AIM

To introduce the candidates to the idea that apostolic action is a way of continuing the mission of Jesus

In the last step, the candidates reflected on the nature of discipleship as a call to continue Jesus' mission through service. Now they will focus specifically on service and learn to define their attitudes toward serving others and identify the valuable qualities they have to bring to service projects in the community. The idea of mission is introduced with the story of two young people who expressed their call to mission by sharing Thanksgiving Dinner with the poor and lonely in the parish.

As part of the Confirmation preparation process, the candidates will become involved in specific service projects. However, before they do so, it is important for them to become aware of their attitudes toward service and the gifts they have to offer the community. A detailed Service Inventory is provided in this step. As the candidates work with the inventory, they will discover both the qualities which best equip them for service to the community, and also the qualities which prevent them from living out the baptismal commitment to Jesus.

By focusing on individual qualities, talents, and attitudes, the candidates will reinforce their growing understanding of themselves as valuable and needed members of their parish.

Resources

You may wish to begin planning for possible service projects in the parish community. The following selections from this guide will be helpful reading:
- Assignments and Service Projects, TM pages 18–19
- Form 27, Sharing the Work of the Lord

AIMS

This step will focus on your call to continue the mission of Jesus through service.

- You and your fellow candidates have certain qualities which make each of you a valuable member of the Christian community.

- Service is learned by serving, and there are real needs in your community which you can serve now.

- Learning your present attitudes toward service can help you appreciate Christian ministry.

- The example of Jesus can help motivate you to fulfill your mission of service.

The Word of God

Jesus returned in the power of the Spirit of Galilee, and his reputation spread throughout the region. He was teaching in their synagogues, and all were loud in his praise.

He came to Nazareth, and entering the synagogue on the Sabbath as he was in the habit of doing, he stood up to do the reading. When the book of the prophet Isaiah was handed him, he unrolled the scroll and found the passage where it was written: "The Spirit of the Lord is upon me; therefore he has anointed me. He has sent me to bring glad tidings to the poor, to proclaim liberty to the captives, recovery of sight to the blind and release to prisoners, to announce a year of favor from the Lord."

Rolling up the scroll he gave it back to the assistant and sat down. All in the synagogue had their eyes fixed on him. Then he began by saying to them, "Today this Scripture passage is fulfilled in your hearing" *(Luke 4:14–21)*.

Group Reunion

Since the last session, you explored your life story to discover the direction it is taking. In outlining your autobiography and reviewing your baptism, reception of the Eucharist, and celebration of Reconciliation, you may have noticed something new about yourself or recalled something you had forgotten. For example, has the Family of God been a major influence in your life? Do you experience a sense of direction (such as long-term goals) in your life? Take a moment to share your insights with the group.

This Scripture passage may be used as an opening prayer, or later as part of the *Reflect* activities on pages 33–34.

GROUP REUNION

Invite volunteers to describe their Reach Out experiences from the past week: How did people respond to the request to share an important event in their lives? How did they feel about sharing a personal story with you?

After the candidates read Group Reunion, ask them to share any insights about themselves or the information about their life stories that they have discovered since last time, such as information about their Baptisms, godparents, and First Communions. Then, ask each one in the group to respond to the last question in the section, "Do you experience a sense of direction (such as long-term goals) in your life?" If there are people in the group who feel no sense of direction, reassure them that it is not unusual to lack a sense of direction at this point in their lives.

The story of Don and Chris happens often in parish communities—people discovering that the simple act of giving their time and talents brings a visible response from others. Ask the candidates to read this section themselves. When they have finished the reading, ask if any of the candidates have ever had a similar experience. Then ask the group to formulate a definition of ministry, based on the story they have just heard.

PREPARE

I Was Hungry and You Fed Me

As part of their ministry in the parish, Don and Chris decided to help with the Thanksgiving meal in the parish hall. Each year, the prayer group and the Saint Vincent de Paul Society sponsored a dinner for the poor and for those who would be alone on Thanksgiving. Many families brought their whole dinners to the church hall on Thanksgiving Day, and Don and Chris helped to receive the food, set up the tables and chairs, and put out the dishes and utensils. Then, they helped pick up the people who had accepted the invitation to dinner.

Serving the meal involved many parishioners, but it was still late in the afternoon by the time Don and Chris and all the other parish volunteers sat down to eat. They agreed that although they were exhausted, they would like to help again the following year. "It was all worth the effort," said Chris, "when one older man told me it was the first time in ten years that he hadn't eaten dinner alone on Thanksgiving Day."

One-on-one

Make certain you understand this story. Spend two or three minutes in silence. Then, answer the following questions. If you wish, share your answers.

1. How would you feel about spending Thanksgiving Day the way Chris and Don did?

2. Share three things for which you are grateful to God.

3. Jot down three ways of showing gratitude to God for what he has given you. Do any of these ways involve serving others?

Direct the group to answer the One-on-one questions. Inform them that their answers will be kept private unless they want to mention them to the group. Provide time for volunteers to share their answers.

STUDY

Your Mission

You have a mission right now. That mission is to live out in the ordinary stuff of your daily life your baptismal commitment to Jesus Christ and to his people. Your answers to the following inventory questions will tell you just what qualities you have going for you in the fulfillment of that calling. Answer all the questions briefly and honestly. Then, discuss your answers.

Service Inventory

1. You are asked to give up everything you own to help make this world a better place. How do you feel about this request?
   a. It is impossible.
   b. It is very difficult.
   c. It is quite easy.

STUDY

The Service Inventory is a useful and important questionnaire. You may wish to spend the rest of the time working with it. The experience will help the candidates define their attitudes toward service and identify their strengths for service. Direct the candidates to work individually on the inventory. After everyone has completed writing, have them form small groups of three or four to discuss their answers. Point out that everyone has a combination of strengths and weaknesses and that not everyone shares exactly the same qualities.

Then, direct each candidate to prepare a list of the particular qualities they have that can help them fulfill their mission. Suggest that they discuss these questions with a family member or friend during the week to identify any additional important strengths they have.

2. What possession of yours would be the most difficult to part with? Why?

3. You are about to leave for a weekend camping trip. A friend calls you and tells you that he or she needs to talk to you at once. What is your response?

4. A good friend of yours is trying out for a school team. You are watching the tryout, and your friend does a really poor job. He or she asks you for your opinion. What would you say?

5. Name at least three activities you can do for long periods of time without getting tired or bored.

6. What mainly motivates you to do something for someone else?
   a. Fear
   b. Hope that the person will like you
   c. Hope that the person will do something for you in return
   d. A sense of "rightness"
   e. A real desire to meet someone's needs
   f. An attempt to be a Christian in action

7. What does the word *service* means to you?

8. How important is it for you to be a Christian? Briefly explain.

9. Describe in one sentence what you think a good Christian is like.

10. What do you feel is your best quality as a Christian?

11. What is your greatest liability as a Christian?

12. Look at the following pairs and circle the item you would prefer to be.
    a. A star or an ordinary member of a team
    b. A follower or a leader
    c. A rock singer or a doctor
    d. A volunteer for a charity or a paid consultant
    e. One who makes decisions or one who carries them out
    f. One who works alone or one who works with others
    g. A filmmaker or a film critic
    h. An aide in a convalescent hospital or a social worker with youth gangs
    i. Behind the scenes or out in front

13. What do you wish to become in your future?

14. List at least three things you will need to do to accomplish this.

┌ REFLECT

From the Holy Father

To understand ourselves as members of a community, as individuals linked together to make up the People of God, as persons responsible for others, is a great insight—an insight that is necessary for fulfilling our mission properly.

As Christians, you have these insights and Christ today wants to reinforce them in you. You speak about "being partners," of sharing and serving and working together. And all of this is linked to God's plan, according to which we are brothers and sisters in Christ—brothers and sisters who belong to the People of God and who are made to live in community, to think about others, to help others. Dear young people of America: in the Church there are many different gifts. There is room for many different cultures and ways of doing things. But there is no room in the Church for selfishness. There is no room in the world for selfishness. It destroys the meaning of life; it destroys the meaning of love; it reduces the human person to a subhuman level. . . .

Your mission as young people today is to the whole world. In what sense? You can never forget the interdependence of human beings wherever they are. When Jesus tells us to love our neighbor, he does not set a geographical limit. What is needed today is a solidarity between all the young people of the world—a solidarity especially with the poor and all those in need. You young people must change society by your lives of justice and fraternal love. It is not just a question of your own country, but of the whole world. This is certainly your mission, dear young people. You are partners with each other, partners with the whole Church, partners with Christ (Pope John Paul II, New Orleans, Louisiana, September 12, 1987).

REFLECT

Note: These sections may be done in class or as "at home" assignments.

The Word of God: Read the passage from Luke on page 27 slowly and meditatively to the group. Ask volunteers to recall incidents from the Gospels in which Jesus fulfilled the prophecy of Isaiah by bringing glad tidings, bringing liberty to captives, and bringing sight to the blind.

From the Holy Father: Read or summarize this section for the group and discuss some of the ways people today help others. Ask: how does a person show responsibility to affect those around him or her? What is the alternative to solidarity?

Dear Candidate

Dear Candidate: Ask a volunteer to read the letter for the group. Then, spend a few moments discussing how service fits into Christian life: Is it possible to be a follower of Christ without the willingness to serve others?

For the past two sessions, you have been exploring your life story to see more clearly who you are and where your personal journey is going. As a follower of Jesus, part of your story includes service. Service or Christian ministry is an extension of Jesus' own mission and ministry to bring glad tidings, to heal, and to proclaim the good news of salvation. From the start, the Apostles and early disciples imitated the works of Jesus through service. Later in the early Church, all members were encouraged to perform actions that would build up the Body of Christ.

Your own service can take many different forms right here in the parish. As Saint Paul teaches, the Spirit gives many gifts to individual members to enable them to serve in selfless ways. Before the next session, take some time to reflect on the special gift for service that *you* have received. And remember, you are a very important person to the members of your parish.

Your Family in Christ

RESPOND

Ask the candidates to answer the questions in the space provided before the next group meeting. Use question 1 for discussion during the session in conjunction with the Service Inventory.

RESPOND

1. Review the results of the Service Inventory. What have you learned about yourself? What, if anything, would you like to change in your answers?

2. Jesus is calling you to a life of service and invites you to become involved in his work. What are some real needs in your community that you can help meet?

3. Name three skills and talents that you have. How could you use these skills and talents to help others?

⌐ PRAYER

My Ministry

Lord Jesus,
I realize that when I am confirmed,
  I will have a job to do.
My job will be one of service.
You said that in your kingdom,
  caring for others is the job of all.
While I am getting ready,
  help me learn my ministry—
  to care for others,
  to help the poor,
  to make sad people happy,
  to heal people who hurt,
  to love even those who don't love me.
Send your Holy Spirit,
  and I will serve you.
We shall renew the face of the earth.

REACH OUT

Encourage the candidates to discuss today's session with family members, close friends, or their sponsors. Ask that they go over their responses to the Service Inventory with another person and ask him or her what strengths of the candidate the inventory reveals.

PRAYER

One suggestion for using this prayer at the end of the session is to begin reading it slowly to the group. Pause after the line, "to love even those who don't love me." Ask the candidates to spend a moment thinking of the people in their lives who need caring. Then ask the group to read the last verses together.

The Parish Family

AIM

To help the candidates expand their understanding of the parish community and examine their feelings about the parish.

To many young people, the parish community is very much like their own families. It is always there. It is familiar. It is somewhat demanding. And there is a bit of mystery as to how it works. It is clear to many that the diverse functions and activities of the parish community—the many roles and ministries of individuals and groups within the parish community—are not shared by most young people. Consequently, it is important to review the variety of ministries within the parish community so that the candidates can begin to see it in a new way. They must be reassured that they can rely on the community for guidance and support as they prepare for Confirmation.

Like a family, the parish needs willing workers to help it grow and flourish. As the candidates continue to focus on service as an expression of ministry, they will work on an inventory of parish needs and formulate some ways to work for the parish.

Resource

You will find the following helpful at this stage of the Confirmation preparation process:
- Program Versus Process, TM pages 23–24

AIMS

This step will help you to review the role of the parish community in the Church and to examine your feelings about your parish.

- The parish is a family in which you are loved and cared for—in which you learn what it means to believe in Jesus Christ.

- As you prepare for Confirmation, the parish community offers you guidance and support.

- Being part of a parish means that you also must give your time and energy to the parish family.

- The focal point of every parish is the celebration of the Mass—the family meal.

The Word of God

Jesus began to address the chief priests and elders of the people, once more using parables. "The reign of God may be likened to a king who gave a wedding banquet for his son. He dispatched his servants to summon the invited guests to the wedding, but they refused to come. A second time he sent other servants, saying: 'Tell those who were invited, See, I have my dinner prepared! My bullocks and corn-fed cattle are killed; everything is ready. Come to the feast.' Some ignored the invitation and went their way, one to his farm, another to his business. The rest laid hold of his servants, insulted them, and killed them. At this the king grew furious and sent his army to destroy those murderers and burn their city. Then he said to his servants: 'The banquet is ready, but those who were invited were unfit to come. That is why you must go out into the byroads and invite to the wedding anyone you come upon.' The servants then went out into the byroads and rounded up everyone they met, bad as well as good. This filled the wedding hall with banqueters" *(Matthew 22:1–10)*.

Group Reunion

In the last session, you discussed how part of your faith story includes ministry. You also discussed that your mission—to keep Jesus Christ present—is not something to be done in the far-off future but something to be lived right now. Review some of the qualities you think are important for Christian service. Can you devise two or three steps you can take now toward learning how to serve? How do you know you are really being of service to others?

This Scripture passage may be used as an opening prayer, or later as part of the *Reflect* activities on pages 41–43.

GROUP REUNION

Direct the candidates to form small groups of three or four. Before they begin this Group Reunion, ask if there are any questions about the nature of ministry. If there are some who need clarification as to how ministry works within the community, read Paul's First Letter to the Corinthians 12:4–11. Then explain that the community of faith is very much like a body, with different members of the body performing different but necessary functions. In the same way, the parish community has many needs, and people with different talents and gifts can fulfill those needs. After the groups have discussed ideas about the qualities important for Christian service, have the candidates make a list of suggestions for learning how to be of service.

PREPARE

Ask a volunteer to read the story of the prayer rug aloud. Then have the candidates read the opening paragraph of the One-on-one questions and pause for a moment.

PREPARE

Tying Knots

In the Persian rug store, there was a magnificent prayer rug, measuring two by three feet. The price was eight thousand dollars. The owner of the store said that the price was so high because the women in Iran who made the rug tied each silk knot by hand. The rug took much time and effort. When it was finished, there was a picture of a lovely garden, symbolic of the perfect happiness that a good Muslim will one day attain with God forever.

Your life is like that prayer rug. Each moment of every day, you tie knots in the relationships that bind you to other people. The tapestry of your life, when it is finished, will tell its own story of who you are and the life you have lived.

One-on-one

Review the candidates' responses to the questions in this section. For question 1, ask for examples of good communication. For question 2, ask the candidates to tell what roles in the parish community these people play. For question 3, try to involve as many of the group as possible in discussing the idea of "tying knots." Ask them to suggest ways of "tying knots" to more people in the parish community.

Spend a few moments in silence thinking about the prayer rug. Then, answer the following questions. Share your responses with your fellow candidates.

1. List the people who are most important in your life. Then, circle the ones with whom you have good communication.

2. Of those people listed, which ones are part of your parish?

3. How can you "tie knots" to more people in the parish community?

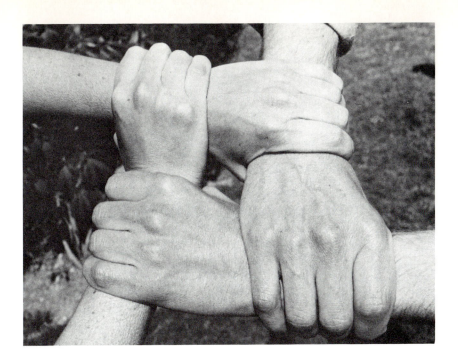

STUDY

The Christian Community

The Christian community is a gathering of people as one under the headship of Jesus Christ. The Christian community is all of us—clergy, religious, laity—ready to give ourselves in service to one another. Just as your family eats, works, plays, and grows together, so, too, does your parish family. Answer the following questions and discuss how your desire to belong to the parish family can be or is being met.

1. Describe three qualities of your parish that demonstrate how it functions as a family, or community.

2. Describe three things that could improve the sense of family in your parish.

3. List five things your parish does for you.

4. List five things you can do for your parish.

5. What are three major committees or organizations in your parish? What is the purpose of each?

6. What does the celebration of Mass mean for your parish community? How do various groups and members take part in the Mass?

Some people find it difficult to admit that they have needs or to express those needs to others. And yet, the ability to admit shortcomings and needs and to ask for help and guidance is fundamental to any human relationship and any living community. If young people are to grow stronger in their faith relationship with the parish, they must see that the community is sympathetic to their needs.

Direct the candidates to read the introductory material and then write their answers to the questions. After the candidates have completed their responses, discuss their answers with them. Use the following questions in your discussion:
■ Are the things you need from the members of your parish family realistic?
■ If so, how can you get what you need?
■ If not, how can you develop a more realistic sense about your needs?
Encourage the candidates to express their needs to the appropriate members of the parish community.

A Helping Family

Preparing for Confirmation is not a task that you must do alone. Your brothers and sisters in the parish family are here to guide, to support, and to sustain you when you have doubts and questions. Yet, you need to look at what you expect from others in order to see if your expectations are too high or too low. You also need to see if you give of yourself to others and if you are giving enough. Giving and receiving are related.

What do you need from others to help you prepare for Confirmation? Take a few moments to answer the following questions.

1. What do you expect from your family to help you prepare?

2. What do you expect from your friends?

3. What do you expect from your fellow candidates?

4. What do you expect from your parish?

From the Holy Father

Dear young people, know how to be witnesses to your faith. Know how to live and proclaim the Christian message in deeds and in words, with simplicity, joy, and daring, without compromises or cowardice. Become persuasive witnesses to your faith before your friends. There are no better apostles for the young than other young people.

The field of your commitment is a vast one: the home, the circle of those of your own age, the different Church communities and organizations for young people, the school, the parish. These are the places in which to proclaim the Lord and the relevance of his Gospel today. In particular, I urge you to take your place in the parish activities of the various organizations for young people. Become intelligent and generous workers within the pastoral plan of your diocese.

Be faithful to your identity. By giving today a consistent and courageous testimony to your faith in Christ and your faithfulness to the Church, you will proclaim and prepare a more just and more serene world for the future (Pope Paul VI, Rome, February 25, 1978).

REFLECT

Note: These sections may be done in class or as "at home" assignments.

The Word of God: Begin by reading the passage from Matthew on page 37 to the group. Pause for a moment and then explain that the wedding banquet given by the king in this parable is similar to the Christian community and their own parish community. Have the group discuss ways or signs that show that the parish community is open to all who are willing to be a part of it. Ask for examples of how the parish community reaches out to all kinds of people in the surrounding neighborhood.

From the Holy Father: Ask three volunteers to read the three paragraphs of this section and then open a discussion on ways in which young people influence other young people, not only in popular styles, but in values and life goals. Then, focus on the sentence, "There are no better apostles for the young than other young people." Ask: "What does the Holy Father mean? In what ways can you communicate your faith to people your own age?"

Dear Candidate

Dear Candidate: Read this section to the group. Brainstorm with them about other organizations that they know about, for example, clubs, political organizations, labor unions, business associations, school organizations. Ask: "How does membership in the parish differ from membership in other kinds of organizations? What does the parish community do for its members that other organizations can't?"

Most of us experience Church in the context of the parish. No parish is perfect, but every parish *is* the Church. As the Church, parishes offer to members and nonmembers the loving hand of friendship. It is a place to go when there is trouble in the family. It offers a sense of identity and belonging. A parish also offers healing and reconciliation to the sinner and the weary or to the member who has wandered away.

The parish is a family that celebrates the joys and sorrows of a loving community. The parish welcomes new members through Baptism. The parish cheers and encourages new young families as it celebrates the joys of weddings. The parish waits and mourns with those who have just encountered the mystery of death.

Life itself is the theme of every parish large or small—life in Christ Jesus. That means your life, too. Stay close to your parish family. Share its life and watch it grow.

Your Family in Christ

▌RESPOND

1. Jesus calls you to share his life and to join your life with the lives of your brothers and sisters. He invites you to Christian community. How does the idea of Christian community strike you? Do you experience it? How? Where?

2. How can you become more fully involved in the Christian community of your parish?

3. Imagine that you and your family moved to a new city and parish. Would you take the initiative to meet the members of the new parish and get involved? Why or why not?

▌PRAYER

Prayer Rug

Lord, we are bound together—
   all my friends and relatives,
   all those who like me,
   and all those who don't.
I watch the news and read the newspapers.
I think about the people I hear and read about.
I think about their needs, their joys, their hopes, and their suf-
   ferings.
They're my brothers and sisters, too.
I feel so helpless, Lord.
I don't know how to help all those I cannot see and touch.
So, Lord, help me to be good to those around me: my friends, my
   family, all the people in my life.
And, Lord, thank you for being patient with me.
Thanks for caring even when I don't.
Praise you, Lord, and thank you.

RESPOND

Remind the candidates to review the questions before the next session. Ask them to determine from their responses whether their attitudes about the parish community need to be changed in any way. Urge them to record any reflections about their present relationship to the community in their journal-notebooks.

REACH OUT

Direct the candidates to investigate the various committees and organizations within the parish community and to draw up a brief profile of each organization's role in the parish, its membership, and its history. These profiles should be shared with the group during the next session. The candidates may work in groups of three or four. Urge as many as possible to attend one of the committees as observers.

PRAYER

You may wish to use this prayer to close the session. Before reading this prayer, have the group spend a moment in silence thinking about all the needs of the people in the world that they know about from personal contact, stories of friends and relatives, and news stories. Then, read the prayer slowly, pausing briefly after each verse.

S T E P   5   Commitment

AIM

To help the candidates appreciate that receiving the sacrament of Confirmation is a free and willing commitment.

Although the candidates prepared for the celebration of First Eucharist and for the sacrament of Reconciliation, they have not been asked to make an adult choice about the sacrament and all that it implies. Now, they are reaching a point where they will be asked to make the choice whether or not to continue the preparation process for the sacrament of Confirmation.

This step calls the candidate's attention to this choice. It also reminds the candidates that the process of preparing is important in itself and requires a commitment. Candidates who are sufficiently prepared and properly disposed will be invited to enter the catechumenate and to continue the preparation process for Confirmation. Not all candidates may be ready for this step. Therefore, it is important that the catechist be sensitive to the uncertainty that some of the candidates may feel. This is not a time of final testing for the reception of Confirmation. Instead, it is designed to assure that those who continue on to the catechumenate are open to the process.

Resources

You may find the following materials in the Resource section helpful in preparing this step:

■ Form 2, Sample Diagnostic Interview
■ Form 3, Sample Diagnostic Test

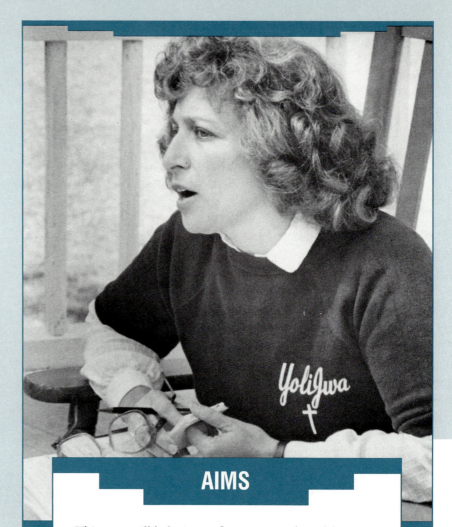

AIMS

This step will help you reflect on your friendship with Jesus and your commitment to him.

■ Jesus is always with you, but you are free to respond to his friendship.

■ Preparation for Confirmation helps you make a free and willing decision to become a full member of the People of God.

■ Just as the People of God will celebrate your being confirmed, they are ready to support you in making a commitment to Jesus.

■ Prayer is one of the best ways to grow in friendship with and commitment to Jesus.

The Word of God

When the Pharisees heard that Jesus had silenced the Sadducees, they assembled in a body; and one of them, a lawyer, in an attempt to trip him up, asked him, "Teacher, which commandment of the law is the greatest?" Jesus said to him: "'You shall love the Lord your God with your whole heart, with your whole soul, and with all your mind.' This is the greatest and first commandment. The second is like it: 'You shall love your neighbor as yourself.' On these two commandments, the whole law is based, and the prophets as well" *(Matthew 22:34–40).*

Group Reunion

During the last session, you saw how the parish community offers opportunities to continue Jesus' mission by serving others. But how can you serve in a practical way? Do you know the needs of members in the parish? Are you aware of the opportunities to serve in the parish? Who can help you find out? Take a few moments to discuss this in the group. See if you can put together a clear profile of your parish family.

This Scripture passage may be used as an opening prayer, or later as part of the *Reflect* activities on pages 49–50.

GROUP REUNION

During the last session, the candidates were introduced to the importance of ministry in the parish community and the importance of the parish community in the life of the Catholic Christian. This theme recurs throughout the Confirmation preparation process. Have the group read the material in this section and begin to discuss the questions. Ask if any of the candidates took the opportunity to attend one of the organizational meetings or work sessions during the past week. Guide them as they put together a profile of the parish family and its different organizations and ministries.

As mentioned earlier, the sacrament of Confirmation is a free and willing commitment to the People of God. The story in this section depicts a young person facing a situation in which he must decide between pursuing a sport leading to a college scholarship and joining the Confirmation preparation classes. The questions which follow the story involve the candidates in the young man's choice and also challenge them to identify their own feelings about the situation. The candidates are further invited to consider some alternatives to the conflict that Bill faces here. It is important to approach this step with a sense of reassurance, especially for those who may be finding difficulties in continuing the preparation process at this time. Read or summarize this section for the candidates and give them a few moments to absorb the details of the situation before going on to the questions.

PREPARE

Making a Move

Bill is about to enroll in the two-year Confirmation process when he discovers that all the meetings are on Thursday nights. Bill, who has been playing ice hockey since he was nine, has practice every Thursday night. The coach has told Bill that he is very talented and that he can probably win a sport scholarship on the basis of his ability. Bill likes that idea very much since his parents could not otherwise afford to send him to college. Eventually, he would like to play professional hockey.

Bill's parents are concerned about the situation and try to help Bill in his decision. Although Bill attends Catholic high school, parish policy is that Bill must attend Confirmation preparation process. According to the National Catholic Directory guidelines, the formation of Christian community is very important, and weekly or biweekly classes support that formation.

Bill's pastor and the director of religious education are understanding but must be fair. If they excuse Bill, what about the students who come to classes faithfully every week?

Finally, Bill's parents tell him to make his own decision. Bill decides to go to hockey practice and to wait a while before receiving Confirmation.

One-on-one

This is not a simple situation. Spend a few moments thinking about Bill's decision. Then, answer the following questions. Share your answers if you wish.

1. Were Bill's parents correct in allowing Bill to make the decision entirely on his own? Why or why not?

2. How do you feel about Bill's decision? Give reasons for your opinion.

3. How would you respond in the same situation? Why? What would make a difference?

4. List some alternatives the parish could have offered Bill.

Direct the candidates to work individually, without discussing the questions with the others. After the candidates have reflected on the situation and answered the questions, discuss question 3. Ask volunteers to share what they would have done in a similar situation and why. After the discussion, draw a chart on the board, newsprint, or transparency with the following columns:

Bill was right
Bill was wrong
Bill's parents were right
Bill's parents were wrong
Alternatives

Then, take a poll of how many people think Bill's decision was right, and how many think he was wrong, and mark the number in columns on the chart. Ask those who think Bill was right to give their reasons. Then, ask whether Bill's parents were right or wrong in allowing him to make his own decision and mark the numbers in the column. Ask volunteers to explain why they answered as they did. Use the column marked "alternatives," and ask volunteers to suggest alternatives the parish could have offered Bill.

Direct the candidates to read the opening paragraph. Discuss the forthcoming interview with the group and answer as many of their questions as you can. Go over the text questions to be sure that everyone understands what is being asked. Stress the fact that this is more of a personal inventory than an objective test. Answers should be expressed in the candidates' own words.

Direct the group to pray and reflect on the questions. Some candidates may wish to work in a quiet area by themselves. Perhaps another classroom, a library, or a reception room is available for this. After the candidates have had time to go over the questions and jot down their personal responses, suggest that they re-

▌STUDY

Some Questions

You will soon be interviewed individually about your readiness to continue the Confirmation process. The chart below covers the questions you should be thinking about. Spend some time praying and reflecting on them. Rehearse your answer to each question. You may wish to jot down some notes. Share your answers if you wish. Finally, evaluate your responses: Is this what I really believe? Does it reflect my true feelings? What have I learned about myself?

QUESTIONS	NOTES
1. What is the effect of Confirmation in the life of a Christian? in the life of the Christian community?	
2. What are your reasons for wanting to receive Confirmation?	
3. What does your participation in the Eucharist and the other sacraments mean to you? to your parish family?	
4. What does prayer mean to you? How would you describe your prayer?	
5. What steps are you taking to make your own Jesus' mission to love and to serve?	
6. How is the Holy Spirit acting in your life right now?	

hearse answering the questions with you or work in pairs with one another. Be sure that each candidate has prepared a satisfactory answer to each question. If any candidate indicates that he or she has particular difficulty with one of the questions, assure the candidate that you will be available to meet with him or her sometime during the week.

┌ REFLECT

From the Holy Father

In the Gospel story of the rich young man, we see that he heard the call—"Follow me"—but that he "went away sad, for he had many possessions." The sadness of the young man makes us reflect. We could be tempted to think that many possessions, many of the goods of the world, can bring happiness. We see instead in the case of the young man in the Gospel that his many possessions had become an obstacle to accepting the call of Jesus to follow him. He was not ready to say *yes* to Jesus and *no* to self, to say *yes* to love and *no* to escape.

Real love is demanding. I would fail in my mission if I did not clearly tell you so. For it was Jesus—our Jesus himself—who said: "You are my friends if you do what I command you" *(John 15:14)*. Love demands effort and a personal commitment to the will of God. It means discipline and sacrifice, but it also means joy and human fulfillment (Pope John Paul II, Boston, Massachusetts, October 1, 1979).

REFLECT

Note: These sections may be done in class or as "at home" assignments.

The Word of God: Read the passage from Matthew on page 45 slowly and meditatively to the group. Then invite the young people to spend a few moments meditating on the love they feel for God and the love they feel for people in their lives. Ask volunteers to share what they think it means to love God "with your whole heart, your whole soul, and with all your mind." Ask: "What are some of the obstacles that prevent you from loving God completely?"

From the Holy Father: Ask a volunteer to read this section aloud and use question 2 on the next page for group discussion.

Dear Candidate: Read this section to the group and allow the candidates a few moments to reflect on the meaning of Jesus' friendship in their lives. Have them respond to question 1 below.

Dear Candidate

Y ou have spent time learning about yourself in relation to Jesus and the Christian community. Preparing for Confirmation means choosing to follow Jesus, and it is important for you to know who you are and where your faith journey is going in order to make that choice. It is also important to realize that you do not stand alone in choosing to follow Jesus. Your brothers and sisters in the community stand behind you. They want to be one with you.

Accepting Jesus is a great challenge but a challenge which can bring great joy. Recall the feelings you had when someone you admired wanted to be your friend. What was it like? Jesus accepts you as a friend and he wants you to accept him—to be his friend. Trust him.

Your Family in Christ

RESPOND

Remind the candidates to answer the questions in this section before the next group meeting. If there is time during the session, discuss question 2 after reading From the Holy Father and question 1 after reading Dear Candidate. Ask volunteers for examples from their own lives in which something meant discipline and sacrifice, but also joy and human fulfillment.

◤ RESPOND

1. Jesus is inviting you to accept him as a friend. What do you think are the first three steps you have to take to accept his friendship?

2. The Holy Father says that following Jesus "means discipline and sacrifice, but it also means joy and fulfillment." In your own words, explain what this message means in your own life.

3. If a fellow candidate decided not to continue with the Confirmation process at this time, what would you say to him or her?

◢ PRAYER

Born Free

Jesus, I keep having to make choices and decisions.
You say, "You have before you life and death. Choose life."
I really want to do that.
But, Lord, there are so many things going on in my life right now.
There are so many pressures and commitments
   —family, friends, school, work.
I know I don't always choose you.
But I want to choose you, to follow you and your Way.
Jesus, without your help, I won't make the best decisions, the best
   choices.
Help me to listen to your Spirit.
Give me wisdom to know what you want.
Give me understanding to do what you want.
Give me courage to be recognized as someone who chooses life.

REACH OUT

This is a very good time to draw the sponsors more closely into the Confirmation process. Direct the candidates to meet with their sponsors sometime before the next group meeting and go over their responses in the section "Some Questions." Remind the candidates that their sponsors are there to guide and support them during the Confirmation process. Refer to Candidate and Sponsor Sharing, TM page 9.

PRAYER

Ask two volunteers to alternate reading verses of this prayer and invite the group to read the last verse together.

Responsible Friendship

AIM

To help the candidates understand the meaning of responsible friendship and assess their own friendships in terms of responsibility.

Step 6 brings the "Getting Ready," or pre-catechumenate, stage of the Confirmation process to a close. This period has provided the candidates with the opportunity to explore the direction of their life stories and to see how those stories involve their family, friends, and the parish community.

The idea of responsible friendship may be new to the candidates. Generally, most young children make their first friends with the children who live in their neighborhoods. As they grow older, they begin to choose friends more on the basis of common interests. These early friendships are often replaced toward the end of high school with relationships that have more depth and dimension.

This step provides stories, questions, and a Scripture exercise for drawing up a personal code of conduct with friends. As the candidates work through the material, they will learn to identify the types of attitudes they currently bring to friendships. They learn to rely on Jesus as an example and guide on whom to base future friendships.

Resources

You may find the following material helpful reading for this point in the Confirmation preparation process:

- Form 6—Sample Candidate and Sponsor Letter
- Form 8—Rite of Becoming a Candidate

AIMS

This step will help you to explore the importance of friendship in the life of a Christian and to use this knowledge to grow in your friendship with Jesus.

- Friendship is a mutual relationship built upon respect, trust, and concern.

- Friendship does not just happen; it is something you must work at.

- The loyalty, faithfulness, and commitment you experience in your human friendships help you understand your friendship with Jesus.

- Friendship with Jesus will help you live a fully human, fully Christian life.

The Word of God

I am the vine, you are the branches. He who lives in me and I in him, will produce abundantly, for apart from me you can do nothing. One who does not live in me is like a withered, rejected branch, picked up to be thrown in the fire and burnt. If you live in me, and my words stay part of you, you may ask what you will—it will be done for you. As the Father has loved me, so I have loved you. Live on in my love. You will live in my love if you keep my commandments. This is my commandment: love one another as I have loved you. There is no greater love than this: to lay down one's life for one's friends. You are my friends if you do what I command you *(John 15:5–7, 9–10, 12–14)*.

Group Reunion

The "Getting Ready" stage of the Confirmation process has given you an opportunity to assess your life story in relation to Jesus and the Christian community. Reflect on some of the ways you have grown during this time. In what ways has your definition of yourself changed? In what ways is Jesus more a part of your life than he was before? How has your sense of mission changed? Share your responses with your fellow candidates.

This Scripture passage may be used as an opening prayer, or later as part of the *Reflect* activities on pages 57–58.

GROUP REUNION

Direct the candidates to read the material in the Group Reunion section. Then ask them to listen and reflect as you reread the text questions. Stop after each question and allow individuals to express their responses. Ideally, at the end of this reunion, each of the members will have shared their responses to at least one of the questions.

Good friendships are important for personal growth and maturity. Yet, even the best of friendships are sometimes tested. As this section points out, such testing need not mean the end of a relationship. When friends face problems in their relationship, they can continue to make it grow and develop.

Have the candidates read the first paragraph of this section and briefly discuss the meaning of friendship given. Then, divide the candidates into two smaller groups and assign one of the stories to each. Direct the candidates to read the stories and discuss the kinds of friendships portrayed. (Remind them to use the questions in the second paragraph to guide their discussion.) Then, ask each group to report on its results.

PREPARE

Testing Friendship

Friendship is both a gift and a treasure. It adds to your sense that life has value and meaning. It teaches you to share and to communicate your thoughts and feelings. It helps you to know what God wants you to do in your life. Because of all you receive from friends, knowing how to take care of your friendships is a giant step in maturity and commitment.

Read the two stories of friendship below. As you read, test the characters with these friendship questions: Is the relationship marked by genuine concern and sensitivity to the other's needs? Is there a dialog and an interest that goes "both ways"? Is there a willingness to share and to receive? Is there loyalty and faithfulness?

Story One
John and Randy are good friends. They are both invited to a Halloween party. Randy doesn't have a car, so he arranges to go with John in his car. The night before the party, John gets an invitation to another party. He accepts the invitation without saying anything to his friend. Finally, on Halloween, John calls Randy an hour before the party and tells him about his change in plans. Randy is stuck without a ride to the party, and it is too late to make other arrangements.

Story Two

Marie and Yolanda are very close friends. Both have an interest in music. Yolanda shows some of her poetry to Marie, and Marie finds a particularly good poem which she puts to music. Soon after, Marie enters the school's yearly talent show. For her performance, Marie decides to sing the song with Yolanda's lyrics. She tells the audience that she wrote the song but doesn't mention Yolanda's contribution.

One-on-one

Briefly review the two stories. Select one of them and write your answers to the following: (1) describe the problem in sentence, (2) analyze why the problem occurred, (3) tell how the situation might negatively affect the friendship, and (4) suggest how the situation could be handled to bring about a growth in friendship.

Direct the candidates to review both stories, to choose one to analyze, and to begin filling in answers to the four points. They should work individually.

1. Problem: _____

_____

2. Reasons for problem: _____

_____

_____

3. Negative results: _____

_____

_____

4. Growth in friendship: _____

_____

_____

_____

Now, choose one of the situations below and with a partner, work out answers to the same four points.

1. Josh feels he has to be superior to everyone else so that Travis will admire and need him. In their friendship, Josh always tries to be the one in control.
2. Carol and Jean have been good friends since grade school. But now, Jean is a member of the school's All-Star Swimming Team, and all her spare time is spent practicing.
3. Tony is always worried that Susan will leave him for another boyfriend. To make sure she will keep liking him, he constantly gives her little presents.

Next, have the candidates choose partners and work in pairs on the second section. Assign the situations to partners to assure that all three situations are covered by the group. Then ask each of the pairs to present its analysis of the situation assigned. If you have time, let the candidates share their reactions to the whole exercise.

Begin by reading or summarizing the first paragraph for the group and opening up a brief discussion on attitudes. Ask the candidates to share problems they may have had because of attitudes—either their own attitudes or those of others.

Then, direct the candidates to read the second paragraph and begin to work using their Bibles. (If it is not possible for each candidate to have a Bible, the work may be done in small groups. However, the activity is most effective when done individually.) Supervise the work closely to be sure that the candidates understand Jesus' attitude in each Scripture passage and how that attitude can apply in their own friendships. If time is short, have each candidate choose two or three passages.

▌STUDY

Growing in Friendship

Christian friendships have to start with an attitude. If you can foster a loving and understanding attitude, you have a good chance of growing in your friendships with others and in your friendship with Christ. Your example and guide for all your relationships is Jesus himself. If you follow him, then you will do as he did. You will be patient. You will be kind. You will be unselfish. You will be honest.

Before you can put your love to work, however, you need a plan of action. Take this opportunity to draw up your own personal code of conduct with regards to friendship. Use the words of your best friend, Jesus, as a basis for your code. Read each of the Scripture passages listed in the chart below. Describe the attitude of Jesus. Then, describe how you can put that attitude to work in your friendships.

SCRIPTURE	ATTITUDE	PERSONAL CODE
1. Matthew 7:1–5		
2. Matthew 7:12		
3. Matthew 17:14–20		
4. Matthew 18:21–35		
5. Mark 9:33–37		
6. Mark 10:13–16		
7. Luke 6:36–38		
8. John 11:17, 32–44		

◤ REFLECT

From the Holy Father

Look for Jesus by reading and studying the Gospel, and by reading some good books. Look for Jesus by taking advantage of the religious instruction lessons at school and of the meetings in your parishes.

Love Jesus! Jesus is not an idea, a sentiment, a memory. Jesus is a person, always alive and present with us! He is our friend. He is everyone's friend and wishes particularly to be the friend and support of you young people on your way through life: you need confidence and friendship so much.

Bear witness to Jesus with your courageous faith and innocence. Do not be afraid to refuse words, acts, and attitudes which are not in conformity with Christian ideals. Be courageous in rejecting what destroys your innocence or wilts the freshness of your love for Christ.

To seek, love, and bear witness to Jesus! This is your commitment! These are the instructions I give you! (Pope John Paul II, Rome, November 8, 1978).

REFLECT

Note: These sections may be done in class or as "at home" assignments.

The Word of God: Read the passage from Saint John on page 53 slowly, meditatively to the group, pausing briefly after a sentence or two to allow the candidates time to reflect on each passage.

From the Holy Father: Give the candidates a few moments to read this excerpt from the Holy Father. Use question 4 on the next page for discussion.

Dear Candidate

Dear Candidate: Read or summarize this section to the group. Then allow time for discussion of any questions the candidates may have about the catechumenate or the Rite of Becoming a Candidate.

The "Getting Ready" stage of the Confirmation process is drawing to a close. You have explored the direction of your life story and seen how that story involves your family, friends, and the parish community. You have heard the call of Jesus to love and to serve, and to be close friends with him. Are you prepared to accept his call? Are you ready to start the journey?

During the weeks and months to come, you will be part of the "Journey" stage, or catechumenate. It will be a time of traveling more closely with the Christian community, of participating in the prayer and worship of the community, and of working actively with others to spread the Gospel and build up the Body of Christ. It is an exciting journey—one that will bring you into full membership with the Christian community. As you travel, remember that the other members of the parish community are supporting you.

Your Family in Christ

RESPOND

Remind the candidates to review the questions in this section before the next meeting. You may wish to discuss question 3 during the session in conjunction with The Word of God, page 53.

RESPOND

1. What do you think are the three most important ingredients of a good friendship? Why did you select these three things?

2. Using the three ingredients you selected as your guide, describe how good a friend you make.

3. Think about your own experiences of friendship. What do you think are the greatest obstacles to friendship?

4. How has your friendship with Jesus helped you *(a)* to grow and to change, *(b)* to be a better friend to others, and *(c)* to participate more fully in the life and worship of your parish family?

▌PRAYER

A Living Gospel

Lord, you seem to hide in my world.
How do I know it's you?
With all the hurry and worry, I don't always recognize you.
But then I remember what you told the followers of John the Baptizer when they asked if you were the Messiah.
"Go and report to John what you hear and see:
the blind recover their sight,
cripples walk,
lepers are cured,
the deaf hear,
dead men are raised to life,
and the poor have the Good News preached to them.
Blest are those who find no stumbling block in me."
Lord, open my eyes so that I may see and understand.
Let me be your Gospel.
Help me share the Good News.

REACH OUT

Urge the candidates to spend some time with a close friend who is not a part of this class discussing what friendship means. Questions 1–3 from the Respond section could be helpful as guidelines for discussion.

PRAYER

If you use this prayer to close the session, ask candidates to close their eyes for a moment. Then read through the prayer slowly until you reach the line, "Lord, open my eyes. . . ." Invite the group to read the rest of the prayer aloud together.

STAGE 2

The Journey

STEPS

The Journey is the second phase of your preparation for Confirmation. During this time, you will be comparing and contrasting your story, your life, with the stories told about Jesus and the Church. By hearing the witness of the other Christians from the larger community around you, you will have the opportunity to reflect daily, weekly, about the place of prayer, study, and apostolic action in your life. This growth in awareness can lead you to a more personal relationship with Jesus and with your Christian brothers and sisters. Your use of time, talent, and treasure can lead you to a greater respect for human rights. And this respect can lead you to a commitment to peace and justice in every stage of your life.

S T E P   7   Watch

AIM

To encourage the candidates to wait patiently for Christ's call and to have the courage to accept personal conversion as part of the answer to the call.

The candidates are probably quite familiar with the role of watching and waiting in their lives. People in their mid or late teens spend their lives in transition, waiting for the time when they will step into adulthood. Some young people use the time well, making good use of the opportunities available. Others, however, fix on the future and lose sight of the value of the present.

Preparing for Confirmation also involves waiting and watching. It is a conversion process which takes place over a period of time rather than immediately. For this, the candidates need patience and an understanding that the journey to full membership isn't always easy. Yet, candidates are not alone in their journey to Confirmation. They must know that the Family of God is with them as they wait for Jesus to come more fully into their lives.

In this step, the candidates will reflect on how the virtues of hope and patience help them to be more aware of what God is asking them to do with their lives. They will see how Saint Paul's own journey to conversion led him to a life of love and service—bringing the Good News to others. Finally, the candidates will think about ways they can make an extra effort to respond to Christ's call to love and service.

Resources

You may find the following forms helpful in preparing for this step:
- Form 23—Suggested Method for Scripture Sharing
- Form 7—First Sponsor Session

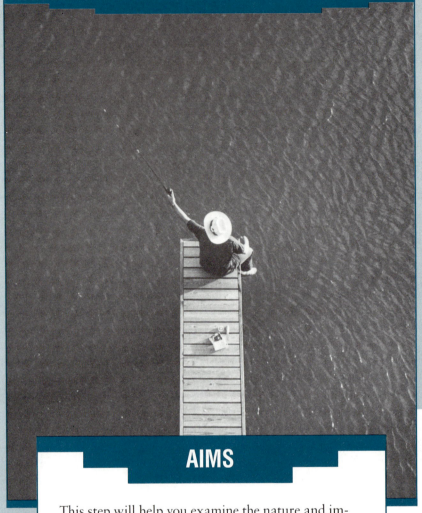

AIMS

This step will help you examine the nature and importance of waiting and of conversion in your preparation for Confirmation.

- Confirmation will strengthen your life in Christ, but you must be ready to respond when you are called.

- The time you spend now watching for the coming of Jesus will help you grow in patience and courage—two important qualities in every disciple's life.

- Saint Paul is an example for every Christian who faces conversion, or change, and answers yes.

The Word of God

Jesus said to his disciples: "Be constantly on the watch! Stay awake! You do not know when the appointed time will come. It is like a man traveling abroad. He leaves home and places his servants in charge, each with his or her own task; and he orders the guard at the gate to watch with a sharp eye. Look around you! You do not know when the master of the house is coming, whether at dusk, at midnight, when the cock crows, or at early dawn. Do not let him come suddenly and catch you asleep. What I say to you, I say to all: Be on guard!" (*Mark* 13:33–37).

Group Reunion

Friendship cannot be forced. It can only be given and received in freedom. Jesus has called you to be his friend, to participate in building up his kingdom. If you choose to accept his friendship, then you need both a sense of urgency and patience. Nothing will happen if you don't get started, but you need a balance because you are still learning. How can you use this time of learning to live out your friendship with Jesus? Where do you think your friendship with Jesus is going? Is it becoming strong enough to last a lifetime? Are you convinced that Jesus' love and support make a difference in your life? What are some of the long-range effects your decision to be friends with Jesus might have on your immediate world? Share your thoughts and responses with your fellow candidates.

This Scripture passage may be used as an opening prayer, or later as part of the *Reflect* activities on pages 68–69.

GROUP REUNION

The first six steps of the Confirmation process have reflected Jesus' call to be friends with him. This Group Reunion asks the candidates to explore what friendship with Jesus means in their lives.

Have the candidates form small groups to discuss the questions. Assign one or two questions to each group to assure that all the questions are discussed. After a few moments of discussion, direct the groups to share the results of their work together. Then, let the candidates talk about what has occurred in their faith lives since the last meeting.

In a world of high technology and instant communications, patience isn't easy. Still, waiting is an experience everyone goes through. And, it is what people do with waiting that counts—letting it be a source of anger, disappointment, and depression, or seeing it as an opportunity to grow in awareness of God's own time.

Give the candidates time to read this section and pause a few moments in silence. Give no hint of directions or of the next move. (Stretch the pause long enough for it to become slightly awkward.) Then spend a moment discussing how the candidates felt: bored? anxious? alert?

Ask the candidates to read the directions and answer the questions. Provide a short time for volunteers to share their responses.

▌PREPARE

Waiting on the Lord

Phee Nguyen had lived in Saint Agatha's parish in Woonsocket, Rhode Island, since she arrived in America with her mother and six children. During those five years, she never lost hope that her husband would eventually join the family. Finally, Phee received word that her husband had left Vietnam and was in Indonesia. The family waited for papers to be processed so that Phee's husband could come to America. Phee said, "God loves us—he's so good! I prayed to Jesus and Mary, and they heard me." She kept waiting in hope.

Meanwhile, the parish, which had supported and sponsored this Vietnamese family for five years, joined Phee and her family in prayer and hope.

One-on-one

Phee knows the value of waiting and watching. Spend a few moments thinking about her story. Then, answer the following questions. Share your answers if you wish.

1. Sometimes, a minute can seem like an hour, and at other times, an hour can seem like several minutes. What do you think causes this distortion of perception?

   _____

   _____

   _____

2. If what you are waiting for does not happen immediately, do you wait patiently or do you begin to lose hope? Why do you react this way?

   _____

   _____

   _____

3. How can the virtues of hope and patience help you be more aware of God acting in your life?

   _____

   _____

   _____

It's Not Always Easy

The path seems easy when we begin.
But then we begin to get tired.
The journey becomes rough.
The road winds up into the mountains, and it isn't much fun anymore.
The journey to Confirmation seems like that, too.
It was easy when we started out because we began by looking only at ourselves.
But as we start looking at the life of Jesus, we realize just where his Way could take us.
We begin to tire out.
We begin to get scared, too.
Do we have what it takes?
Can we face the challenge?
Jesus lived every moment the way the Father wanted.
Now, he's asking us to do the same thing.
We don't know if we can, Lord.
We want to, but we don't know if we can.
Help us to continue our journey.
You want that journey to be more intense, more perfect.
That means not to stop at the point at which we have arrived, but with your help, to progress in love.

Listen and Pray

A good way to learn what Jesus wants of you is to spend five minutes a day with him in meditating on the Scriptures. Begin by taking a minute to quiet yourself. Close your eyes. Remember that God is present with you.

Next, look up one of the Scripture passages listed below. Read the passage about three times. Let each word sink in. Think of its meaning for your life. How can you *do* what God asks of you? Listen and pray. Then, read the passage one last time.

Scripture passages: Isaiah 49:14–15, 6:3, 9:6, 9:7, 11:1–2, 11:5–6, 12:5–6, 22:22, 25:1, 28:16, 30:18, 33:17, 33:23, 35:4, and 40:31; Luke 1:28, 1:32–33, 1:35, 1:38, 1:45, 1:52, 1:54, 1:78–79, 2:4–6, 2:7, and 2:9–11; Romans 8:22–23; 1 Corinthians 1:4–9; Ephesians 1:3–4, 1:5–6; 1 Timothy 1:15; and Philemon 2:6–7.

Circle the passage you chose. Write what the passage means in your life.

STUDY

Ask a volunteer to read this reflection aloud. After the reading, have the candidates spend a few minutes silently reflecting on times in their lives when they have experienced difficulty in completing a task or project. Provide some time for the candidates to recount stories of their difficulties.

Read or summarize the opening paragraphs for the candidates and direct them to look up one of the Scripture passages and work with it as suggested. If there are individuals who are not familiar with the Bible, spend a few moments explaining its organization into Old and New Testaments. (Note: It may be necessary to review the meaning of the reference numbers of each Scripture passage. It is important for the candidates to be familiar with the organization of the Bible so that they can work with it independently in future lessons.) After they have completed the exercise, encourage them to spend five minutes a day during this Advent season meditating on the Scriptures. Suggest that they list the Scripture passages they have worked with in their journal-notebooks.

Ask the candidates to read the first two paragraphs for the group. Ask how many are familiar with the story of Paul's conversion. Have volunteers indicate what they mean by the term "conversion."

Have the candidates read the remaining material. Then, ask them to close their eyes and imagine the impact Paul's conversion had on his life as you read Acts 9:1–9. After a brief pause, read the passage in the text from Romans and invite volunteers to share a spontaneous prayer in response to the passage.

The Call of Paul

God has often been a God of surprises. Who would have thought that God would choose Paul to preach the Good News of Jesus? How could a man like Paul change so completely in such a short time? How could a person who was so determined to arrest and punish the followers of Jesus become an Apostle?

The story line reads like that of an adventure novel. On the road to Damascus, Paul is thrown to the ground by a great flash of light and finds himself face-to-face with Jesus. He is blinded by this encounter and has to be led into Damascus. There, Ananias, who is sent by the Lord, heals Paul's eyes and frees him from his struggles and doubts. Paul is now filled with the Holy Spirit and can face the Jesus he was afraid of, the Jesus he had persecuted. Thus begins Paul's new way of life, a journey which will eventually lead him to martyrdom in Rome.

Conversion

Paul's conversion may seem like a sudden event, but actually he was already living a life devoted to God. Paul was brought up a Jew and knew well the traditions and customs of Judaism. He studied the Law and the commandments. He tried to live out God's will in every facet of his life. He thought he knew what conversion meant—until that day on the road to Damascus.

The risen Jesus called Paul to turn around his life, to believe in the Gospel. Once Paul said yes and believed in Jesus' power to save all people, nothing could stop Paul in bringing the Good News to others.

> Who will separate us from the love of Christ? Trial, or distress, or persecution, or hunger, or nakedness, or danger, or the sword? In all this, we are more than conquerors because of him who has loved us. For I am certain that neither death nor life, neither angels or principalities, neither the present nor the future, nor powers, neither height nor depth nor any other creature, will be able to separate us from the love of God that comes to us in Christ Jesus, our Lord.

(Romans 8:35, 37–39)

Alone, you cannot love others as you should. You cannot pray or speak or act as you should. But God not only calls you, he also gives you the means to live in his love—the Holy Spirit. Through the Spirit, you, like Paul, can say yes to God's life and his love within you. You can show through your honesty, selflessness, and service to others that the kingdom of God is alive in the world. You can make the Gospel of Jesus Christ happen.

You are being called by Christ to make a conversion—to live a life of love and service. To discover Christ's call, you need to develop the skill of listening for that call. Reflect for a moment on the areas of your life in which Christ's call can be heard. In the chart below, indicate how Christ is calling you to share his love. Then, write a check mark next to the area in which you will make an extra effort to respond during the coming week.

Read and discuss the last two paragraphs with the candidates. When you feel that the group understands the meaning of conversion, direct them to write an answer to question 3 in the Respond section on a separate sheet of paper. Collect these answers.

AREA	LOVE	SERVICE
At home		
At school		
At Confirmation class		
With friends		
In the parish		

The Word of God: Ask a volunteer to read the passage from Saint Mark on page 63 to the group.

From the Holy Father: Read this section to the group. Open up a brief discussion on how the candidates have observed the season of Advent in the past: What changes in their lives did Advent preparation mean? How is this Advent the same as or different from previous Advents?

Dear Candidate: Ask a volunteer to read this letter to the group and have them use question 2 on the next page for discussion.

REFLECT

From the Holy Father

Christ says to each of you, "Watch!" because the moment is not known but it is certain that it will come. The most important thing is fidelity to the task entrusted to you and to the gifts that make you capable of carrying it out. To each of you, there has been entrusted a duty which is specifically yours, that "house" which you must look after. This house is you, it is your family, the environment in which you live, work, and rest. It is the parish, the city, the village, the Church, the world, for which each of you is jointly responsible before God and all people. What is your solicitude for this "house" entrusted to you, that there may reign in it the order willed by God, which corresponds to the deepest human aspirations and desires? What is your contribution in this work, which calls for constant putting into order, renewal, fidelity? Here are your questions and tasks for Advent (Pope John Paul II, address to the parish of Saint Frances of Rome, November 29, 1981).

Dear Candidate

Phee's husband, Thieu, has finally come to America from Indonesia. The night he arrived home, the whole parish welcomed him with praise and celebration. God is so good! Thieu's parish family had prayed and waited for five years, and then this brave father was united with his wife and children.

The Church teaches that as you pray and wait during Advent, you are preparing in a special way for the coming of Jesus into your life. May your waiting and watching bring you even closer to accepting Jesus as Lord of your life.

Your Family in Christ

RESPOND

Remind the candidates to review the questions in this section before the next meeting. If there is time during class, discuss question 2 after reading Dear Candidate.

RESPOND

1. Review some of your attitudes toward waiting on the Lord. What are some words which describe how you feel about waiting? Why do you use these words?

2. How can your Family in Christ make it easier for you to watch for the coming of Jesus?

3. Describe what you feel is Christ's call to you right now. How can you answer that call? What things stand in your way? What things will help you?

▌PRAYER

Don't You Know?

Wait! Wait!
It seems like all I ever do is wait.
I wait for lunch.
I wait in line for the show.
I wait to grow up.
I'm not sure I like waiting.
Everytime I turn around, someone is telling me that life is a journey, a search, or a process.
Father, I am not very patient.
There is so much I want right now!
Please, teach me that waiting is important.
Help me to see that while I am waiting, I have the time to learn about myself and to learn about others.
I want to be loved and cared for.
Doesn't everybody?
Well, maybe if I am just a bit more patient, you might get through to me.
And when you do, I'll hear you saying,
    "Don't you know?
    I love you—all the time—
    even while you are waiting."

REACH OUT

The Scripture passages listed on page 65 under "Listen and Pray" are especially suitable for Advent reading and meditation. Urge the candidates to offer to read one of these passages to the family before or after a family meal.

PRAYER

One way to use this prayer to close the session is to ask the candidates to read it silently to themselves and pause a moment. Then, ask volunteers to pray individually for things that they are waiting for right now in their lives. Close by having the group pray the Lord's Prayer together.

Prepare

AIM

To reinforce for the candidates the need to prepare for the coming of Jesus.

While preparing to receive the sacrament of Confirmation, the candidates are also preparing for another event—the coming of Jesus. Since earliest Christian times, the community realized what impact future events have on the present. While waiting for Jesus' Second Coming, the community of faith struggled with the question, "What does it mean for us today?" Preparing for the Lord means seeing his face in every human being today. Serving others is the key. Paul reminded his early converts of this when they shunned their responsibilities and awaited "the end of the world."

Resources

When preparing this step, please refer to the following forms:

- Form 26, The Prayer of Contemplation
- Form 13, Prayer and Planning Session—Advent

AIMS

This step will give you the opportunity to explore what it means to always be prepared for the coming of Jesus.

- You need to take time to pray and to think in order to find out how you can best serve God and his people.

- Living your life according to God's plan takes a good sense of values, rooted in faith.

- Faith in Jesus and awareness of his presence in your life will help you meet the challenge of being a Christian.

- Jesus is always with you, ready to help through his words and example, his sacraments, and his Church.

The Word of God

Here begins the Gospel of Jesus Christ, the Son of God. In Isaiah the prophet, it is written: "I send my messenger before you to prepare your way: a herald's voice in the desert, crying, 'Make ready the way of the Lord, clear him a straight path.'"

Thus it was that John the Baptizer appeared in the desert proclaiming a baptism of repentance which led to the forgiveness of sins. All the Judean countryside and the people of Jerusalem went out to him in great numbers. They were being baptized by him in the Jordan River as they confessed their sins. John was clothed in camel's hair, and wore a leather belt around his waist. His food was grasshoppers and wild honey. The theme of his preaching was: "One more powerful that I is to come after me. I am not fit to stoop and untie his sandal straps. I have baptized you in water; he will baptize you in the Holy Spirit" *(Mark 1:1–8)*.

Group Reunion

Focus on the importance of patience and hope in the life of a Christian. What would it be like if every time you tried to do something new, your best friend lost patience with you or didn't believe in you? How would your friend's reaction affect you? Would you give up? try harder? How does knowing that God believes in you make you feel? What is the relationship between hard work and patience? between courage and hope? Can you ever be too patient? too hopeful? What are some practical ways you can grow in the virtues of patience and hope?

This Scripture passage may be used as an opening prayer, or later as part of the *Reflect* activities on pages 76–77.

GROUP REUNION

Advent is a season of hope. The last step asked the candidates to consider the role of patience and hope in their lives. Here, the Group Reunion reflects on that theme. Use the questions in this section to generate a discussion on the importance of faith and hope in the life of the Christian. Ask volunteers if they have ever experienced a loss of hope and, if so, what feelings were caused by the experience. How did they regain their sense of hope? As the discussion progresses, list on the board, newsprint, or a transparency the candidates' suggestions for practical ways to grow in the virtues of patience and hope.

PREPARE

Direct the candidates to read this section and work on the questions. After sufficient time, ask for volunteers to share their responses to having to prepare for company in a special way.

Make the point that both Advent and these sessions are examples of preparation. The candidates are preparing to make a deeper commitment to Christ, a commitment that necessitates conversion. Have the candidates read the opening paragraph and answer the questions. Invite volunteers to share.

PREPARE

Getting Ready

Preparing for the arrival of Pope John Paul II involved the work, skill, and talent of hundreds of thousands of people. For the members of the press, preparing to travel throughout the United States with the Pope meant applying for credentials and clearance from the Secret Service. For many of those who were to travel with him, preparation meant reading all there was to know about Pope John Paul II. Travel arrangements and hotel reservations had to be made. Preparation even involved learning as much as possible about the background of the papacy itself.

How would you go about preparing for the arrival of a famous person?

_____

_____

_____

How do you prepare for the arrival of company? How do you feel about having company?

_____

_____

_____

Share a time when you prepared for company in a special way.

_____

_____

_____

_____

_____

One-on-one

The journey to Confirmation is a long one. To prepare for the journey, we have to make sure we have everything we need: the desire to make the journey in the first place, and the courage to allow the Lord to convert us from our way of thinking to his.

Part of the meaning of conversion is "to turn against." But against what? Conversion means to turn against anything in our lives that keeps us from God.

1. What are the things in your life that keep you from God?

_____

_____

_____

2. Name three things in your life right now that may be obstacles between you and God.

_____

_____

_____

3. What can you do to remove those obstacles?

_____

_____

_____

STUDY

Read or summarize the first paragraph for the group. Ask if anyone has ever experienced such excitement over an event about to happen that they lost all sense of their present responsibilities. Continue reading or summarizing the material. Then, direct the candidates to read the opening material in the next section.

⌐ STUDY

Be Alert

The earliest Christians expected Jesus to return very soon after his resurrection and ascension. There was a real sense of urgency about the Second Coming. Some believed so strongly that the end of the world would come soon that they stopped working altogether. They shunned their responsibilities to serve the community and began living according to the philosophy, "Eat, drink, and be merry, for tomorrow we may die." Saint Paul had to remind these Christians that no one knows the day of the Lord's return.

Today, centuries after the time of the first Christians, it is still important to await the Second Coming and the completion of the building of the kingdom of God. But it is also important to develop an awareness of Jesus acting in your life right now. Through his Spirit, he is calling and strengthening you. One way to respond is by translating your awareness into action. As Jesus did, you can reach out to others. You can share what is best in you.

Meeting the Challenge

Respond to the following statements which are related in some way to your Christian mission. Mark each statement by circling the number which most accurately describes your reactions: 1–agree strongly, 2–agree, 3–agree somewhat, 4–disagree somewhat, 5–disagree, 6–disagree strongly. Be prepared to discuss the reasons for your responses.

1. It's all right to be rich as long as you use some of your money to help others.

    1   2   3   4   5   6

2. There is little I can do to improve the quality of life for those who go to bed hungry

    1   2   3   4   5   6

3. Sure, I want to help others, but first there are things I want to do for myself.

    1   2   3   4   5   6

4. Caring about others is important, but there should be some kind of return on your investment.

    1   2   3   4   5   6

5. I can get burned once and forget it. I can get burned twice and forget it. But the third time, watch out!

    1   2   3   4   5   6

6. There are some things I shouldn't go along with in my crowd, but what's worse than being left out.

    1   2   3   4   5   6

7. Sometimes, it's better to fight back instead of turning the other cheek.

    1   2   3   4   5   6

8. If I were really courageous, I would never be afraid.

    1   2   3   4   5   6

9. To be honest, I don't think it's possible to love everybody, all the time.

    1   2   3   4   5   6

10. Happiness is something that can be a permanent part of my life.

    1   2   3   4   5   6

Have the candidates read each statement carefully and work individually on their answers. Then divide the class into groups of three or four and assign three questions to each group for discussion. Do not assign question 2. After the groups have discussed their questions for about five minutes, ask a spokesperson from each group to report on his or her group's response. Later, involve the entire group in a discussion of question 2. Elicit some practical suggestions for action against hunger in the world.

REFLECT

Note: These sections may be done in class or as "at home" assignments.

The Word of God: Ask a volunteer to read the passage from Saint Mark on page 71 to the group. Then, use question 1 below for discussion. Ask: "What did John ask the people of his time to do in order to prepare for Jesus' coming?" (Repent, change their lives, confess their sins.)

From the Holy Father: Do a meditative reading of this message from the Holy Father. Read a phrase at a time, pause a few moments to allow the candidates to reflect on it, then continue reading.

Dear Candidate: Read or summarize this letter for the group and then use question 2 on the next page for discussion.

REFLECT

From the Holy Father

Keep Jesus Christ in your hearts, and you will recognize his face in every human being. You will want to help him out in all his needs: the needs of your brothers and sisters. This is the way we prepare ourselves to meet Jesus, when he will come again, on the last day, as the judge of the living and the dead. And he will say to us: "Come, you have my Father's blessing! Inherit the kingdom prepared for you from the creation of the world. For I was hungry and you gave me food, I was thirsty and you gave me drink. I was a stranger and you welcomed me, naked and you clothed me. I was ill and you comforted me, in prison and you came to visit me. . . . I assure you, as often as you did it for one of my least brothers and sisters, you did it for me" (Matthew 25:34–35, 39) (Pope John Paul II, New York City, October 3, 1979).

Dear Candidate

As you prepare for Confirmation, spend some time recalling your baptism and how your parents and godparents helped you in becoming a Catholic Christian. Someone can introduce you to a new person, but it is up to you to take the time and effort to become a friend. Your family introduced you to Jesus, but now you must make your own commitment and respond to his friendship.

Confirmation will seal your baptism, your friendship with Jesus. Through Confirmation, you will experience not only the joys of that friendship but also the responsibilities of being a living witness to his Gospel. You will share in Jesus' ministry to bring joy, unity, and love into a world that cries out for peace. Be prepared by opening your mind and heart to his Spirit, and by believing in yourself as much as he does.

Your Family in Christ

RESPOND

Remind the candidates to review these questions between sessions. You may wish to use question 1 in conjunction with The Word of God and question 2 with Dear Candidate for discussion during this session.

RESPOND

1. Do you feel that the values of Jesus—honesty, selflessness, and service—conflict with the values of your peer group? In what ways have you experienced this conflict? How did you resolve the situations?

2. How can the sacraments and the Church help you meet the challenge of being a Christian?

Preparing Well

Lord, help me prepare for your Second Coming the way I prepare for the arrival of all great people in my life: by tidying up, cleaning the corners, putting all in order.

Help me clear the cobwebs out of my mind and dust the selfish areas of my heart to make ready for you.

Help me recognize you in those around me—the hungry, the thirsty, the stranger.

And, Lord, when you come again, let me see that being present to you is the most important part of my hospitality.

Lord, I await your Second Coming.

Let me be here for you.

REACH OUT

For many, the term *peer group* automatically means teenagers . Yet, adults have peer groups, too. Encourage the candidates to use question 1 in the Respond section as a discussion starter with a parent, sponsor, or adult friend. Have them ask, "How do the values of your (adult) peers conflict with the values of Jesus—honesty, selflessness, and service?"

PRAYER

Ask a volunteer to read the prayer to the group. The rest of the group should respond by reading the last two lines of the prayer aloud.

Rejoice

AIM

To help the candidates focus on the forgiveness of sins and the importance of celebrating that forgiveness in the sacrament of Reconciliation.

The candidates may differ in their understanding of the sacrament of Reconciliation. For some, the sacrament may be a regular part of their lives. Others may tend to avoid the sacrament or not realize the important role it plays in helping their faith remain strong and alive.

Having a sense of direction is important for the candidates as they accept life's responsibilities as young adults. This step will help the candidates understand that Reconciliation can help them have that direction. The candidates will reflect on their own experience in receiving the sacrament and discover how forgiveness can help them grow closer to God. They will also read Jesus' own words on forgiveness and discuss situations where they needed his healing in their own lives.

The emphasis in this step is not the damage done by sin, but the healing and restoration available through the sacrament of Reconciliation. In order to put this lesson into practice, you might schedule a prayer service using the themes in this step. Ask volunteers to help you with the selection of prayers, songs, and readings from the Scripture.

Resource

You will find the following material helpful at this point in the Confirmation preparation process:
■ Form 29, Celebration of a Penitential Rite

AIMS

This step will help you grow in your understanding of the sacrament of Reconciliation.

■ In the sacrament of Reconciliation, you encounter the healing and forgiving Christ.

■ As a follower of Jesus, you are called to have the same healing and forgiving attitude toward others.

■ Celebrating the sacrament of Reconciliation will strengthen you to be a healer in the way you think and act.

■ Through commitment and conversion, you will experience the true joy of redemption.

The Word of God

Rejoice always, never cease praying, render constant thanks; such is God's will for you in Christ Jesus. Do not stifle the Spirit. Do not despise prophecies. Test everything; retain what is good. Avoid any semblance of evil. May the God of peace make you perfect in holiness. May he preserve you whole and entire, spirit, soul, and body, irreproachable at the coming of our Lord Jesus Christ. *(1 Thessalonians 5:16–23).*

Group Reunion

In the last session, you discussed what it means to always be prepared for the coming of Jesus. An important aspect of preparing for Jesus is to examine your life to see if you are acting positively. Spend a few minutes meditating on the Corporal Works of Mercy. Then, as a group, discuss possible ways you can respond to these needs in your everyday life. Be practical and specific. Remember, the Christian response to another's need is always a personal one.

This Scripture passage may be used as an opening prayer, or later as part of the *Reflect* activities on pages 83-84.

GROUP REUNION

During the last step, the candidates had the opportunity to reflect on the importance of preparing for the Lord's coming. They also saw the importance of being responsible to others as part of that preparation. After members of the group take their places for Group Reunion, refer them to page 186 of A Catholic Treasury. Give them a moment to review the Corporal Works of Mercy. Then, ask them to read the material in this section and discuss possible ways in which they can respond to the demands of the works of mercy.

PREPARE

This story of a young man's visit to a renewal center and the invitation extended to him and others to receive the sacrament of Reconciliation stresses two points. First, forgiveness is a gift. It cannot be forced; it can only be freely accepted. For those who do not celebrate the sacrament of forgiveness regularly, a sincere invitation often encourages them to celebrate the sacrament on a more regular basis. Second, Reconciliation provides a person with a better sense of direction and helps the individual move away from whatever keeps him or her separated from God.

Direct the candidates to read the material in this section. After they have finished, spend a few moments discussing Scott's situation and the point made by Father Raymond. Ask: "Do you think Scott's initial fear about receiving the sacrament of Reconciliation is unusual? Why or why not? In your own words, describe what Father Raymond was saying. How important is it to have a sense of direction in your life? How can the sacrament of Reconciliation help you to find that direction?"

Invitation to Forgiveness

Scott's best friend invited him to come along on the parish weekend renewal. Although Scott knew about the weekend, he hadn't given it any thought. He accepted, partly because his friends would be there and partly out of curiosity. So, he got on the parish bus headed for the Franciscan Renewal Center with mixed feelings.

The Friday evening session was very enjoyable. The theme for the evening was friendship. After the formal session, the young people got together informally to meet one another. Scott began to relax. He found himself enjoying the process of meeting new people. He also discovered that others in the group had felt a little hesitant about coming and were also beginning to relax.

Saturday morning's group discussion centered on God's love and forgiveness. The leader, Father Raymond, pointed out the reason for making an examination of conscience. "One of the ways we know where we are is by comparisons," he began. "We cannot know up without a down or a left without a right. In the same way, we use comparisons to see where our lives are going." Father Raymond was careful to point out that the world is not simply black and white. It is better to see it as a spectrum. "We examine our actions to see the direction in which we are moving. In order to move closer to God, we try to move away from what keeps us from him."

At the end of the session, the group was invited to celebrate the sacrament of Reconciliation. All of a sudden, Scott got frightened. It had been almost a year since he last celebrated the sacrament. But as he looked around, he realized the others might be frightened, too. The more he thought about it, the more he realized that his life was somewhere in the grays, and he did not have a sense of movement or growth in his personal life. He hoped that the sacrament would help him get back some of that direction. Scott smiled an anxious smile and joined the others in receiving the sacrament.

One-on-one

For a few moments, review Scott's experience. Try to identify some of the feelings Scott may have had. When you have finished your reflection, answer the following questions. Share your answers if you wish.

1. Describe your personal experience in receiving the sacrament of Reconciliation.

2. In your own words, what value do you see in confessing your sins to a priest?

3. Why is it said that people "celebrate" the sacrament of Reconciliation?

Ask the candidates to read the opening paragraph and to work individually on the questions. When they have finished, ask volunteers to share their responses to questions 1 and 2. When discussing question 3, remind the candidates that forgiveness is a gift from God. People "celebrate" the sacrament of Reconciliation because it is a source of joy and happiness.

STUDY

Come Back to Me

The preaching of Jesus often took up the same themes of conversion and repentance that John the Baptizer preached. "This is the time of fulfillment. The reign of God is at hand! Reform your lives and believe in the Gospel!"

STUDY

This section points out God's unending offer of forgiveness and presents a summary of Jesus' message about God's forgiveness and love for each person. Begin by asking the candidates to read the first three paragraphs.

After they have finished, explain that the Old Testament sometimes uses stories about people to reveal God's love for his people. In this example, just as Hosea could not give up on his wife even when she kept running away from him, so God cannot give up on his people even when they turn away from him through sin.

Ask the candidates to read the rest of the material in this section and to spend a moment reflecting on Jesus' fourfold message about God's forgiveness. Ask the candidates to work individually on the Scripture exercise. Be sure there are Bibles available for the candidates to use. When they have completed the exercise, divide the candidates into groups of three or four and have them discuss their responses.

(Mark 1:15). That message is addressed to all who encounter the saving power for the first time. It calls for a change of mind, heart, intention, and attitude. It asks for complete conversion, sorrow for sin, and the beginning of a new life in Christ.

Even people who have accepted the saving power of Jesus in their lives can turn away from Christ and sin. No one is spared temptation. But the miracle of God's love keeps any sin from being fatal. God forgives everyone who wants to try again.

In the Old Testament, there is a powerful example of God's forgiveness—the story of Hosea the Prophet. Hosea was married to a woman who was a failure in everybody's eyes. Gomer, his wife, was a wicked woman. She kept running away from Hosea. But every time she ran away, Hosea went after her and urged her to come back. Hosea really loved Gomer, and nothing she could do would ever change that.

The story of Hosea and his wife has a very simple lesson: Nothing you do can change the simple truth of God's love. Jesus came to tell people more about God's love and forgiveness. He wanted his followers to see that being forgiven by God is part of their identity. In all the teaching Jesus did, he had a simple fourfold message about God's forgiveness and love for each person: (1) No matter what happens, come back home to God. (2) Try always to see the good in yourself that God your Father sees in you. (3) Accept as a gift the care, love, and concern of God your Father. (4) Always be willing to forgive others.

The four Scripture passages listed below give examples of each part of Jesus' message of forgiveness. Read each passage. Then, briefly write what the passage means to you. Finally, describe a time when you needed this message of forgiveness. Discuss the exercise with the other candidates.

PASSAGE	MEANING	TIME OF NEED
Luke 15:11–20		
Luke 7:36–47		
Luke 5:17–25		
Matthew 18:23–35		

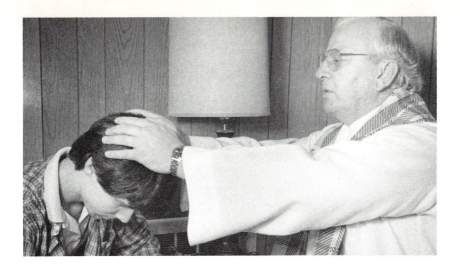

REFLECT

From the Holy Father

Christ said, "No longer do I call you servants. I call you friends. This is my commandment, that you love one another." Purify your hearts in the sacrament of Reconciliation. Sacramental confession is not a repression but a liberation. It does not restore the feelings of guilt. It cancels the guilt, dissolves the evil done, and bestows the grace of forgiveness.

The causes of evil are to be found in the heart, and the remedy for evil starts also from the heart. Christians, through the sincerity of their commitment and conversion, must proclaim with their own lives the joy of true liberation from sin by means of Christ's forgiveness (Pope John Paul II, Rome, April 5, 1979).

Dear Candidate

Jesus calls you to rejoice in all the events of your life. Rejoicing is easy when you are fulfilling your responsibilities and getting along with everyone. But when you withdraw into yourself or fail in your Christian commitment, being joyful isn't so easy. However, reconciliation is always possible. When you restore your friendship with Jesus and follow the will of the Father, you can rejoice again.

As you become more aware of the signs and wonders of the Lord in your everyday life, you will experience a peace which nothing can disturb. You begin to become holy, not because of anything you do on your own, but because the Lord changes you and draws you into his life. You become holy when you accept your baptism and decide to live as a child of God. And remember, happiness and joy are signs of a truly holy person.

Your Family in Christ

REFLECT

Note: These sections may be done in class or as "at home" assignments.

The Word of God: Ask a volunteer to read this passage slowly for the group. Then, open a brief discussion using question 3 on the next page.

From the Holy Father: Have the candidates read this section silently by themselves, then point out the following three sentences: "Sacramental confession is not a repression but a liberation. It does not restore feelings of guilt. It cancels the guilt, dissolves the evil done, and bestows the grace of forgiveness." Open a discussion on this point using question 4 as a discussion starter.

Dear Candidate: Read or summarize this section for the group and give a few moments to reflect quietly. Then, open a brief discussion on young people's attitudes toward the sacrament of Reconciliation. Ask: "Do young people your age frequently receive the sacrament of Reconciliation? Why or why not? If someone hesitates to go to the sacrament, what do you think his or her reasons might be?"

RESPOND

Urge the candidates to review these questions before the next session. You may wish to use question 4 in conjunction with From the Holy Father for discussion during the session.

RESPOND

1. Read the following Scripture passages: Psalm 51:3–4 and Isaiah 11:6. How do these passages represent what the sacrament of Reconciliation does for you?

2. In what ways does the sacrament of Reconciliation help you continue your journey to Confirmation?

3. In your relationships with other people, what is the importance of being able to say, "I'm sorry"? being able to say, "You are forgiven"?

4. In what ways does knowing that your sins are forgiven give you feelings of joy?

Again I Say, Rejoice

To rejoice in hope is to know with incredible certainty that I am
loved: not for what I do, but for who I am.
To rejoice in hope is to believe that I am cherished: not for what I
say, but for being myself.
I rejoice in you, Lord, and in your promises to me.
I praise you for the wonder of each day's newness and real po-
tential.
Help me, Lord, to seek your forgiveness.
Help me to rejoice always.

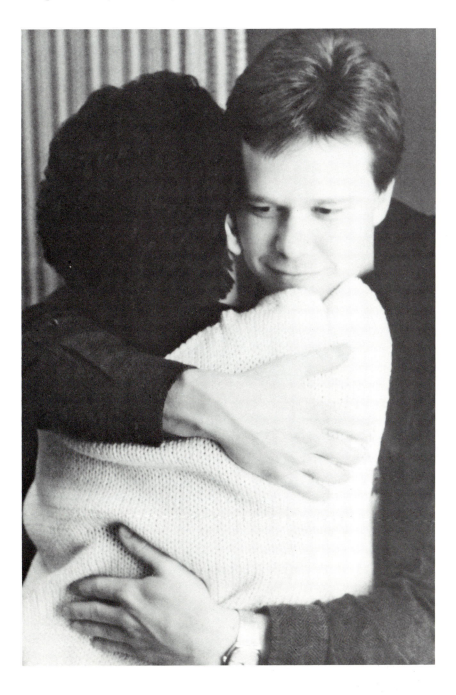

REACH OUT

The would be a good time for the candidates to participate in prayer service
which included the celebration of the sacrament of Reconciliation. Schedule the
service at a time convenient for other
members of the Parish community. Ask
the candidates to help with the selection
of prayers, songs, and readings from the
Scripture. Each candidate should invite
close friends, family members, and sponsors to the celebration. Some might want
to work on posters or other decorations
using the theme of joy and forgiveness.

PRAYER

If you decide to use this prayer to end the
session, begin by reading it aloud slowly
and meditatively for the group. Then,
have the candidates recite together the
Act of Contrition, which can be found in A
Catholic Treasury, page 187.

Christ with Us

AIM

To bring the candidates to a more mature understanding of the Incarnation and to encourage them to share themselves with God's People.

The *National Catechetical Directory* states that "the Church considers the Christmas season, which celebrates the birth of our Lord and his epiphanies (Magi, Cana, Baptism), 'second only to the annual celebrations of the Easter mystery'" (#144c). The material in this step emphasizes the importance of the Christmas event. It will help the candidates to understand Christmas as a time for sharing themselves, both spiritually and practically, with God's People.

On their way to Bethlehem, the Wise Men experienced an important *epiphany*—moment of revelation. Such moments have the power to transform the lives of those who experience them. In this step, the candidates will explore the meaning of epiphany and reflect on some of the moments of revelation that they have had in their own lives. They will also examine the symbolic nature of gift-giving and assess their own attitudes toward Christmas.

It is important for the candidates to integrate service to the community into their lives of faith. The Christmas season is an ideal time for the candidates to work as a group on some service project that aids the needy in the parish. This step will involve the members of the group in the actual planning of a project to be carried out sometime before the next step. To prepare for this lesson, determine some of the actual needs in the parish community and inform the appropriate organizations and committees, as well as the pastor or associate pastor, of the nature of this step.

Resources

The following materials will be helpful for you in preparing this step.
- Assignments and Service Projects, TM pages 18–19
- Literature and the Arts, TM page 24

AIMS

This step will help you grow toward a new and more mature understanding of Christmas.

- In Jesus, God revealed himself to his People in a very special way because Jesus is God in Person.

- Learning to know Jesus and understanding his message does not happen all at once but usually occurs through a series of *epiphanies*—moments of revelation.

- By using your special gifts and talents to reach out to others, you can continue the revelation of God to his People.

- Christmas reminds God's People of his great love for them and gives them an opportunity to give more of themselves as a gift to others.

The Word of God

After Jesus' birth in Bethlehem of Judea during the reign of King Herod, astrologers from the East arrived one day in Jerusalem inquiring, "Where is the newborn king of the Jews? We observed his star at its rising and have come to pay him homage." At this news, King Herod became greatly disturbed and with him all Jerusalem. Summoning all of the chief priests and scribes of the people, he inquired of them where the Messiah was to be born. "In Bethlehem of Judea," they informed him. "Here is what the prophet has written: 'And you, Bethlehem, land of Judah, are by no means least among the princes of Judah, since from you shall come a ruler who is to shepherd my people Israel.'" Herod called the astrologers aside and found out from them the exact time of the star's appearance. Then he sent them to Bethlehem, after having instructed them: "Go and get detailed information about the child. When you have found him, report it to me so that I may go and offer him homage, too."

After their audience with the king, they set out. The star which they had observed at its rising went ahead of them until it came to a standstill over the place where the child was. They were overjoyed at seeing the star, and on entering the house, found the child with Mary his mother. They prostrated themselves and did him homage. Then they opened their coffers and presented him with gifts of gold, frankincense, and myrrh *(Matthew 2:1–11).*

Group Reunion

The last three sessions helped you prepare for the coming of Jesus. Now, the moment has come. Christmas is here. How has your preparation changed the way you feel about Christmas? the way you will celebrate? What steps have you taken to help the other members of God's Family be ready for the coming of Jesus? How have the sacraments of Reconciliation and Eucharist strengthened you in your resolve to be born again in Christ Jesus?

This Scripture passage may be used as an opening prayer, or later as part of the *Reflect* activities on pages 92–93.

GROUP REUNION

The point of this Reunion is to help the candidates appreciate the transition from Advent to Christmas. Begin by summarizing for the group the discussion on Sacred Time (especially the first five paragraphs) on pages 183–184 of the text. Then briefly review the last three sessions with the candidates, stressing the idea of preparation.

Continue by having the candidates read this section quickly and discuss the questions. Place special emphasis on the question of how their preparation has changed the way they feel about Christmas and the way they will celebrate it.

PREPARE

Although the candidates may be familiar with the story of the Epiphany, they may not realize that epiphanies are important moments of revelation that can occur in their own lives. Work closely with the candidates on this section of the text, and provide some time for questions and discussion. Have the first paragraph read aloud, and then discuss it briefly. Have the next paragraph read aloud and spend a few moments in discussion before directing the candidates to begin work on the questions below.

PREPARE

Revelations

In his book of short stories entitled *The Dubliners*, James Joyce, an Irish author, used the word *epiphany* to indicate a moment which is very special because it gives meaning to the other moments of life. For example, in the short story "The Dead," the epiphany occurs when Gabriel, one of the main characters, suddenly realizes that he does not really know his wife as well as he thinks he does. As he comes to grips with his false perceptions of himself and his wife, he is overcome with embarrassment at his own vanity.

The history of God's People is filled with epiphanies, or moments of revelation. In the story of the Wise Men who follow the star to Bethlehem, the epiphany occurs when they realize that the child before them is the Messiah, the Son of God. As you travel on your own journey of faith, remember the experience of the Magi. Christmas is celebrated on only one day a year, but if you have a Christmas attitude, then you will have epiphanies throughout the year—moments when you know Jesus is your Messiah. You may have these moments when you participate at Mass or talk with a friend or reach out to help someone. Each epiphany you experience will strengthen your faith and help you take a more active part in the People of God.

One-on-one

Use the questions in this section to explore further the nature of epiphany in the lives of the candidates. Use questions 1 and 3 for class discussion.

Carefully reread the material above. Think about the meaning of epiphany. Then, answer the following questions. Share your answers if you wish.

1. Since beginning the journey to Confirmation, how have you experienced an epiphany in self-knowledge? What did you learn? How did you feel at that moment?

2. How have you experienced an epiphany in your relationship to Jesus? What effect has this insight had in your Confirmation process?

3. What does it mean to have a Christmas attitude all year through? In what way can this Christmas be an epiphany for you?

STUDY

Christmas Giving

When the Magi found Jesus, they offered him gifts of gold, frankincense, and myrrh. These were the kinds of gifts that would be offered to a king in the time of Jesus. The gifts symbolized Jesus' kingship. In a sense, all gifts are symbols. For example, a husband and wife celebrating their wedding anniversary might exchange very personal gifts—an engraved watch or ring—to symbolize their intimacy and oneness. A student graduating from high school, on the other hand, might receive a typewriter to help him or her in a career or in college. The typewriter is a practical gift that is symbolic of the giver's best wishes for success.

1. Suppose you could purchase any gift you wanted for your best friend. What gift would you give? What would you want your gift to show about your friendship?

_____

_____

_____

2. A gift need not be an object. It could also be a service, a part of your time, or a helping hand. What gift other than an object would you like to receive? What would it symbolize to you?

_____

_____

_____

3. Christmas can be an especially difficult time for the poor, the sick, and the elderly. During this time, the parish family makes a special effort to reach out to these people—sometimes with food or clothing, sometimes with services or a helping hand. How do these actions, or gifts, continue the mission of Jesus? How can they help both the giver and the receiver experience an epiphany?

_____

_____

_____

4. How do you feel about giving your time and effort to others in need during Christmastime?

_____

_____

_____

The purpose of this exercise in class is to have the candidates themselves work out the details of a Christmas project which they can carry out during the time between Steps 10 and 11. You should not simply assign a project with all the details worked out. However, it would be a good idea to survey the various service groups and organizations in the parish to determine what projects they are undertaking in order to avoid duplication of efforts. Some Confirmation classes may opt to work in conjunction with a project already in operation. For example, the collection of canned goods and the distribution of food baskets is a traditional Christmas project in many parishes.

Begin this activity by reading or summarizing the introductory paragraph for the group. Then have the group brainstorm ideas for a project. Have one of the candidates record the suggestions on the board, newsprint, or transparency. Be

Christmas Project

Work out a project in which your group can assist the needy of your parish. Each candidate should suggest at least one way he or she would like to help the poor. Then, as a group, choose one of the suggested projects to do together. Discuss how you will go about it and list specific steps you will need to take. What resources will you need? Where will you go for support? How much time will the project take? Use the following worksheet as a guide. (Note: Be sure to evaluate the project when it is completed.)

1. Project: _____

_____

2. What is to be done: _____

_____

sure that each member of the group contributes. Next, have the candidates form groups of three or four to discuss and evaluate the projects listed. Finally, bring the group together again and have them vote on a project that could be carried out easily. For their project, they should consider the place, time, steps to be taken, resources necessary, and extent of the project.

3. Where: _____

_____

4. When: _____

_____

5. Steps to be taken: _____

_____

_____

_____

_____

6. Resources you will need: _____

_____

_____

7. Extent of the project: _____

_____

_____

8. Follow-up on the project: _____

_____

_____

REFLECT

Note: These sections may be done in class or as "at home" assignments.

The Word of God: Ask the candidates to read the passage themselves and then use question 1 for discussion during the session.

From the Holy Father: Read this section from John Paul II to the group and discuss how existence, redemption, and faith are genuine gifts from God. Refer the candidates to question 2.

Dear Candidate: Ask the candidates to read this letter themselves. Then have them spend a few moments discussing what it means to be a source of strength, joy, and peace for others.

REFLECT

From the Holy Father

People today—young people—meet God when they open up to him their very selves (which are gifts) in order to accept and reciprocate the immense gifts which God bestowed in the first place: the gift of existence, the gift of redemption, the gift of faith. And that child who accepted the gifts of the Magi is still the one before whom whole peoples "open their treasures." In the act of this opening before God-Incarnate, the gifts of the human spirit take on particular value. They become the treasures of the various cultures, the spiritual riches of the peoples, of the nations, the common heritage of the whole world. He is the center of this exchange: the same one who accepted the gifts of the Magi. He himself, who is the visible and Incarnate Gift, causes the opening up of souls and that exchange of gifts from which live not only individuals, but also peoples, nations, the whole of humankind (Pope John Paul II, Rome, January 24, 1979).

Dear Candidate

The Church calls you to offer the gift of yourself to God, just as the Magi offered gold, frankincense, and myrrh—symbols of honor in the Orient. "But how?" you ask. "How do I offer myself?" First, you try to see Christ working in every situation of your life. You offer him praise for your family, your friends, your school, your neighborhood. You try to see Christ in everyone and pray that his love becomes a real part of your life.

Then, having followed the star, you take the love of Jesus back into the world. You become more concerned about the problems of other people, and your family and friends begin to find in you a source of strength and joy and peace.

Your Family in Christ

RESPOND

Remind the candidates to review the questions in this section before the next session. You may wish to use question 2 with From the Holy Father.

RESPOND

1. As you celebrate feast days and holidays from year to year, the meaning of those celebrations changes because you change and grow. What new meaning does Christmas have for you this year?

2. How can you become more aware that your life—your existence, your family and friends, your faith—is a gift from God? Write a short prayer thanking God for this gift. Use the prayer in the closing service.

3. What are some of the commercial aspects of Christmas that annoy you the most? How can you de-emphasize the commercial side of Christmas in your own life?

▌PRAYER

Gifted

Thank you, Lord, for the epiphanies in my life.
These are the moments when you have revealed yourself to me through nature or other people, or through your sacraments.
Thank you, Lord, for making yourself known, too, through my conscience.
Thank you, Lord, for the times when, seeing myself as I can be, I have been overwhelmed by your love and your mercy.
I have seen myself act bravely and lovingly.
But I have also seen myself act cowardly and hatefully.
Always, though, you have been here loving me as I am.
Teach me, Lord, to see in all the moments of my life times when I can come to know you better.
Help me to realize that every second is a gift from your hands.
Teach me to act accordingly.
Amen.

REACH OUT

The Christmas project for this session serves as the Reach Out exercise for the week. Encourage each of the candidates to give his or her best effort in carrying out the project chosen. Ask them to record reflections, reactions, and suggestions in their journal-notebooks for the next Group Reunion.

PRAYER

Choose a song appropriate to the Christmas season to sing together, and then have one of the candidates read the prayer aloud to the group as the others listen with their eyes closed.

Stewards in the Kingdom

AIM

To help the candidates learn the meaning of Christian stewardship and to express it in their faith lives.

The life of Archbishop Oscar Romero is an example of Christian stewardship. He was an advocate of peace and justice in El Salvador and gave his life rather than compromise his beliefs. The story is used in this step to show the candidates that there are people in the world who willingly make sacrifices, endure suffering, and even give up their lives to keep their baptismal promises.

Most young people are inspired by the stories of courageous people like Archbishop Romero. They are at an age when they keenly feel the injustices that exist in the world and they are generally willing to involve themselves in activities to help overcome those injustices. However, the candidates cannot take effective social action until they recognize and value the special talents and gifts God has given them. This step asks the candidates to consider how they use their time, talents, and possessions to answer God's call to be caretakers of others. An outline for a project which can be turned into an ongoing ministry is provided for the candidates to use as a focus for their enthusiasm and willingness to help others. It can be used for individual or group projects.

You may find the following material helpful in preparing this lesson:
- Assignments and Service Projects, TM pages 18–19
- Film and Television Analysis, TM page 19

AIMS

This step will focus on the importance good works play in the lives of members of the People of God.

- Archbishop Oscar Romero was an outstanding example of a Christian who was willing to give everything—even his life—for what he believed in.

- Every Christian is called to use his or her gifts and talents to build up the kingdom of God on earth.

- Christians' stewardship—their saving mission—has a priestly aspect, a prophetic aspect, and a ruling aspect.

- Christians can work together to help build up the kingdom of justice and peace on earth.

The Word of God

My brothers and sisters, what good is it to profess faith without practicing it? Such faith has no power to save one, has it? If a brother or sister has nothing to wear and no food for the day, and you say to them, "Goodbye and good luck! Keep warm and well fed," but do not meet their bodily needs, what good is that? So it is with the faith that does nothing in practice. It is thoroughly lifeless.

To such a person one might say, "You have faith and I have works—is that it?" Show me your faith without works, and I will show you the faith that underlies my works! Do you believe that God is one? You are quite right. The demons believe that, and shudder. Do you want proof that without works faith is idle? Was not our father Abraham justified by his works when he offered his son Isaac on the altar? There you see proof that faith was both assisting his works and implemented by his works. You also see how the Scripture was fulfilled which says, "Abraham believed God, and it was credited to him as justice"; for this he received the title "God's friend" *(James 2:14–23)*.

Group Reunion

Since the last session, you have worked on the Christmas project which was to benefit the poor in the parish. Spend a few moments completing an evaluation of what you have done. First, describe your reactions to the project. Then, describe how you felt working with the other members of the group. Finally, make a fairly detailed list of suggestions for improving the project and making it more effective in the future. It would be a good idea to write out your suggestions so that they will not be forgotten.

This Scripture passage may be used as an opening prayer, or later as part of the *Reflect* activities on pages 100–101.

GROUP REUNION

This time should be devoted to an evaluation of the Christmas project. Allow a few moments for the candidates to read the material in this section and to reflect on the questions. Divide the group into smaller groups and have each group discuss their reactions to the project and make a list of suggestions for improving the project. Put the following list of questions on the board, newsprint, or transparency and refer the candidates to them during their analyses:

- Did we do what we set out to do?
- Did everyone in the group take part in the project?
- Did everyone bring a "Christmas attitude" to the project?
- What aspect of the project was the most effective and satisfying?
- What was the least successful part of the project?
- What should we do differently next time?

After the smaller groups have made their examinations of the project, bring them together and make a final list of suggestions.

PREPARE

Read this section aloud to the group or have volunteers read two or three paragraphs each. Direct the candidates to begin work on the questions before discussing the story with others so that their responses to the questions reflect their immediate personal reactions to Archbishop Romero's life.

⌐ PREPARE

Archbishop Oscar

On March 24, 1980, a shot rang out in the cathedral of San Salvador. Archbishop Oscar Romero lay dead on the floor. He had been preparing to celebrate Mass for his people. But assassins wanted to silence the loving man who was rallying his flock to be real signs of hope in the war-torn country of El Salvador.

Archbishop Romero was appointed to his post by Pope Paul VI in 1977. One of his first acts as archbishop was to preside at the funeral of one of his priests who had been killed. During the first months of the year, a cruel repression had been unleashed against the Church. Priests and sisters were jailed and threatened. The archbishop would bury seven of his priests before he himself met death.

But Archbishop Oscar discovered something even worse than persecution of the clergy. He discovered that the government was repressing the poor, the farmers, the suffering families. The archbishop saw that he had to side with the people. He decided to join them in their suffering.

In the name of God, Archbishop Romero spoke to all. To his people he proclaimed a "dangerous" message of conversion. He spoke out against everyone who was hurting the poor. He could not rest while some people were making the lives of so many miserable.

The outspoken archbishop received many death threats. The powerful and selfish did not want Oscar Romero to rally the poor.

His priests asked him to be more careful—more security-minded. The archbishop refused. He said, "The shepherd does not want security when security is not given to his flock."

Two weeks before he was assassinated, Archbishop Romero preached a sermon in the cathedral. In that sermon, he said, "As a pastor, I am obliged by divine command to give my life for those I love—and that is for all Salvadorans, even for those who may assassinate me." As an advocate of justice and peace for all his people, Archbishop Oscar was willing to risk and to lose his life in order to preach a Gospel without compromise.

One-on-one

For a few moments, reflect in silence on how the poor people of El Salvador must have felt when Archbishop Romero was killed. Then, answer the following questions. You may share your responses with your fellow candidates if you wish.

1. What is your personal reaction to the life and death of Archbishop Oscar Romero?

_____

_____

_____

Direct the candidates to reflect quietly on what the feelings of the people of El Salvador were, and then to answer the questions themselves. After they have completed their work, invite volunteers to discuss their responses. After sharing, discuss the important points of the story, stressing Archbishop Romero's strong faith and willingness to die for it. Help the candidates understand that although they may never be asked to die for their beliefs, they need to develop an attitude of willingness to make sacrifices in order to actualize their Christian stewardship. Point out, also, that as they grow in their faith, they will grow stronger in their ability to sacrifice and endure suffering for the faith.

2. Archbishop Romero took his stewardship of God's kingdom very seriously. How do you see yourself caring for God's People?

_____

_____

_____

3. Who are the truly needy in your life? What can you do to meet their needs?

_____

_____

_____

4. What is one gift or talent you have been given which would help you be a steward of God's kingdom on earth?

_____

_____

_____

STUDY

Summarize this section for the group and write the three statements of paragraph 2 on the board, newsprint, or transparency:

■ When I have extra time, I choose to . . .
■ When I have extra money, I use it to . . .
■ I try to help others by . . .

Then, go through the questions one at a time and ask each individual to respond as quickly and honestly as possible. Jot down responses and note any patterns. Explore what the responses indicate about the group's readiness to act as stewards—taking care of God's gifts and resources.

Spend a few moments at the end of this session discussing the statement, "Through Baptism, you are a priest, prophet, and ruler." Ask volunteers to give examples of how they can find and express the qualities of the priest, the prophet, and the ruler in their own lives.

Direct the candidates to read the material under "A Ministry" and then read through the outline before they begin work. Ask if there are any questions about what they are to do. They should work on question 1 as part of the large group and then form smaller groups for the questions which follow. As an alternative, have the candidates begin work on the outline in class and then arrange to meet with their small group members sometime during the week to complete the work.

┌ STUDY

Use Your Talents

Jesus told the parable of a master who gave out silver pieces to his servants according to each one's ability: two of the servants invested the silver pieces, but one buried it in the ground. While the master praised the first two servants for using his resources properly, he was very unhappy with the one who buried the money (*see* Matthew 25:14–30).

God has made his People responsible for his kingdom on earth. He meant them to use everything he has given them—within them and around them—as a means of knowing, loving, and serving him. Your stewardship, then, means not only taking care of God's gifts and resources but also giving an account of how each gift and resource has been used. Test your stewardship by honestly completing the following statements: (1) "When I have extra time, I choose to . . ." (2) "When I have extra money, I use it to . . ." (3) "I try to help others by . . ."

Following Christ means looking carefully at the way you use your material possessions, the way you spend your time, and the way you use your gifts. It means that you use your time, talents, and possessions to answer God's call to be a caretaker of others. In imitation of Jesus, you can decide how best to use all that you are and all that you have to further God's kingdom on earth.

Being God's steward also means that you participate in the saving mission of the Church. Through Baptism, you are a priest, prophet, and ruler. As a *priestly* person, you can become involved in the worship of the Church. As a *prophetic* person, you can help spread the Gospel. As a *ruling* person, you can help build up God's kingdom by working for social justice and peace.

A Ministry

Draw up a list of how caring for the needs of God's People is being done in your parish. Some activities such as reading and distributing the Eucharist are apparent. But perhaps there is much more going on behind the scenes, such as visiting the elderly or doing housework for families in which both parents work.

Use the outline below to help you find a project which you can turn into an ongoing ministry. It can be something that you work on individually or with the other candidates.

1. As a group, list some of the specific tasks you could do in each of the following areas:

   Liturgy: _____

   Education: _____

   Family life: _____

   Social justice: _____

Other: _____

_____

_____

2. Now, describe a project in which you think your talents would be best used. You may wish to work in small groups.

_____

_____

_____

_____

3. Who is the person you should contact to find out more information about the project?

_____

4. How much time per week can you offer?

_____

5. When could you begin working on the project?

_____

Note: These sections may be done in class or as "at home" assignments.

The Word of God: Ask a volunteer to read this passage from the Epistle of James aloud to the group. After a moment of silence, refer the candidates to question 2 for discussion during this session.

From the Holy Father: Read this section aloud to the group. Ask: "What is the difference between doing something for others just to feel good and performing service for others in union with Christ?"

Dear Candidate: Ask volunteers to read this letter to the candidate and then use question 1 for discussion on the meaning of stewardship.

⌐ REFLECT

From the Holy Father

The Church has always proclaimed a love of preference for the poor. Perhaps the language is new, but the reality is not. Nor has the Church taken a narrow view of poverty and the poor. Poverty, certainly, is often a matter of material deprivation. But it is also a matter of spiritual impoverishment, the lack of human liberties, and the result of any violation of human rights and human dignity. There is also a very special and pitiable form of poverty: the poverty of selfishness, the poverty of those who have and will not share, of those who could be rich by giving but choose to be poor by keeping everything they have. These people, too, need help.

The Christian view is that human beings are to be valued for what they are, not for what they have. (Pope John Paul II, San Antonio, Texas, September 13, 1987).

Dear Candidate

In Baptism, you were anointed with oil and given the responsibility to be "priest, prophet, and ruler." Living out your baptismal promises is not always easy. Sometimes, it requires sacrifice and suffering. But as you grow in faith and in understanding of your mission, you become stronger and more willing to offer your time and talents to God and his People. You begin to relate to all people as your brothers and sisters in Christ, and you look upon your gifts as belonging not just to you but primarily to God and to those with whom you share your life.

In these ways, you become a good steward of all of creation. You become more careful of the way in which you help conserve and protect the earth's natural and human resources. You realize that religion is not something apart from life but a way of helping you relate to God so that you recognize your dependence on him for everything. Your time, talent, and treasure belong to him, since he gave you all that you are and have. Think carefully about how you can best serve him, and make your daily plans according to his plan for you.

Your Family in Christ

RESPOND

1. In your own words, define the term *stewardship*. How will the sacrament of Confirmation help you be a good steward of God's kingdom on earth?

2. Stewardship and service often require sacrifice. Archbishop Romero, for example, was asked to give the ultimate gift—his life. How do you feel about being called to take care of, to serve, and to sacrifice because of your membership in the Church?

PRAYER

Spirited

Lord, you call me to look around my world and to see that my life has meaning.
My presence here can make a difference.
I look at myself, and I know that you have given me many gifts—my sense of humor, my ability to serve you, my capacity for being happy.
I want to use all my gifts for you, Lord.
I offer you all that I am and all that I have—not just what I think I have but everything you have given me.
Help me to discover every day, Lord, new and better ways of serving you and all people.
Give me the strength I need to fight against poverty and injustice, in all their forms.
Give me the vision I need to see what you see and to do what you want done.
Here I am, Lord.
Send me.

RESPOND

Remind the candidates to review the questions in this section before the next class session. You may wish to use question 2 with From the Holy Father and question 1 with Dear Candidate for discussion during this session.

REACH OUT

Encourage the candidates to review their responses to the ministry outline on pages 98–99 or to complete those outlines with their small working group sometime before the next session. Suggest that they talk about their responses with their sponsors and record reflections on that conversation in their journal-notebooks.

PRAYER

Have the candidates gather together in a group as you read the Corporal Works of Mercy on page 186 of the text. Then invite individuals to take turns reading individual verses from the prayer.

Taking a Stand

AIM

To review with the candidates the steps for forming conscience and to help them reflect on the importance of making correct moral choices.

The formation of conscience is a process which begins during childhood and continues throughout life. As children mature and grow, they move beyond their early childish understanding of the reasons some actions are right and others are wrong, to a fuller appreciation of moral principles and God's law. It is important, therefore, to help maturing young people see their responsibility for developing their consciences according to the teaching of the Christian community.

Contemporary culture and peer pressure help young people see self-honesty as the primary moral issue in decision making. Though self-honesty is indeed an important part of decision making, the Christian community also shares a tradition of moral teaching and a common sense of conscience formed by the faith of the community. This step takes the opportunity to remind the candidates of this communal dimension of conscience.

Candidates' understandings of the nature of conscience may be at different stages. So, this step will introduce them to the fundamentals of good moral decision making. There will be opportunities later on in the Confirmation process to develop some of these themes further.

No special materials are recommended for this step.

AIMS

This step will focus on your ability to make faith decisions and moral choices. It will help you review the steps involved in forming a good Catholic conscience.

- It is important for everyone to have sound moral principles on which to form moral judgments.

- Forming and following your conscience is a personal responsibility—one you cannot delegate to others.

- Every Catholic must form his or her conscience based on God's Law as it is interpreted by the Church.

- Every moral decision should have several characteristics in order to be a good decision.

The Word of God

People even brought babies to Jesus to be touched by him. When the disciples saw this, they scolded them roundly; but Jesus called for the children, saying: "Let the little children come to me. Do not shut them off. The reign of God belongs to such as these. Trust me when I tell you that whoever does not accept the kingdom of God as a child will not enter into it."

One of the ruling class asked him then, "Good Teacher, what must I do to share in everlasting life?" Jesus said to him, "Why call me 'good'? None is good but God alone. You know the commandments: You shall not commit adultery. You shall not kill. You shall not steal. You shall not bear dishonest witness. Honor your father and your mother." The man replied, "I have kept all these since I was a boy." When Jesus heard this, he said to him: "There is one thing further you must do. Sell all you have and give to the poor. You will have treasure in heaven. Then come and follow me" *(Luke 18:15–22)*.

Group Reunion

Since the last session, you have been trying to establish an ongoing service project, or ministry, in your parish. Take a few moments to report on how you are progressing. Have you already discovered something to do? Have you begun your project? What opportunities have surfaced? Have you encountered any difficulties in establishing a ministry? Those who have not yet begun may wish to establish a support group to make the task easier.

This Scripture passage may be used as an opening prayer, or later as part of the *Reflect* activities on pages 107–109.

GROUP REUNION

During the last session, the candidates were asked to give some serious thought to becoming involved in long-term service projects with the parish community. It is not expected that each of the candidates will have made final plans for such service projects, but this is a good time to help them to continue the planning stage.

Direct the candidates to read this section and to discuss the questions about their progress in establishing an ongoing ministry in the parish. If there are candidates who are having difficulty finding a project or implementing one, take them aside and work with them directly in solving their problems. Those who have not yet found a project may be able to join a group in the parish that is already established. Try to involve each candidate in a project.

PREPARE

Begin by reading the opening sentence aloud to the group and pausing for a moment for spontaneous responses to the question (How easy is it to stick to your moral principles and religious convictions?). Direct the candidates to read the rest of the section to themselves.

⌐PREPARE

Convictions

How easy is it to stick to your moral principles and religious convictions? In his Gospel, Saint Matthew describes the time when Jesus returned to the town in which he grew up—Nazareth. Jesus spent time teaching in the local synagogue, but the reaction of his former neighbors was not good. "Where did this man get such wisdom and miraculous powers? Isn't this the carpenter's son? Isn't Mary known to be his mother? Where did he get all this?" In other words, they were saying, "Isn't he just like us? What makes him so special?" Jesus responded, "No prophet is without honor except in his native place."

Sometimes, the people closest to you—your friends and peers—are the greatest challenge to your beliefs and principles. It isn't always easy to take a stand. Consider the following situation: Carla and Teresa went to the shopping mall with Anna. Anna picked out a gold chain and paid the cashier, but Carla and Teresa also saw Anna take a pair of gold earrings and put them in her coat pocket.

One-on-one

Spend a few moments imagining the scene you have just read. Then, answer the following questions. If you care to, share your answers with your fellow candidates.

1. What are some of the different approaches Carla and Teresa might take to the shoplifting incident?

   _____

   _____

   _____

2. Briefly describe an incident in your life like the one in the shopping mall. What kind of pressure did you feel? What did you do?

   _____

   _____

   _____

Forming Your Conscience

A conscience is very personal. It is fitted to you. Forming and following your conscience is a *personal responsibility*. Like many other responsibilities, it is not one that can be delegated. While conscience is not your intellect, it is the *use* of your intellect on moral questions.

Very simply stated, your conscience is your mind making a judgment here and now as to whether or not an action is right or wrong. You look at an action, and your judgment is "That's a good thing to do!" Or your judgment is "That's a bad thing to do!" Then, you *choose* to follow or not to follow the judgment you have made. You are free to act morally rightly or wrongly.

Forming your conscience includes attention to every detail which influences your moral judgment—the practice of good deeds, prayer, sensitivity to the Spirit, consultation, peer pressure, family customs, society, etc. But to be more specific, the formation of conscience means knowing and understanding the most important sources of moral knowledge: *(a)* God, *(b)* God's Law as outlined and interpreted by his Church, and *(c)* God's Law as seen in the norms and standards of good people.

Read the paragraph and go through each of the six qualities involved in making a moral judgment. Ask candidates to suggest specific examples to accompany each. Then, direct the candidates to begin work on the chart individually by filling in the first two columns: describing the ways they are *now* using the quality, and ways they can *improve* their use of the quality. When they have completed the first two columns, have them form small groups and discuss ways in which the group can support each other in using the qualities of good moral judgment. Ask the group which quality they think is the most difficult to use. Finally, urge the candidates to reread their responses to the chart at home and to reflect on ways they can grow in taking moral stands.

In learning to make accurate moral judgments, you open yourself up to the truth and are willing to learn from certain norms outside yourself what is right and what is wrong. As your knowledge and understanding grow, you are more able to act in a morally right way—to act according to your conscience. You are able to act freely and without guilt because each of your decisions includes the following:

1. *A good intention.* You analyze fully and sincerely the action, your motivation for wanting to do the action, and the effects of the action on your own growth and on the growth of others.
2. *Knowledge of Christ's teachings.* You study not only Jesus' words but also his actions. You listen to his representatives as they have applied the parables to the present times. You take to heart not just the letter of the law but the spirit of the law.
3. *The advice and counsel of others.* You ask others for help in times of doubt and at times of decision. You care about what the other members of the People of God think, and you try to use their experience and knowledge in your own life.
4. *An awareness of current moral issues.* You read both the pros and cons in the debates on important social and moral issues. You learn how the Catholic Church views these issues. You understand that your knowledge is not absolute—that you must keep your mind open in order to sift facts, weigh opinions, and form judgments.
5. *Prayer.* You ask for God's help not only in making a particular decision but also for help in making all your decisions and actions a response to his love.
6. *Honesty.* You admit to God, to yourself, and to the other members of the People of God that you have made mistakes and will probably do so again. But with God's help and his People's help, you will continue to grow.

Now, use the chart on the following page to outline your own approach to taking a moral stand. For each of the qualities listed below, describe one way you are now using the quality to make moral choices. Then, describe one way you can improve. Finally, describe a way your group can support and encourage each quality.

QUALITY	NOW	IMPROVE	GROUP SUPPORT
1. Good Intention			
2. Knowledge			
3. Counsel			
4. Awareness			
5. Prayer			
6. Honesty			

REFLECT

From the Holy Father

The Church needs you. The world needs you, because it needs Christ, and you belong to Christ. And so I ask you to accept your responsibility in the Church, the responsibility of your Catholic education: to help—by your words, and above all, by the examples of your lives—to spread the Gospel.

Dear young people, by a real Christian life, by the practice of your religion, you are called to give witness to your faith. And because actions speak louder than words, you are called to proclaim, by the conduct of your daily lives, that you really do believe that Jesus Christ is Lord! (Pope John Paul II, New York City, October 3, 1979).

REFLECT

Note: These sections may be done in class or as "at home" assignments.

The Word of God: Ask two volunteers to take turns reading the passage on page 103 to the group. Then, open a discussion on the role of Jesus in making decisions by using question 3 on page 109 as a primer.

From the Holy Father: Ask the candidates to read this section to themselves. When they have finished, discuss the role of the Christian community in helping its members form mature consciences.

Dear Candidate: Read or summarize this letter for the candidates and use question 1 for a discussion starter.

Dear Candidate

Perhaps the most difficult challenge you face is in the area of right and wrong. At the same time as your peers are telling you that "anything goes," you may be experiencing a realization that you have choices to make. At the same time as you may be experiencing conflict in your desires, you might also be questioning every aspect of your Christian faith. But even when you are confused, you can rely on God to provide for you. Not only can you measure the morality of your actions by Scripture, but you also have Tradition—the Word of God handed down through the Church.

Catholic Christians believe that the pope and bishops are descendants of the Apostles. When Jesus spoke to these Apostles before he ascended to the Father, he said: "Go therefore and make disciples of all the nations. Baptize them in the name of the Father, and of the Son, and of the Holy Spirit. Teach them to carry out everything I have commanded you. And know that I am with you always, until the end of the world." When God's People read those words, they are filled with the knowledge that their faith is based not only on words but also on actions. Throughout the history of the Church, Christ has remained faithful. Despite the mistakes of men and women, Christ has kept the doctrine of the Church free from error.

So, your faith and moral decisions are not just yours to make. For if you belong to the larger Family called the Catholic Church, you must care what the Family thinks. And as you measure your decisions against the Word of God in Scripture and Tradition, you learn how loved you are by the Living God.

Your Family in Christ

RESPOND

Remind the candidates to review the questions before the next session. If there is time during the session, you may wish to discuss question 1 with Dear Candidate and question 3 with The Word of God.

RESPOND

1. Give an example of how your moral choices are influenced by pressure from others your age or by popular culture (television, music, and films).

2. If the influence described above is negative, how can you bring more positive influences into your moral decision making?

3. How does your friendship with Jesus affect your decision making? Do you ever pray about a decision before you have to make it?

Shared Growth

A friend is a friend when all is well and you agree.

A friend is also a friend in darkness and pain, and—yes, even in disagreement.

A friend is a person you love no matter what: somewhere in the middle region of time where nothing is clear or definite and so much is hard to figure out.

The Spirit gives trust to hope for a future time of reconciliation and peace.

Time teaches that love must be stringless and with no conditions: not even returned love, returned care.

Arguing and parting of ways is sometimes a way to understand and grow.

In coming back together in truth and trust, friends can be reborn.

Then, friends who have disagreed can lean on one another, help one another, and support one another in the friendship, the love of Jesus Christ.

Help us, Lord.

We want to know and to follow your Law—together.

REACH OUT

Encourage the candidates to discuss with their sponsors the material on conscience and taking a stand. They may wish to present their responses to the chart exercise. Suggest that they ask sponsors to share examples of situations where they had to stick to moral principles in a difficult situation.

PRAYER

Invite the candidates to meditate silently on a wrong moral judgment they have made in the past and to think of how they will make a different judgment in the future. Then, ask a volunteer to read the prayer aloud to the group. Group members should say the last two lines of the prayer aloud as their response.

Justice

AIM

To help the candidates reflect on the importance of justice in the life of the Christian and the duty to help build a just society.

Justice is a virtue which leads a person to respect and be concerned for another person's rights and well-being. It applies to personal relationships and to the political, social, and economic structures and organizations that people create. Christians are called to help build the kingdom of God here and now, and the promotion of justice is an important part of that mission. True love and charity cannot exist without justice.

The virtue of justice is not contrary to the spirit of the Beatitudes—blessed are the lowly, the persecuted. Jesus calls each Christian not only to an attitude of faith, trust, and acceptance, but to a readiness to reach out and help others in need. As Saint John warns, "Let us love in deed and in truth and not merely talk about it" (1 John 3:18).

In this step, the candidates will examine the virtue of justice as it applies to both personal relationships and social, political, and economic issues. They will see that it is not always easy to find a just solution. Still, with reflection and consideration of another person's rights, a person can act justly in a difficult situation. The candidates will also examine some of the social justice issues that Christians are concerned about and reflect on their own willingness to respond to those needs.

Resource

The following material will be helpful at this point in the Confirmation preparation process: Form 15, Prayer and Planning Session—Lent.

AIMS

This step will help you reflect on the importance of justice in the life of the Christian and the duty to help build a just society.

- Justice is a virtue which leads a person to look out for another person's rights and well-being.

- The virtue of justice also applies to the political, social, and economic structures and organizations that people create. Christians help build the kingdom of God by promoting social justice.

- Justice goes hand in hand with love. There cannot be true justice without love.

The Word of God

Jesus said to his disciples, "When the Son of Man comes in his glory, escorted by all the angels of heaven, he will sit upon his royal throne, and all the nations will be assembled before him. Then he will separate them into two groups, as a shepherd separates sheep from goats. The sheep he will place on his right hand, the goats on his left. The king will say to those on his right; 'Come. You have my Father's blessing! Inherit the kingdom prepared for you from the creation of the world. For I was hungry and you gave me food. I was thirsty and you gave me drink. I was a stranger and you welcomed me, naked and you clothed me. I was ill and you comforted me, in prison and you came to visit me.' Then the just will ask him: 'Lord, when did we see you hungry and feed you or see you thirsty and give you drink? When did we welcome you away from home or clothe you in your nakedness? When did we visit you when you were ill or in prison?' The king will answer them; 'I assure you, as often as you did it for one of my least brothers or sisters, you did it for me!'" *(Matthew 25:31–40).*

This Scripture passage may be used as an opening prayer, or later as part of the *Reflect* activities on pages 115–117.

Group Reunion

Over the past few sessions, you have been learning that you need to have something to believe in, you need to take a stand, and you have a ministry of service to perform in the Church. As you start this new season, look back for a moment in order to discover how you are identifying with the People of God. How have the past few sessions made you feel about being a Catholic? What questions do you still have about being a fully initiated member of the Church? What is one accomplishment in the Family of God that you would like to have made before your time of preparation for Confirmation is completed? How can you work toward that accomplishment during this coming Lent?

GROUP REUNION

Direct the candidates to read this section and spend a few moments in silence reflecting on how they identify with the People of God. Keep a quiet tone in this reunion, and ask candidates to take turns sharing their responses to the text questions. Answer any of their questions about being fully initiated members of the Church. Suggest that they pay special attention to the last two questions as they describe the accomplishment in the Family of God that they would like to make.

PREPARE

This section presents a situation in which a woman must decide whether or not to have her elderly mother move in with her family. It is the kind of issue that many families face and it sometimes raises strong emotions. Allow the candidates a few moments to read this section and to review the details of Joan's situation.

▌PREPARE

A Dilemma

Joan faces a decision. Her mother, who is seventy-five years old, is finding it difficult to live in the city and to maintain her own apartment. It is a struggle for her to do all the shopping and cleaning herself. Although Joan visits her mother on weekends, her full-time job prevents her from giving her mother the care she needs. Yet, the job is important, and the family depends on Joan's income to help pay the bills. With four children, family expenses are high. Quitting her job is out of the question.

Joan sees two alternatives. The first is to place her mother in a retirement home. Although this would ensure her mother's physical well-being, Joan knows that her mother would find the adjustment difficult. On occasions when she raised the issue of a retirement home, her mother got very upset. Furthermore, the only suitable facility is miles away.

Joan's second alternative is to have her mother live with the family. This, too, has its problems. Two of the children would have to share the same bedroom. The house would have to be quieter, and they would all have to adjust to the needs of an older person. Joan is afraid that additional restrictions on activities around the house would be unfair to the teenagers. The house would be more crowded, and the little privacy that Joan and her husband do enjoy might be jeopardized.

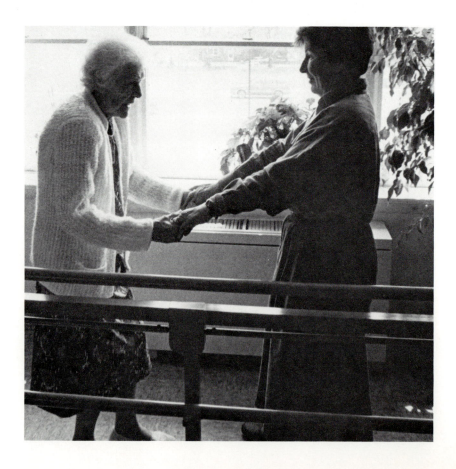

One-on-one

For a few moments, review Joan's dilemma. Try to imagine what the most just solution might be. Remember, justice is a virtue which leads a person to look out for another person's rights and well-being. Then, answer the following questions. Share your answers if you wish.

1. Do you think that Joan's mother has a right to be cared for in her old age by Joan and her family? Why or why not?

2. What are the rights of Joan's children in this situation? Should they be expected to alter their life-styles if their grandmother moves into the house? Explain.

3. Given the two alternatives Joan faces, what would you decide? Can you think of any other solutions that would protect the rights of Joan's mother and of the family?

4. What is your own definition of *justice*?

After the candidates have had time to review the above section, have them work individually on the questions in this section. To help the candidates get a clearer picture of the dilemma, suggest that they note the consequences of each of the alternatives (placing Joan's mother in a retirement home or having her live with the family). When they have finished, ask them to share their answers.

This section has two aims: to help the candidates understand the nature of justice as a personal virtue, and to reflect on justice as it applies to social situations. Begin by asking the candidates to read the first three paragraphs. Discuss the material with the following questions:

- What is a virtue?
- Describe the virtue of justice.
- Describe the two ways justice works.

Ask the candidates to review their answers to question 4 on the previous page and to make a note of any changes in their definitions of justice.

Next, have the candidates read the material in "Social Justice." Ask them to describe in their own words what social justice means. Then, direct them to work individually on the exercise. After they have finished, invite them to share ideas on what the group can do to address the social justice issues listed. Make a list of their responses on the board, newsprint, or transparency and ask the candidates to select one or two issues for which they might work.

STUDY

Habits of Justice

A virtue is a strength or good habit which helps people to do what is morally good and to avoid what is evil. When practiced regularly, the strength becomes almost second nature. The virtue of justice is sometimes described as the minimum measure of charity. In other words, no matter what situation you find yourself in, justice is the bottom-line Christian response. If you are not responding to another person justly, you are not following Jesus' commandment of love.

Justice begins with respect for another person's rights. Justice demands that you constantly avoid denying another person his or her rights. Justice works in two ways. First, it keeps you aware of another person's rights. You understand more clearly how another person should be treated as a child of God. Second, justice provides a perspective on the relative importance of different rights. For example, people have a right to speak and communicate. But in a library setting, other people have the right to peace and quiet in order to study. Justice helps a person see that one right is more important than another.

Justice also brings with it a desire to combat injustice when possible. Christians strive to see that society is just. It is not enough simply to avoid injuring another person's rights. In situations where Christians have the opportunity to prevent or eliminate injustice, they are called to do so.

Social Justice

In the early days of the Church, the followers of Jesus tried to be as close to one another as members of a family. If one family had no oil for their lamps, the family that had more than enough oil would share. If children lost their parents to sickness or accidental death, another family would take those children in.

Whenever the followers of Jesus forgot about the care and concern they were supposed to have for the rights of others, someone would try to remind them. Down through the centuries, many saints and heroes in the Church have given their lives for the rights of others.

In the simplest of terms, social justice means that the followers of Jesus cannot worry just about themselves. Jesus taught his friends to be aware of the needs of others and to help and care for one another. What people do in Poland affects the people in El Salvador. What people in the United States choose to do affects people in Asia. It is important for Christians to know the world and its problems. Knowing world problems helps people make just and loving decisions.

What motivates the Christian community to work for social justice is the call to build up the kingdom of God. It is the vocation of every Christian. Your actions—and failure to act—affect others. Either you help build God's kingdom of justice and peace as the opportunities arise, or you stand as an obstacle to it. There is no neutral ground.

Behind every issue of social justice, there are basic rights of people at stake. For each of the issues listed below, describe the rights of people involved in that issue. Then, determine what you as an individual can do about it. Finally, offer some suggestions as to what the group can do to address the issue.

ISSUE	RIGHTS	YOUR RESPONSE	GROUP RESPONSE
World hunger			
Nuclear war			
Discrimination			
Poverty			
Protection of the environment			

REFLECT

From the Holy Father

Basic human and Christian values are challenged by crime, violence and terrorism. Honesty and justice in business and public life are often violated. Throughout the world great sums are spent on armaments while millions of poor people struggle for the basic necessities of life. Alcohol and drug abuse take a heavy toll on individuals and on society. The commercial exploitation of sex through pornography offends human dignity and endangers the future of young people. Family life is subjected to powerful pressures; fornication, adultery, divorce and contraception are wrongly regarded as acceptable by many. The unborn are cruelly killed and the lives of the elderly are in serious danger from a mentality that would open the door wide to euthanasia.

REFLECT

Note: These sections may be done in class or as "at home" assignments.

The Word of God: Ask a volunteer to read this passage aloud. Allow a few moments for reflection and use question 2 for group discussion.

From the Holy Father: Ask the candidates to read this message to themselves and to spend a few moments reflecting on question 1. Ask volunteers to share responses.

In the face of all this, however, faithful Christians must not be discouraged, nor can they conform to the spirit of the world. Instead, they are called upon to acknowledge the supremacy of God and his law, to raise their voices and join their efforts on behalf of moral values, to offer society the example of their own upright conduct, and to help those in need. Christians are called to act with the serene conviction that grace is more powerful than sin because of the victory of Christ's Cross (Pope John Paul II, Miami, Florida, September 11, 1987).

Dear Candidate: Have one of the candidates read this letter aloud to the group. Refer to question 3 and give the candidates a few moments to work on their personal pledges to try to be just. Ask them to share their pledges with another candidate.

Dear Candidate

The quest for justice is not something new to the Christian. It was a concern for the Apostle and the early Church. "I ask you, how can God's love survive in a person who has enough of this world's goods yet closes his or her heart to someone in need? Let us love in deed and in truth and not merely talk about it" *(1 John 3:17–18).*

By reflecting on the virtues of justice, moderation, courage, and prudence, you will see more clearly the importance of loving in deed and in truth and not merely talking about it. A life of faith does not come easily. It takes patience with yourself and confidence in God's ways. But time and God are on your side.

Your Family in Christ

RESPOND

Remind the candidates to review these questions before the next session. If there is enough time, discuss question 2 after The Word of God, question 1 after From the Holy Father, and question 3 after Dear Candidate.

RESPOND

1. Being just often requires thought and reflection. Sometimes, as in the case of Joan's mother moving in with the family, the rights of individuals are not always clear. It is a good idea in such instances to seek help before making a decision. If you were not clear as to how to be just in a particular situation, with whom would you talk? Why would you value that person's advice?

2. What justice issues do you think are most important in your own neighborhood right now? What can you do to work on these issues?

3. Write a personal pledge to try to be more just a person. Include in your pledge at least three areas in which you feel you need improvement.

◤ PRAYER

Tunnel Vision

I went through a tunnel once.
I was really scared at first, because all I could see was darkness.
Then, all of a sudden, I saw a tiny spot of sunlight.
I knew that I was getting there.
I knew that pretty soon I would come through the tunnel out onto the other side.
Even though I had a ways to go, I was happy.

When I look at this weary world and its injustices, I get tunnel vision.
I feel that the justice journey will never end.
Sometimes, I have felt as if I haven't done anything that amounted to anything.
But you'll be here with me, Lord, for the whole trip.
Stay with me, Lord—or (I should say) keep me with you.
Let me have a peek at the light of your justice.
Then, I can travel toward that light.
I can touch the weary world and refresh it a bit.
I know the kingdom of justice can come!
Keep my eyes on the light, Lord!

REACH OUT

Ask the candidate to explore the justice issues in their neighborhoods. Encourage them to ask friends and family members about the needs of people they are aware of. The candidates should list the issues and possible ways to work on each one. Tell them that this information will be used during the next Group Reunion.

PRAYER

If you use this prayer to close the session, ask two volunteers to read it aloud to the group. Invite the class to respond by reading together the Beatitudes, page 185 of the text.

Moderation

AIM

To help the candidates see that moderation, or temperance, is a Christian responsibility and is essential to be a well-balanced and healthy person.

Moderation, or temperance, is a virtue that affects the well-being of a person's body, mind, and spirit, by helping one control and direct his or her energies and emotions. As the candidates approach full initiation into the Christian community, they should spend time reflecting on how the virtue of moderation applies to all aspects of their lives—their physical health, their emotional well-being, and their relationships with others.

This step focuses on moderation as the balance and harmony of an individual within him or herself, and in relationships with others. The candidates will think about the role of balance and harmony in their lives and consider some of the threats to moderation—especially drugs and alcohol. They will fill out a brief survey which will help them clarify their own attitudes toward the use of drugs and alcohol. The questions are presented in such a way that the candidates can discuss the matter without revealing personal involvement with the substances.

Resource

You may wish to celebrate the sacrament of Reconciliation either at the end of this session or sometime in the near future. Refer to Form 29, Celebration of a Penitential Rite.

AIMS

This step will help you see that moderation, or temperance, in all that you do is part of your responsibility as a Christian and essential for you to be a well-balanced and healthy person.

- Moderation is a virtue which helps you to control and to direct your energies and emotions.

- Drugs and alcohol are powerful chemicals. The use of drugs or excessive drinking is contrary to moderate behavior and can cause serious physical and emotional harm.

- Christians apply the virtue of moderation to all aspects of their lives—their physical health, their emotional well-being, and their relationships with others.

- It takes desire and practice to develop the habit of moderation in behavior.

The Word of God

Put aside now all the anger and quick temper, the malice, the insults, the foul language. Stop lying to one another. What you have done is put aside your old self with its past deeds and put on a new self, one who grows in knowledge as you are formed anew in the image of your Creator.

Because you are God's chosen ones, holy and beloved, clothe yourselves with heartfelt mercy, with kindness, humility, meekness, and patience. Bear with one another; forgive whatever grievances you have against one another. Forgive as the Lord has forgiven you. Over all these virtues, put on love, which binds the rest together and makes them perfect. Christ's peace must reign in your hearts, since as members of the one Body you have been called to that peace. Dedicate yourself to thankfulness. Let the word of Christ, rich as it is, dwell in you. In wisdom made perfect, instruct and admonish one another. Sing gratefully to God from your hearts in psalms, hymns, and inspired songs. Whatever you do, whether in speech or in action, do it in the name of the Lord Jesus. Give thanks to God the Father through him (*Colossians 3:8–10, 12–17*).

This Scripture passage may be used as an opening prayer, or later as part of the *Reflect* activities on pages 125–126.

Group Reunion

During the last session, you explored the importance of the virtue of justice in the life of the Christian. Christians constantly work to eliminate injustice from social, political, and economic structures that threaten people's basic human rights. Since last session, what human needs have you noticed? How have you been more aware of people's rights? How have you tried to be more just? In what ways have you supported one another in practicing the virtue of justice? Spend a few moments sharing your responses.

GROUP REUNION

For the Reach Out assignment of the last session, the candidates were asked to explore the justice issues in their neighborhoods and to ask family and friends about the needs of others that they have noticed. Direct the candidates to read the material in this section and to discuss the questions. For the first two questions, ask them to refer to their findings from Reach Out.

PREPARE

This story about Glenn and the school orchestra introduces the notion of balance and harmony and how it is achieved through work and patience. Direct the candidates to read this section. When they have finished, ask volunteers for other examples where balance and harmony (control and direction) are important.

⌐ PREPARE

Harmony

Glenn had the opportunity of a lifetime. Mr. Jefferson, the conductor of the school orchestra, was going to be out of town for a whole week. He had asked Glenn to take over the rehearsals during his absence. The orchestra had only fifteen practice days left before the spring concert. Although Glenn had helped Mr. Jefferson rehearse the brass and strings before, he had never taken charge of the whole orchestra. Glenn was an excellent musician. He felt confident that he could handle the job.

But the first practice was a disaster. Glenn tapped the orchestra to attention and led them through a simple exercise. What noise! The horns were too loud. The piano sounded out of tune. The timpani were off rhythm. The strings could scarcely be heard.

Glenn was worried. He could not decide whether his conducting or the individual musicians were at fault. With the principal's permission, Glenn organized extra practice sessions during lunch hour and after study hall. For the next three days, he worked with each section of the orchestra separately. The violins grew stronger. The brass toned down. The drums caught the beat. The piano was tuned. Most of all, Glenn gained confidence.

On Friday, Glenn brought the whole orchestra together again and worked on timing and blend. After a few false starts, everything began to click. The result was very encouraging. There was balance and harmony. The music was strong and clear.

When he returned, Mr. Jefferson commended both Glenn and the orchestra for what they had accomplished together.

One-on-one

Spend a few moments reviewing the story of Glenn and the school orchestra. Try to capture some of the feelings and frustrations the orchestra might have had. Try to imagine how Glenn felt during the experience. Then, answer the questions below. Share your answers if you wish.

1. Recall a time in your life when you felt out of balance. Describe what had happened to cause the feeling. How did you react? What did you do?

2. Why is balance and harmony important for living? How can a person gain balance if it has been lost?

3. List two or three things which can throw someone out of balance. Why are these things threats? What can be done about them?

Personal Balance

Christian living is a call to balance and harmony within yourself and with others. Moderation, restraint, and control are important tools for membership in the Body of Christ. By thinking about your life—body, feelings, mind, and spirit—as an orchestra, you can get an idea of the importance of integrating all the different aspects of yourself into a balance and a harmony.

Moderation, or temperance, is the Christian virtue which helps you achieve harmony and balance in your life. Just like in an orchestra, some aspects of your life need to be highlighted, others toned down. But moderation is not gloomy self-denial. It is positive discipline—the ability to bring the best out of yourself at all times. Also, moderation is a way of looking at yourself and making sure that everything is working smoothly.

Like every other virtue, moderation has enemies. It is important for you as a maturing member of the Family of God to be aware of some of these enemies. It is important for you, too, to have some very firm attitudes about these enemies so that you will be able to face them squarely and to help others face them, too.

STUDY

This section summarizes the importance of moderation, restraint, and control for membership in the Body of Christ. It leads to a discussion of drugs and alcohol as threats to the virtue of moderation. Since there might be candidates whose families face a problem with drugs or alcohol, approach this material sensitively. Try to reach out to the candidates without invading their privacy.

After the candidates read this section, divide the class into groups of three or four and assign questions to each group. When they have finished, invite each group to report its conclusions and have the class as a whole discuss the findings.

As an alternative, have each candidate work individually on all the questions and ask volunteers for responses.

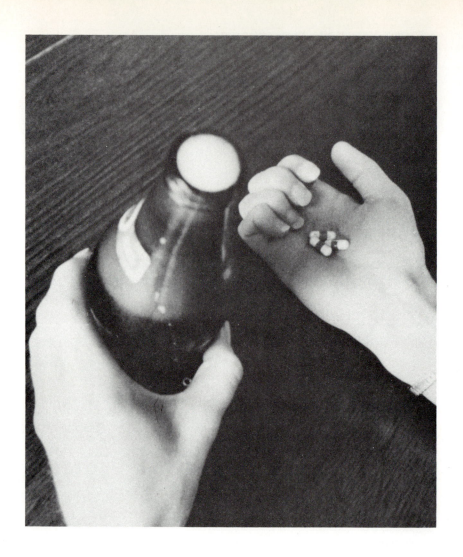

Drugs and Alcohol

The use of drugs and alcohol are serious threats to moderation. The widespread use of these chemicals does not minimize the fact that they are powerful, have both physical and psychological effects, and are potentially addictive. They can throw everything in you out of balance. Even if there were no dangers of physical addiction, studies have shown that the high risk of psychological addiction can be even harder to handle. Not only are there personal dangers connected with the use of substances which affect your brain, your nervous system, or your bodily chemistry, but there also are dangers for the innocent bystander. For example, there is an extremely high incidence of drug and alcohol abuse in automobile accidents and accidental deaths.

Members of the Christian community strive for moderation and temperance in their lives. As members of Christ's Body, they see life not only as a gift but as the visible presence of Christ in the world. They take responsibility for their own health and well-being and that of others. As you approach initiation into full membership in the Christian community, you should be clear about your own values and principles. Now is a good time for you to check your attitudes toward drugs and alcohol, and toward the people who use them. Complete the following survey and discuss the results.

1. Why do you think people use drugs? What role does peer pressure play in the use of drugs and alcohol?

2. What is the most dangerous aspect in the use of alcohol?

3. Are there any drugs which are not dangerous? Why do you think this way?

4. Do you discuss with people your own age the problem of drug use? Why or why not?

5. Do you think that the use of drugs is a moral problem? What is the morality of drug and alcohol use?

6. What is the relationship between your faith and the use of drugs and alcohol?

7. How do you feel when you see someone who is drunk or high on drugs?

8. Have you ever had anyone pressure you to drink or to use drugs? How did you react to the pressure?

9. In your own mind, is there a difference (other than legality) between drugs and alcohol? Why or why not?

10. What responsibility do friends of people who use drugs have? What should they do?

Modesty

Moderation also involves modesty. Clothing, speech, gestures, and actions directly affect the people around you. Modesty is not prudishness. However, the modest person is always aware of the effect his or her behavior has on others and strives for appropriate behavior. While it is appropriate, for example, to wear a bathing suit at the beach, it would not be fitting to do so in the classroom. Simply put, a modest person is one who is sensitive to the feelings and perceptions of others in the way he or she dresses, talks, and acts.

Moderation is a virtue of respect—respect for God's creation, for yourself, and for those around you. Like other virtues, it grows stronger the more you practice it. Moderation allows you to control and direct your energies as a mature and whole person, and it helps you to live out your call to holiness in God's Family.

Listed below are areas of behavior that call for balance and moderation. For each area, analyze your own situation and describe what needs moderation and balance. Then, sketch out a plan of action to make improvements. It is not necessary to share these answers.

AREA OF BEHAVIOR	WHAT NEEDS BALANCE	PLAN OF ACTION
Diet		
Exercise		
Emotions		
Modesty		

▌REFLECT

From the Holy Father

A temperate person is one who does not abuse food, drink, or pleasures, and who does not deprive him or herself of consciousness by using drugs or narcotics. A temperate person is one who is in control, one in whom passions do not prevail over reason, over will, and even over the heart. We understand, therefore, how the virtue of temperance is indispensable in order that the person may be fully human. The sad and degrading spectacle of an alcoholic or a drug addict makes us understand clearly that to be human means, before everything else, to respect one's own dignity, that is, to let oneself be guided by the virtue of temperance.

Temperance requires from each of us specific humility with regard to the gifts that God has placed in our human nature. There is the humility of the body and that of the heart. This humility is a necessary condition for a person's interior harmony and beauty. A young man or a young woman must be beautiful first and foremost inwardly. Without this interior beauty, all other efforts aimed only at the body will not make him or her a really beautiful person. And my wish to you, dear young people, is that you will always be radiant with interior beauty! (Pope John Paul II, Rome, November 22, 1978).

REFLECT

Note: These sections may be done in class or as "at home" assignments.

The Word of God: Invite a volunteer to read the passage from Colossians. Use question 3 for group discussion.

From the Holy Father: After the candidates read this message from the Holy Father, have them discuss question 2 in groups of three or four.

Dear Candidate: Ask a volunteer to read this letter aloud to the group. Use question 1 for group discussion.

Dear Candidate

The problem that many people have with moderation is not in understanding the virtue but in practicing it, in making it a natural part of their lives. People who are not in control of themselves and their desires lose sight of the balance and harmony that can be part of their lives. They are, in effect, out of touch with themselves, with others, and with God.

Saint Paul says that your body is a temple of the Holy Spirit and that you should present your body as a living sacrifice, holy and pleasing to God. Both your body and your mind are sacred trusts given to you by God. Misusing either one is a violation of God's generous love and a violation of your own integrity as a person. Still, moderation is indeed attainable. You always have God's grace and the support of the Christian community to help you.

Your Family in Christ

RESPOND

Remind the candidates to review these questions before the next session. If there is time during class, discuss question 3 after The Word of God, question 2 after From the Holy Father, and question 1 after Dear Candidate.

RESPOND

1. How do you deal with both the expression and control of your feelings and emotions? Would you consider yourself a moderate person in these areas? Why or why not?

2. The Holy Father says that a person should be beautiful first and foremost inwardly. What do you think he means by interior beauty? Describe a person that you know whom you think has interior beauty.

3. How can the members of your group help one another develop habits of moderation? How effective can group support and pressure be for moderation in behavior?

⌐ PRAYER

Rushing Water

Lord, I love water.
I love the taste and feel of clear, cold water rushing out of the faucet.
I really enjoy the sight of a still, clear, blue lake.
Sometimes, I have a laugh at a plucky stream bubbling through the woods.
I am thrilled by ocean waves pounding against the rocks.

But, Lord, there is a big difference between a gentle rain and a raging storm.
There is a big difference between the cresting surf and a tidal wave.
There is a difference, too, between a sparkling river and one bursting its banks to deal death in a flood.

Lord, teach me the water's lesson.
Inside of me, there are many hopes, dreams, fears, and feelings.
Let me know the power of them.
Let me know the gentleness of them.
But, Lord, please help me know the control of them.
It may take my whole life before I really get the knack of it.
But in my learning times, give me the living water of your love.

REACH OUT

During this session, the candidates had the opportunity to reflect on the use of drugs and alcohol and on their own responsibilities as Christians. Ask the candidates to research some of the drug and alcohol rehabilitation centers in their area. If possible, they should interview staff members of such facilities to get a better understanding of the problem of addiction and the effect it has on the people who are addicted as well as the effect on their family and friends. The candidates might prefer to work in small groups.

PRAYER

This prayer has three sections. Ask volunteers to read the first two sections and invite the group to read the third section together as a response.

STEP 15 Courage

To help the candidates appreciate courage as a virtue which helps them overcome fear and take the risk of Christian living.

The call of the Christian is a call to courage. Christians act courageously because they are aware of their dignity as children of God. They are engaged in building a world of justice, honesty, and peace. In facing the challenges to the building up of the kingdom, Christians need the virtue of courage to help them overcome fear and to strengthen the resolve to put their faith into action.

This step helps the candidates explore the virtue of courage as it is lived out by members of the Christian community. They will learn that courage is not the absence of fear, but the ability to overcome fear, to take risks, and to act when something worthwhile is at stake. They will also find that courage is something Christians share with one another and that it grows as they overcome the fears in their lives.

No special materials are recommended for this step.

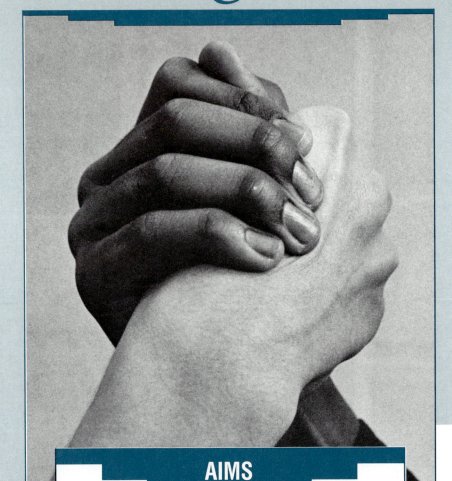

AIMS

This step focuses on courage as the virtue that helps you overcome fear and take the risk of Christian living.

- Not everyone is called to martyrdom, but all Christians are called to face the challenges to faith with courage, or fortitude.

- Courage is not the lack of fear but the overcoming of fear when something worthwhile is at stake.

- Courage enabled the early Christians to endure many trials and persecutions. Today, you need courage to overcome the challenges to faith that you encounter.

- Christian courage has great witness value because the courageous act invites imitation.

The Word of God

Five times I received forty lashes less one; three times I was beaten with rods; I was stoned once, shipwrecked three times; I passed a day and a night on the sea. I traveled continually, endangered by floods, robbers, my own people, the Gentiles; imperiled in the city, in the desert, at sea, by false friends; enduring labor, hardship, many sleepless nights; in hunger and thirst and frequent fastings, in cold and nakedness. Leaving other sufferings unmentioned, there is that daily tension pressing on me, my anxiety for all the churches. Who is weak that I am not affected by it? Who is scandalized that I am not aflame with indignation? If I must boast, I will make a point of my weakness. The God and Father of the Lord Jesus knows that I do not lie.

As to the extraordinary revelations, in order that I might not become conceited, I was given a thorn in the flesh, an angel of Satan to beat me and keep me from getting proud. Three times I begged the Lord that this might leave me. He said to me, "My grace is enough for you, for in weakness power reaches perfection." And so I willingly boast of my weaknesses instead, that the power of Christ may rest upon me. Therefore, I am content with weakness, with mistreatment, with distress, with persecutions and difficulties for the sake of Christ; for when I am powerless, it is then that I am strong (*2 Corinthians 11:24–31, 12:7–10*).

This Scripture passage may be used as an opening prayer, or later as part of the Reflect activities on pages 134–135.

Group Reunion

In the last session, you saw the importance of maintaining a sense of balance and harmony in everything you do. Moderation helps you to respect your limits—both physical and emotional—and to remove excesses and discord from your life. Since last session, what have you noticed about the effect an individual's immoderate behavior has on others? How can you help friends or family members who may have an addiction problem? How can you help others avoid the traps of drugs and alcohol? Spend a few moments sharing your responses with the other candidates.

GROUP REUNION

In the last session, the candidates were asked to Reach Out by researching some of the drug and alcohol rehabilitation centers in their neighborhoods. They were challenged to learn more about addiction and how it affects not only those addicted but also the family and friends of the addict. Although addiction is an extreme form of immoderate behavior, it illustrates how one person's irresponsible behavior can seriously affect those close to him or her.

Have the candidates read the material in this section. Ask them to report on their experiences as a result of the Reach Out assignment. If the candidates worked in small groups or pairs, ask a representative from each to report on the group's findings.

The story of Father Maximilian Kolbe is an example of extraordinary courage. His ability to overcome the fear of death in order to save the life of a fellow prisoner at Auschwitz shows that it is possible to confront evil with love and faith. Allow the candidates a few moments to read this section and to reflect on the details of the story.

▌PREPARE

Courage for Others

Father Maximilian Kolbe was a Franciscan priest in Poland at the time of the Nazi invasion of that country in 1939. For years, he had been involved in publishing a number of Catholic magazines. The Gestapo, however, watched Kolbe closely, and in February, 1941, they arrested the priest and jailed him just outside Warsaw. In late May, suffering from tuberculosis, Kolbe was sent to the concentration camp at Auschwitz where he was forced to haul heavy carts of gravel for the construction of a gas chamber. Like the other inmates, he suffered beatings and insults by the Nazi guards. Yet, no one was able to break his spirit, and Father Kolbe continued to share his faith and encouragement with the others.

In order to tighten security and to discourage prisoners from escaping the camp, the Nazis had the policy of starving to death ten men for every prisoner who got free. On July 30, the word spread that someone had escaped, and the Nazis ordered all of the men in Father Kolbe's cell block to stand in the center of the prison yard. From these men, the guards selected the ten who would be placed in the starvation bunker. Kolbe was not one of the men chosen. However, when one of those who were chosen broke down at the thought of not seeing his family again, Kolbe stepped before the commandant and offered to take the man's place in the bunker. "Who are you?" the commandant snapped. "I am a Catholic priest," Father Maximilian answered.

Inside the bunker, the priest helped the other doomed inmates to keep their faith in God in the face of hatred and despair. During the third week of starvation, only Kolbe and three others were still alive. Driven by impatience, the commandant ordered the camp executioner to inject the four survivors with carbolic acid. On August 14, 1941, Father Kolbe and the others died by injection. Today he is Saint Maximilian Kolbe—a model of Christian courage.

The call to Christian witness and courage goes back to the Apostles. Not everyone is called to martyrdom, but all Christians are called to face the challenges to faith with courage, or fortitude. Father Kolbe's story shows that hatred and despair are not the only possible responses to human cruelty and injustice. When confronted with evil, it is still possible to love and to have faith.

One-on-one

Silently review the story of Maximilian Kolbe. Try to imagine what he felt like when he accepted death for another human being. Imagine, too, the feelings of those who saw this act of courage. Then, answer the questions below. Share your answers if you wish.

Ask the candidates to work individually on these questions. After they have finished, ask volunteers to share their responses.

1. Describe a person whom you know personally and whom you think of as courageous. What qualities make that person courageous? How does he or she demonstrate courage? What influence does that person have on your own life?

_____

_____

_____

_____

2. How do you react to suffering or the threat of suffering?

_____

_____

_____

_____

3. In your own words, what is the most courageous act a Christian can perform in today's world?

_____

_____

_____

STUDY

This section explains how courage works to help a person overcome fear and be able to deal with new situations. Direct the candidates to read to themselves the first four paragraphs. When they have finished, ask volunteers to summarize this section in their own words.

Ask the candidates to continue reading the material under "Courage to Live." Spend a few moments discussing some of the challenges to Christian values today that require a courageous response.

▛ STUDY

What Is Courage?

Courage is a state of mind, an attitude with which you approach life. It allows you to go from day to day without living in complete fear—and being frozen by fear—of the possible risks and consequences that each day brings. At the same time, courage brings you in touch with reality. A courageous person does not act rashly. Rather, he or she takes risks in line with principles and goals. A courageous person is fully aware of the consequences of an action.

From birth, a child is confronted with a complex and mysterious reality which is not always safe and reassuring. As a person grows and learns, new horizons, opportunities, and risks open up. A new acquaintance, neighborhood, school, or job brings with it a risk—the possibility of failing or not being accepted. These are natural occasions for fear. From time to time, extraordinary situations arise in which the possible risks and dangers are far greater. The need to act under these circumstances is often very frightening. Courage is not lack of fear but the ability to overcome fear when something worthwhile is at stake. Without some courage, a person might be unable to deal with any new situation.

Hiding one's fear, especially in dangerous situations, is not a sign of courage. Instead, it can lead to rash and foolhardy action. Courage admits fear, encounters fear, and overcomes it. A person who simply walks around in full sight of a deranged sniper to show a lack of fear is rash, not courageous. But the person who exposes him or herself to sniper fire in order to rescue a friend is courageous. Although fearful, that person weighs the risks and acts because something worthwhile is at stake. Courage puts the person in touch with the reality of the situation.

You may or may not be called on during your life to make a heroic decision. You are, however, constantly faced with new situations which require you to act with courage. Like the other virtues, courage gets stronger the more you practice it. With enough practice, being courageous can become a way of life.

Courage to Live

After the death and resurrection of Jesus, the Apostles faced a crisis of courage. Although their initial confusion was turned into faith and confidence in the risen Lord, they remained fearful and felt unable to share the Good News with others. Only the coming of the Holy Spirit on Pentecost gave them the courage to emerge from hiding and proclaim the Gospel to all who would listen.

Courage enabled the early Christians to endure many trials and persecutions. Jesus warned that his followers would be treated as he had been: "They will manhandle and persecute you, summoning you to synagogues and prisons, bringing you to trial before kings and governors, all because of my name" (*Luke 21:12*). In the Acts of the Apostles, there is a description of the first martyrdom in the infant Church—that of Saint Stephen. Eventually, all of the apostles, except John, were killed for their faith and for preaching it to others. Courage helped them to overcome the fear of death, to remain true to their faith in Jesus, and to pass on their faith and courage to others.

There are still places today where the Christian community is persecuted or discouraged from practicing its faith. Although you do not encounter direct persecution for being a Christian, there are many forces within contemporary society that challenge you. Television, music, books, and films often portray values contrary to your Christian faith. Advertising sends out the message that happiness and human fulfillment can be found in a product— whether a granola bar or a sports car. Peers can challenge your faith by disagreeing with your moral values or by arguing that faith in God really is not important. Whatever obstacle you meet in living out your faith, the fear that obstacle brings—fear of rejection or embarrassment—can be overcome by courage. And courage is something that Christians share with and strengthen in one another.

What are the challenges to faith that you encounter? Below, list five specific trials or challenges that you have experienced. Explain why the incident is a challenge to your faith. Then, describe your personal response to the challenge. Finally, describe how you can get community support to help you face the challenge. Share your responses if you wish.

Finally, direct the candidates to work individually on the exercise involving challenges to faith. When they have completed the exercise, divide the group into pairs and ask the candidates to share their responses with their partners. If time is short, ask the candidates to complete the exercise as a home assignment.

CHALLENGE	WHY	RESPONSE	SUPPORT
1.			
2.			
3.			
4.			
5.			

REFLECT

Note: These sections may be done in class or as "at home" assignments.

The Word of God: Ask a volunteer to read the passage aloud for the group. Use question 2 for group discussion.

From the Holy Father: Read this message from the Holy Father aloud to the group. Ask the candidates to spend a few moments reflecting on question 3. Allow them time to compose their own short prayers for courage. Invite volunteers to share their prayers with the group.

Dear Candidate: After the candidates read this letter, use question 1 for group discussion.

REFLECT

From the Holy Father

Christ's victory in our hearts calls for the exercise of the virtue of fortitude, the third cardinal virtue. This virtue, which enables us to face dangers and bear adversity, permits us to fight courageously for the ideals of justice, honesty, and peace. It is not possible to think of constructing a new world without being strong and courageous in overcoming the false ideas of fashion, the world's principles of violence, and the promptings of evil.

You see, dear young people, to follow Christ and to help others to do so entails courageous resolutions and the tenacious strength to put them into practice, sustaining one another also with forms of community, which make it possible to unite your efforts, deepen your convictions mutually, and encourage one another with reciprocal and loving help. Entrust yourselves to the grace of the Lord who cries within us: courage! (Pope John Paul II, Rome, November 15, 1978).

Dear Candidate

Christians act courageously because they are aware of their dignity as children of God. This sense of dignity brings with it genuine pride—a conviction that God creates people in his image and that acting as anything less than his son or daughter is just not right. This pride at being a child of God is the motivation to be courageous.

Another reason why Christians act courageously is because courage is an infectious virtue. People admire courageous people and imitate them as heroes and heroines. They want to participate in the sense of self-worth and enthusiasm for life that a courageous person has.

Your courage continues to grow the more you overcome the fears in your life. The Church is full of people who overcome fear and reach out to grasp God's gift of life. Remember, the Christian community is behind you and willing to help you live your life with courage.

Your Family in Christ

RESPOND

Remind the candidates to review these questions before the next session. Discuss question 2 after The Word of God, question 3 after From the Holy Father, and question 1 after Dear Candidate.

RESPOND

1. How courageous are you in your faith? How well do you compare to the courageous Christians of the early Church?

2. In what situations do you feel your greatest need for courage? What do you do when your courage fails you?

3. What relationship do good habits of regular prayer have to do with the virtue of fortitude, or courage? Compose a short prayer for courage which you can use when you are in real need of courage.

PRAYER

The Lion's Den

I really know how Daniel felt.
He was a good man who was just trying to do what was right.
All of a sudden, he found himself in a den of hungry lions.

There are lions in my life, too.
The lion of selfishness tries to keep me from being kind and generous.
The lion of pride keeps me from admitting that I am wrong.
The lion of fear keeps me from taking the chances I need to take to follow Jesus.
The lion of laziness keeps me from going out of my way for others.

But there is always hope.
You, Lord, have offered me the perfect whip to keep these lions away.
That whip is the virtue of Christian courage.
Please, Lord, help me to use that weapon.

Being trapped in a lion's den is no way to live!
Your courage will rescue me.

REACH OUT

As this step pointed out, courage is an infectious virtue. People admire courageous people and emulate them as heroes and heroines. Direct the candidates to survey at least five people they know and to ask them about the people they think of as courageous. The candidates should use the following questions:
- Name two or three people whom you admire for their courage.
- How have the people you named affected your own life?
- How would you define courage?

Tell the candidates that the results of the survey will be part of the next Group Reunion.

PRAYER

If you use this prayer to close the session, ask volunteers to read the first three sections aloud and have the group read the last two lines together as a response.

Prudence

AIM

To help the candidates appreciate prudence as a virtue which helps them make good choices in life.

More than ever, people need the virtue of prudence. In a fast-paced society with access to a wide range of values, young people are confronted with a multitude of choices on how to live their lives now and what direction their lives should take for the future. In the midst of the many options and the flood of information available, young people look for personal freedom as they pursue personal commitment in life. In practical terms, this means that they look forward to establishing their independence as adults and preparing for their life goals. Both objectives involve choices and decisions, and the virtue of prudence is essential for accomplishing them.

This step focuses on the virtue of prudence as the ability to take responsibility for one's actions. The candidates will take a look at some of the distractions in life that make it difficult to make prudent decisions and to stick to one's life goals. They will see how people can be swayed by false messiahs promising sure and easy answers to life's difficulties. They will also examine the three qualities of a prudent decision—mature deliberation, wise choice, and correct action—and see how these qualities can work in situations in the candidates' own lives.

No special materials are recommended for this step.

AIMS

This step focuses on prudence as the virtue which helps you make good choices in life.

■ People today are confronted by false messiahs promising sure and easy answers to life's difficulties. Without the virtue of prudence, a person can be led away from God's Family.

■ In order to make good decisions, three qualities are necessary—mature deliberation, a wise choice, and correct action.

■ Fascination with the occult and extreme political groups are examples of the traps that imprudent people can fall into.

■ A key to Christian prudence is the ability you have to take full responsibility for your actions.

The Word of God

Jesus said to his disciples, "If anyone tells you, 'Look, the Messiah is here,' or 'He is there,' do not believe it. False messiahs and false prophets will appear, performing signs and wonders so great as to mislead even the chosen if that were possible. Remember, I have told you all about it beforehand; so if they tell you, 'Look, he is in the desert,' do not go out there; or 'He is in the innermost rooms,' do not believe it.

"The coming of the Son of Man will repeat what happened in Noah's time. In the days before the flood, people were eating and drinking, marrying and being married, right up to the day Noah entered the ark. They were totally unconcerned until the flood came and destroyed them. So will it be at the coming of the Son of Man. Two men will be out in the field; one will be taken and one will be left. Two women will be grinding meal; one will be taken and one will be left. Stay awake, therefore! You cannot know the day your Lord is coming" (*Matthew 24:23–27, 37–42*).

Group Reunion

In the last session, you saw the importance of courage in living a Christian life. One of the tasks that Christians have is to build up God's kingdom of peace and justice in this world—to challenge the selfish structures of society and to replace them with those which respect the dignity of the person. What are your dreams for a better world? Describe one major goal or improvement in the world that you consider worth working for. What hesitations, doubts, or fears do you have about committing yourself to that goal? How can what you have learned about courage unlock your energies so that you could commit yourself to your goal?

This Scripture passage may be used as an opening prayer, or later as part of the *Reflect* activities on pages 141–142.

GROUP REUNION

During the last session, the candidates were encouraged to interview five people and to ask them about the people they admire for their courage. Ask the candidates to share their results with others in the group. Then, ask them to read the material in this section and to work in groups of three or four as they respond to the questions.

PREPARE

This section presents a situation in which a young woman searching for happiness and meaning in life is persuaded to join a cult. It is an example of the kind of false solutions to life's difficulties that young people encounter today. Ask the candidates to read this section and allow a few moments for them to review the details.

⌐ PREPARE

Cults

Kathy feels trapped! She is a member of the One Life Institute. Members of the Institute center their lives around the Book of the Master by Maharishi Sumi, its founder. Kathy's days are busy with early morning chanting and meditation, hours of soliciting money on street corners, daily self-criticism in front of other members, and manual labor. The institute demands complete and unquestioning commitment. Maharishi Sumi does not allow his followers to marry, to maintain family ties, or to own even personal belongings.

At one time, Kathy enjoyed the feelings of belonging and challenge the Institute gave her. But now she is just going through the motions. Her days are exhausting. She has cut herself off from her friends, her family, and her past. She can't even think about leaving the Institute. There is nowhere else to go.

While in her freshman year at Brown University, Kathy was looking for direction in her life. Up until then, she lived with her family in the security of familiar surroundings and friends. Getting out of high school was her only goal. She didn't have to make any life decisions. Nor did she really think about college. Her parents had hoped she would go to Brown as other family members had. Once there, Kathy felt empty. She really did not know for sure why she was in college.

When Kathy met Jim and Pam, things seemed to get brighter. They were members of the One Life Institute, and they told Kathy that it was dedicated to building a new world and changing human

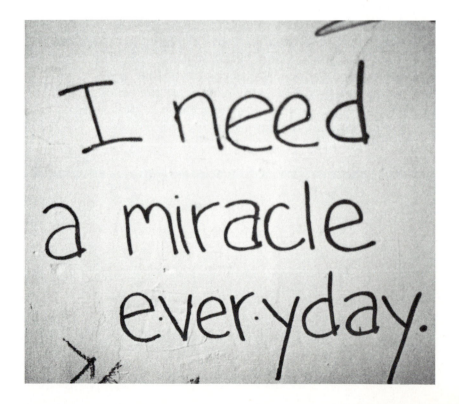

relationships. Under the guidance of Maharishi Sumi, members were unlocking their deepest selves and finding happiness—now! They explained how their own lives had been transformed by the master's teachings. It was her life, they told her. She could continue living her life for her parents, or she could pursue her own goals and join the Institute.

It didn't take much to persuade Kathy to join. Her first encounter with the other members convinced her that the Institute would give her the meaning in life that she sought. Everyone was warm and friendly. No one seemed lonely or confused. But after she left Brown and moved to the Institute, she learned that the Maharishi demanded more than she expected. The group made her feel guilty when she asked questions. Now, whenever her commitment weakens, she is disciplined and told to try harder. While some members of the Institute become group leaders, Kathy remains a follower. She has nowhere to turn.

One-on-one

Review the story of Kathy and the One Life Institute. Try to imagine the feelings she had when she joined. Imagine her feelings of being trapped. Then, answer the questions below. Share your answers if you wish.

Direct the candidates to read this section and to work individually on the questions. Try to involve as many candidates as possible in discussing question 1. Use question 1 on page 142 for further discussion.

1. Why do you think people are attracted to and join cults? Have you ever felt attracted to one? How did you feel?

_____

_____

_____

_____

2. How do you go about making important decisions? What steps do you take to make sure you are doing the right thing?

_____

_____

_____

_____

3. Once you have made a decision, what are two or three things which might get in the way of your carrying out that decision?

_____

_____

_____

This section is divided into three parts. The first two paragraphs describe the nature of prudent decisions. The second part, "Distractions," presents some of the distractions in life that challenge prudent decision making. The last part, "Using Prudence," is an exercise to help the candidates use the virtue of prudence in their own lives.

Begin by asking the candidates to read the first two paragraphs. When they have finished, review the three qualities present in a prudent decision: (1) mature deliberation, (2) a wise choice, and (3) correct action. Refer to Kathy's situation in the section above and ask the candidates to analyze what qualities were missing from Kathy's decision to join the One Life Institute.

Direct the candidates to read the material under "Distractions" and ask volunteers to give examples from films and music where the occult and satanic imagery are used.

Finally, direct the candidates to read the introductory material under "Using Prudence" and to work individually on the exercise. When they have finished, ask volunteers to share their results. If time is short, ask the candidates to complete the exercise as a home assignment.

⌐ STUDY

The Value of Prudence

Prudence, one of the four moral virtues, helps a person make good choices and decisions in order to attain his or her aim in life. In a prudent decision, three qualities are always present: (1) mature deliberation, (2) a wise choice, and (3) correct action. Mature deliberation is the weighing of all sides of an issue and the careful examination of all the options. Wise choice is the selection of the best means to achieve a goal or objective. Finally, correct action is the carrying out of a choice to the best of one's ability.

The story of Kathy and the One Life Institute shows that Kathy ignored the first two steps. She was looking for something special in her life, but she did not explore her options. Kathy failed to determine exactly what it was she was looking for. She did not deliberate. Kathy chose the Institute foolishly. She rushed ahead of herself and grasped the very first option which seemed attractive and good. Instead of growing and developing as a person, Kathy got lost in an organization which took everything and gave nothing.

Distractions

Life is seldom what it appears to be. If it were, there would be no need for prudence. On television, in popular music, on the movie screen, in contemporary magazines, there are many distractions—elements which make it very difficult to make prudent choices or decisions.

Many of these distractions promise more than they can ever deliver. They make people believe that by choosing a distraction, they can take shortcuts to their greatest goals and ambitions. One example of such a distraction is the current fascination with the occult.

Most people view the occult—Ouija boards, witchcraft, fortune-telling, and astrology—as a form of entertainment. And often the setting for such things is that of recreation or diversion. There is an atmosphere of a circus sideshow or carnival about them. However, there is a kind of fascination with the occult that leads away from entertainment and toward a relationship with Satan and with the cult of evil. In Satan worship, evil is set over good. The images of truth, justice, peace, loyalty, and faith are lost.

There is much satanic imagery in popular cult-type music and certain horror films. The difference between a good scary movie and a satanic film is simple. In the old-fashioned horror story, good triumphs over evil. In satanic films and music, evil triumphs over good.

Another distraction is political extremism. The current fascination with neo-Nazi parties, the Ku Klux Klan, the Red Brigade, or other terrorist groups like the Symbionese Liberation Army takes people's attention away from the real evil in the world. These groups demand absolute loyalty to a cause. For the most part, they deal in death, not in life.

Using Prudence

There are other distractions which are not as extreme as cults, political extremists, and a fascination with the occult. These are the little choices you make every day which could somehow distract you from your goals and purpose in life. Whenever you are attracted to something new or different, you need to use the virtue of prudence. You need to stop to review all the options, to make certain that your choice is a wise one, and to act in such a way that you will grow in your faith as well as in your love of God and neighbor.

On the chart below, list three distractions you have experienced personally. For each distraction, show how you could use mature deliberation, make a wise choice, and follow a correct course of action. Be sure to discuss the results in the group. Discuss, too, how you can support one another in the virtue of prudence.

DISTRACTION	DELIBERATION	WISE CHOICE	CORRECT ACTION
1.			
2.			
3.			

⌐ REFLECT

From the Holy Father

Today, people yearn to free themselves from need and dependence. But this liberation starts with the interior freedom that people must find again with regard to their goods and their powers. They will never reach true liberation except through a transcendent love for humankind and a genuine readiness to serve. Otherwise, as one can see only too clearly, the most revolutionary ideologies lead only to a change of masters. Once installed in power, these new masters surround themselves

REFLECT

Note: These sections may be done in class or as "at home" assignments.

The Word of God: Note for the candidates that the early followers of Jesus were also confronted with promises by false messiahs. Ask a volunteer to read this section aloud to the group. Then, use question 1 on the next page for group discussion.

From the Holy Father: Allow the candidates a few moments to read this section to themselves and to reflect on the Holy Father's message. Then have them discuss question 3 on the next page.

with privileges, limit freedoms, and allow other forms of injustice to become established.

Thus, amid the diversity of situations, functions, and organizations, each one must determine, in his or her conscience, the actions which that individual is called to share in. The Christian must make a wise and vigilant choice, and avoid involving him or herself in commitments contrary to the principles of a true humanism.

Examine yourself to see what has been done and what ought to be done. It is not enough to recall principles, state intentions, point to crying injustices, and utter prophetic denunciations. These words will lack real weight unless they are accompanied for each individual by a livelier awareness of personal responsibility and by effective action (Pope Paul VI, Rome, May 14, 1971).

Dear Candidate

Dear Candidate: Read or summarize this letter for the candidates and review with them the five tips to help them grow in prudence. Use question 2 for group discussion.

The gift of prudence is planted in you like a seed. As with the other virtues, it must be practiced in order for it to grow strong and become a part of you. There is no list of prudent behavior that can be memorized. However, it can be imitated.

Here are a few tips to help you to grow in prudence. First, when you are confronted with a decision or a choice, slow down and be patient. Jumping to conclusions is the best way to act imprudently. Second, ask questions. Explore the consequences of each option. Third, never look for quick and easy solutions. Life is more complicated than that. Fourth, think about others. Consider what effect your choice or decision will have on them. Finally, talk to others. Ask for advice if you need it before making a decision. And even if you already have made a bad choice, never be afraid to ask for help and forgiveness. Your family and friends in the Christian community are always ready to help.

Your Family in Christ

RESPOND

RESPOND
Remind the candidates to review these questions before the next session. If there is sufficient time, discuss question 1 after The Word of God, question 3 after From the Holy Father, and question 2 after Dear Candidate.

1. As Jesus warned, there are many false messiahs in the world. The leaders of cults and extreme political groups are two examples. What are some other false messiahs in contemporary society? What does each one promise?

2. Describe someone you know personally whom you would consider to be a prudent person. Explain your choice.

3. How can you help one another grow in the virtue of prudence? Why is good group support important in avoiding distractions from your goal, or purpose in life?

▌ PRAYER

On the Track

Lord, you put me on the track that is guaranteed to lead to you.
But I have a difficult time staying on the track.
I am all too anxious to go on little side trips.
I look for shortcuts.
I try different fads or fancies.
I stall a bit and forget which direction I am going.

Lord, along the way, you have given me signposts and warnings.
They help me get through the difficult switches and over the dangerous gorges.
You gave me the Family of Faith to remind me of the truth.
You gave me the sacraments to keep your love fresh in my mind.
You gave me prayer so that I can keep my eyes on the goal.

Thanks for the help, Lord.
I have to know where I am going.
I have to choose my route wisely.
And, Lord, I need to keep moving toward you.
No siding or spur line is worth trading for my final destination
Lord, keep me on the track to you!

REACH OUT

Ask the candidates to recall their responses to question 2 above which asked them to describe someone whom they consider prudent. Encourage them to compose a short poem or personal letter to that person explaining why the candidate thinks he or she is a prudent person and what that person's example means to the candidate. The poem or letter may be written in the candidate's journal-notebook or actually sent to the person.

PRAYER

Ask volunteers to take turns reading individual verses from the first two sections of the prayer. Invite the group to read the last six lines as a group response.

From Death to Life

AIM

To help the candidates examine their feelings about death and develop an awareness that death is the beginning of everlasting life.

Death is a forbidden subject in contemporary society. Today, the topic is avoided, covered up, talked around, and denied much the same way that sexuality was handled during the Victorian period. Even those who are more straightforward about the reality of death try to soften its impact by speaking of someone who has "passed away" or "departed." Young people in particular are sheltered from discussions of death.

Lent is a good time for the candidates to share their own feelings and fears about dying. By doing so, they come to the realization that an awareness of death can bring greater meaning to life. The candidates will learn that Jesus expressed fears of his own death, but that he willingly accepted it in order to bring everlasting life to all of his followers.

It is important to come to grips with death. During this step, the candidates will share with one another their memories of their first experience with death, and explore what they think death is all about. A series of questions follow the discussion on the acceptance of death. These will help the students judge their own acceptance of death.

A prayer service celebrating Jesus' death completes the step. It is suggested that you involve the group in decorating the area for the prayer service and in choosing some recorded music or songs for the group to sing during service.

You will find the following material helpful in preparing this session:
- Planning a Prayer Service, TM page 17
- Respecting Individual Differences, TM pages 22–23

AIMS

This step will help you become more aware of death as the beginning of life everlasting.

- It is important to examine your feelings about death.

- By sharing some of those feelings in the group, you can become more aware of everyone's attitude toward death.

- The experience of suffering or hardship can lead to an awareness of the meaning your life has and the trust in God you need to have.

- Jesus faced his own death with complete trust in the Father.

The Word of God

Among those who had come up to worship at the feast of Passover were some Greeks. They approached Philip, who was from Bethsaida in Galilee, and put this request to him: "Sir, we should like to see Jesus." Philip went to tell Andrew; Philip and Andrew in turn came to inform Jesus. Jesus answered them: "The hour has come for the Son of Man to be glorified. I solemnly assure you, unless the grain of wheat falls to the earth and dies, it remains just a grain of wheat. But if it dies, it produces much fruit. The one who loves life loses it, while the one who hates life in this world preserves it to life eternal. If you would serve me, follow me; where I am, there will my servant be. Anyone who serves me, the Father will honor. My soul is troubled now, yet what should I say—Father, save me from this hour? But it was for this that I came to this hour. Father, glorify your name!"

Then a voice came from the sky: "I have glorified it, and will glorify it again." When the crowd of bystanders heard the voice, they said it was thunder. Others maintained, "An angel was speaking to him." Jesus answered, "That voice did not come for my sake, but for yours. Now has judgment come upon this world, now will this world's prince be driven out, and I—once I am lifted up from earth—will draw all to myself" *(John 12:20–33).*

Group Reunion

During the past four sessions, you explored the four cardinal virtues: justice, moderation, courage, and prudence. They are the signs of a mature Christian life. Moreover, all four virtues are interrelated. When one virtue is missing from a person's life, he or she will have difficulty practicing the other three. For example, it takes courage to live a moderate life in face of peer pressure. With a partner, discuss the interrelationship of the four virtues. Then spend a few moments sharing the results of your discussion with the group.

This Scripture passage may be used as an opening prayer, or later as part of the *Reflect* activities on page 151.

GROUP REUNION

This group-sharing session looks again at the cardinal virtues discussed in the last four Steps: justice, moderation, courage, and prudence. After the candidates read this section, briefly review the meaning of each virtue. Then proceed with the discussion of the interrelationship of the four virtues.

PREPARE

Read the material aloud to the group. Direct the candidates to note the varying and sometimes contradictory feelings expressed by Paul Beauchamp. When the reading is completed, ask if anyone wishes to comment.

PREPARE

Paradox

"The Lord has a perfect plan for me. He cares for me. I put my heart in his hand. Lord, I love. When you ask, *believe*. He does hear you. He is there. The Spirit of the Lord is your life."

Paul Beauchamp, twenty-two, taped these words shortly before he died of Hodgkin's disease. The doctors and nurses, his relatives, and the members of the prayer group to which Paul belonged were amazed at Paul's faith and courage.

On the same tape, Paul added: "Seeing my friends with all their goals being accomplished is tough. Here I am with water around my lung, having difficulty climbing stairs. It's hard relying on the Lord in these circumstances. I keep on praying and there's no answer." Then he said, "I couldn't fall asleep, trying to figure out what the Lord wants me to do in my life—If it's worth it to go back to college or if I should work with my father. I pray to the Lord that he gives me his answer."

Later on the same tape, Paul prayed, "I'm truly sorry I have not totally turned to you. I'm twenty-two, life's going on. I can't see the future. I pray you show me the way and give me strength. I'm scared and I'm sick. Thank you, Lord. Thank you, Jesus. The more time I spend with you, the better things look."

One-on-one

Spend a few moments reviewing the story of Paul Beauchamp. Imagine how you would cope with the knowledge that you were going to die soon. Imagine yourself, too, having a conversation with Paul about his feelings, longings, and prayers. Then, answer the following questions. Share your answers if you wish.

Direct the candidates to review the story and then to work individually on the questions. Since the topic of death is one that is highly emotional and often generates fear or avoidance, many people gloss over it. To help the candidates come to terms with their emotional responses, spend as much time as needed to discuss fully each of the questions. There may be people in the group who have not had a direct experience with death. Those students may share experiences, stories, or movies about death which moved them in a special way. It would be appropriate and helpful if you shared with the group your own feelings about death.

1. What was your first experience of death? How did you feel? How did you act?

2. If you had the opportunity to talk with Paul, what questions would you ask him?

3. In your own words, describe what death is all about.

STUDY

It is important for the candidates to develop an attitude of acceptance toward death. Read the material aloud and direct the candidates to answer the questions individually. Spend sufficient time to discuss the candidates' responses. When the discussion is completed, prepare the room for the prayer service.

STUDY

Accepting the Father's Will

For most people, death is not easy to talk about. Many people find it difficult to offer their sympathies or talk freely with someone who has lost a wife, a father, a grandparent, or a friend. It is even harder to talk to someone who is dying. The reasons are simple. Everyone fears death. No one can hide from it.

When he faced his own death, Jesus did not escape the fear of dying. "He advanced a little and fell to the ground, praying that if it were possible this hour might pass him by. He kept saying, 'O Father, you have the power to do all things. Take this cup away from me. But let it be as you would have it, not as I'" *(Mark 14:35–36)*.

By accepting death, Jesus showed that God the Father was the absolute center of his life. By giving himself on the cross, Jesus breathed God's Spirit and life into every person willing to accept the gift of faith. Through his death and resurrection, Jesus conquered people's worst fear and promised eternal life.

1. Recall a time in your life when suffering or hardship led you to a new awareness of the meaning of your life. Describe the event. What new awareness did you come to? Why was the suffering or hardship necessary for you to come to this new awareness?

_____

_____

_____

2. Although Jesus agonized over his impending death, he accepted it as his Father's will. How does Jesus' acceptance of death affect your attitude toward the pain and suffering in your life? your own death?

_____

_____

_____

Before you begin, have the students skim through the service in order to familiarize themselves with the format. Choose a leader and a reader. If possible, darken the room somewhat and have a lighted candle in a prominent place. Allow a few moments of silence after each reading of Scripture. You may wish to supplement the readings with additional prayers or Scripture.

Prayer Service

Sometimes it is important to pray and celebrate even such frightening events as death. The following prayer service is a celebration of death—the death of someone with great faith, hope, and love. Try to make this service a very special time. Do your best to create an atmosphere for celebration. If you wish, you may play some recorded music or sing some familiar songs during the service.

Reading One

Since, then, we have a great high priest who has passed through the heavens, Jesus, the Son of God, let us hold fast to our profession of faith. For we do not have a high priest who is unable to sympathize with our weakness, but one who was tempted in every way that we are, yet never sinned. So let us confidently approach the throne of grace to receive mercy and favor and to find help in time of need.

In the days when he was in the flesh, he offered prayers and supplications with loud cries and tears to God, who was able to save him from death, and he was heard because of his reverence. Son though he was, he learned obedience from what he suffered; and when perfected, he became the source of eternal salvation for all who obey him, designated by God as high priest according to the order of Melchizedek.

(Hebrews 4:14–16, 5:7–9)

Leader: In you, O Lord, I take refuge; let me never be put to shame.

All: Father, I put my life in your hands.

Leader: Into your hands, I commend my spirit: you will redeem me, O Lord, O faithful God.

All: Father, I put my life in your hands.

Leader: For all my foes, I am an object of reproach, a laughing-stock to my neighbors, and a dread to my friends; they who see me abroad flee from me.

All: Father, I put my life in your hands.

Leader: But my trust is in you, O Lord; I say, "You are my God." In your hands is my destiny; rescue me from the clutches of my enemies and my persecutors.

All: Father, I put my life in your hands.

Leader: Take courage and be stouthearted, all you who hope in the Lord.

All: Father, I put my life in your hands.

Reading Two

Though he was in the form of God, he did not deem equality with God something to be grasped at. Rather, he emptied himself and took the form of a slave, being born in the likeness of men. He was known to be of human estate, and it was thus that he humbled himself, obediently accepting even death, death on a cross! Because of this, God highly exalted him and bestowed on him the name above every other name, so that at Jesus' name every knee must bend in the heavens, on the earth, and under the earth, and every tongue proclaim to the glory of God the Father: Jesus Christ Is Lord!

(Philippians 2:6–11)

Leader: Whoever sees the Son and believes in him will live forever, and I shall raise him up on the last day, alleluia.

Side 1: Blessed be the Lord, the God of Israel; he has come to his people and set them free.

Side 2: He has raised up for us a mighty Savior, born of the house of his servant David.

Side 1: Through his holy prophets, he promised of old that he would save us from our enemies, from the hands of all who hate us.

Side 2: He promised to show mercy to our fathers and to remember his holy covenant.

Side 1: This was the oath he swore to our father Abraham: to set us free from the hands of our enemies, free to worship him without fear, holy and righteous in his sight all the days of our life.

Side 2: You, my child, shall be called the prophet of the Most High; for you will go before the Lord to prepare his way, to give his people knowledge of salvation by the forgiveness of their sins.

Side 1: In the tender compassion of our God the dawn from on high shall break upon us to shine on those who dwell in darkness and the shadow of death, and to guide our feet into the way of peace.

Side 2: Glory be to the Father . . .

All: Whoever sees the Son and believes in him will live forever, and I shall raise him up on the last day, alleluia.

From the Holy Father

The Eucharist that we celebrate constantly confirms our living and dying in the Lord: "Dying, you destroyed our death; rising, you restored our life." In fact, St. Paul wrote: "We are the Lord's. That is why Christ died and came to life again, that he might be Lord of both the dead and the living" *(Romans 14:8–9)*. Yes, Christ is the Lord!

The Paschal Mystery has transformed our human existence, so that it is no longer under the dominion of death. In Jesus Christ, our Redeemer, "we live for the Lord" and "we die for the Lord." Through him and with him and in him, we belong to God in life and in death. We exist not only "for death" but "for God." For this reason, on this day "made by the Lord" *(Psalm 118:24)*, the Church all over the world speaks her blessing from the very depths of the Paschal Mystery of Christ: "My soul, give thanks to the Lord; all my being, bless his holy name. Give thanks . . . and never forget all his blessings" *(Psalm 102:1–2)* (Pope John Paul II, San Antonio, Texas, September 13, 1987).

Dear Candidate

Suffering remains a mystery. But somehow, the whole human family is tied into the mystery through the death and resurrection of Jesus Christ. Look carefully at the life and death of Jesus. In that story is hidden the key to the mystery of suffering for you. Jesus died to take away sin. He died to make sure that your life and your death have meaning. Taking up your cross daily and following Jesus is your way of responding—of making sure that your life and your death are linked with the great sacrifice of the Son of God.

Remember, however, that you are not alone in carrying your cross. As you may be noticing throughout this preparation for Confirmation, following Jesus is a family affair. Together with your brothers and sisters in God's Family, even cross-carrying can be easier, even suffering can have meaning, even death can be the promise of eternal joy.

Your Family in Christ

REFLECT

Note: These sections may be done in class or as "at home" assignments.

The Word of God: If there is time during the prayer service, you may wish to read this passage immediately following Reading Two.

From the Holy Father: If you wish to expand the material in the prayer service, use this section as a preparatory reading at the very beginning of the service.

Dear Candidate: After the candidates complete the questions under "Accepting the Father's Will," ask them to read this letter to themselves. Use question 3 for class discussion.

RESPOND

Remind the candidates to review these questions sometime before the next session.

RESPOND

1. Before he died, Paul Beauchamp experienced both fear and trust. The Gospels record similar mixed emotions in Jesus' agony in the garden. Recall a situation in your life story where both emotions were present. In the face of fear, what caused you to persist in trust?

2. Jesus' prayer to the Father, "But let it be as you would have it," is a prayer of trust. Is trust an important part of your relationship to God? How do you express your trust in God?

3. Lent is the season of preparing yourself to celebrate the death and resurrection of Jesus. How have you made use of this special season? How has it helped you to see more clearly into the saving mission of Jesus?

Death's Sting

I do not like to think about dying.
Lord, I am not so strange for feeling that way.
Even though I love you very much, it is very hard for me to believe
    that something goes on after death.
But every once in a while I feel like a forever person.

Remind me, Lord, that death is the beginning of life, not the end.
Remind me, Lord, that those I love will share heaven with me.
Remind me, Lord, that you have destroyed death.
Death can never, ever, win again.

One last thing, Lord.
Let everybody who looks at me see someone who believes in life.
Let everyone see someone who is brave enough to carry the cross.
Let my every action say that I believe the sting of death will bring
    the happiness of loving you for all the ages to come.

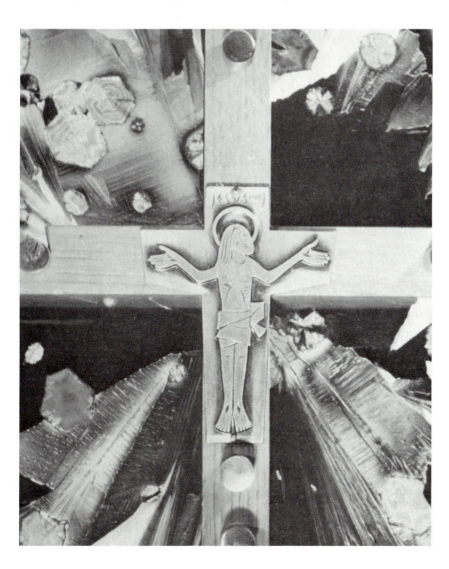

REACH OUT

The celebration of the passion, death, and resurrection of Jesus is the high point in the liturgical year. It is a time when the community puts out its best efforts to celebrate the Paschal Mystery as fully as possible. This is a good opportunity for the candidates to become directly involved in the work of the parish as it prepares for Holy Week and Easter. Encourage the candidates to find out what contributions they can make this week. There is always need for help—the liturgy, cleaning, decorations, transportation for the elderly, the parish day-care center. Urge the candidates to contact the parish liturgical committee, the youth ministry director, or the parish priest and to offer their services during this week.

PRAYER

If you wish to incorporate this reflective prayer into the service, ask the candidates to pause a moment after Reading Two and ask a volunteer to read this prayer slowly to the group.

Resurrection

AIM

To help the candidates explore the meaning of the resurrection in their lives and grow in their faith in the risen Lord.

As the candidates grow into mature faith, they begin to see more clearly how their friendship with Jesus is a relationship with the risen Christ, which even death cannot destroy. They come to realize that they have moments of resurrection in their own lives—the experience of coming to life in Jesus.

When going through the material on the resurrection, the candidates will not be prepared to understand many aspects about the mystery of Jesus' resurrection. This should not come as a surprise. The Apostles and disciples had to struggle with their faith in the risen Jesus before they could proclaim this great event to anyone who would listen. An important approach to this step is to help the candidates understand that it takes time, patience, and desire to learn about the mystery of Jesus.

This step helps the candidates to see the impact of the resurrection on other people's lives and to reflect on the joy of Easter that the early disciples experienced in their contact with the risen Jesus. As they work through this session, they will have a closer sense of resurrection in their own lives today.

Resource

As you begin the Easter season with the candidates, it is a good idea to gather with others on the Confirmation team to strengthen one another in the Good News. Refer to Form 16, Prayer and Planning Session—April.

AIMS

This step will help you explore the meaning of the resurrection in your life and grow in your faith in the risen Lord.

- Suffering and difficulty can lead to a stronger and more active faith.

- The resurrection of Jesus is a promise that not even death can destroy a relationship with him.

- The risen Jesus showed humanness in his appearances as well as the transformation which resurrection brings.

- There are "resurrection" moments in your life. You can learn to recognize them.

The Word of God

Early in the morning on the first day of the week, while it was still dark, Mary Magdalene came to the tomb. She saw that the stone had been moved away, so she ran off to Simon Peter and the other disciple (the one Jesus loved) and told them, "The Lord has been taken from the tomb! We don't know where they have put him!" At that, Peter and the other disciple started out on their way toward the tomb. They were running side by side, but then the other disciple outran Peter and reached the tomb first. He did not enter but bent down to peer in, and saw the wrappings lying on the ground. Presently, Simon Peter came along behind him and entered the tomb. He observed the wrappings on the ground and saw a piece of cloth which had covered the head not lying with the wrappings, but rolled up in a place by itself. Then the disciple who had arrived first at the tomb went in. He saw and believed *(John 20:1–9)*.

Group Reunion

In each of the sessions during Lent, you discovered how change, suffering, and even death have meaning. A good way to begin the celebration of Easter is to review briefly how those discoveries are making a difference in your life. With the group, list ways in which you have experienced meaning in change and suffering. Then, list ways in which you can help and support one another in moments of change, suffering, and even death.

This Scripture passage may be used as an opening prayer, or later as part of the *Reflect* activities on pages 159–160.

GROUP REUNION

The candidates are very familiar with the dramatic effect that change can have on their lives. However, not all change is easy to understand. Within the Christian community, all change and suffering have meaning through Christ. Have the candidates read the section and begin making their lists of ways in which change and suffering have been meaningful in their lives. Ask the candidates to work individually for a few moments and then discuss their lists with one another. Suggest that the candidates record in their journal-notebooks some of the ideas for helping and supporting others during times of change, suffering, or death.

PREPARE

Have two candidates read the stories of Mary and George. Ask if they understand what "coming to life" means. If they are having difficulty with the idea, ask them to consider examples of people who don't grow and change, or who feel trapped because they lack the trust and faith to reach out. Explain that the power of the risen Jesus helps us to see the possibilities of new life in each day.

▌PREPARE

Coming to Life

The two stories below are examples of people "coming to life"—changing for the better. The key in each story is faith, but in each, the experience of coming to life is very different. Read the stories. Let the stories remind you of moments when you came to life.

Mary, thirty-five, recently lost her husband. Jim was driving home from work when he pulled over to the side of the road and died of a heart attack. It had been a difficult marriage. Jim was not a very understanding man, and he often drank too much. But Mary loved him and tried always to communicate with him. Now, Mary was left with a child to support and with many legal struggles to face. She reflects that without her faith, she could not have made it through the tough days. That faith, nourished from infancy, survived a difficult marriage and death itself. Not only is she stronger than ever, but she has come to rely on the Lord for everything in her life. Mary is happy.

George couldn't tell you the precise moment when he made his decision. No flash of light or sudden burst of recognition occurred. No serious tragedy struck his life, nor did he "turn away from a life of sin." He had always tried to be a good person, and in so doing, he gradually came to know and love Jesus until he became the Lord of his life. One day, however, George sat at his desk and wrote the following note to his family and friends.

"This summer, I am going to El Salvador as a missionary with the Jesuit Lay Volunteers. My job will be to work with the refugees around San Salvador, the capital. As a missionary, I need your prayer support. I have never done anything like this before. I am both excited and nervous. But I know I want to serve the Lord. I would like to ask you to pray for me and the team. Pray for our spiritual growth, financial support, missionary burden, good health, traveling safety, and for the refugees of that country."

One-on-one

Spend a few moments reviewing these two stories. Then, answer the following questions. Share your answers if you wish.

1. What are the similarities and differences in the two stories?

Ask the candidates to review the two stories and answer the questions. Allow them a few minutes to share their answers with one other person. Then, open a discussion on the candidates' answers to question 3. Be sure to share the meaning of the resurrection in your own life.

2. What in your own life has helped you come to life?

3. In your own words, what does the resurrection of Jesus Christ mean to you?

STUDY

Unsettling News

Faith is a source of strength and confidence. It is a way of seeing God's plan to share a new and eternal life with him. Yet, faith is not a tidy little package of beliefs that you buy once and for all. Instead, faith in the risen Jesus is a gift you care for and nourish.

Sometimes you need to challenge your faith and struggle with it, much the same way that you come to grips with your own body as it changes and develops from childhood through adolescence to maturity. Sometimes you resist faith, and yet it is a part of you.

STUDY

Read the text aloud to the candidates. Go over the ideas in each paragraph and use the two questions for discussion. Help the candidates accept the idea that the resurrection of Jesus is real, but that it is sometimes difficult to understand. It was a shocking event even for the disciples. Point out that it is sometimes necessary to be patient with themselves in trying to understand aspects of their faith.

Compared to the relatively uniform presentation of the passion and death of Jesus in the Gospel accounts, the resurrection narratives are much shorter and present a variety of situations where the disciples encountered the risen Lord. However, all appearance narratives show that Jesus was still human while at the same time showing signs of transformation.

The early followers of Jesus knew what it meant to grow in faith in the risen Jesus. The Gospel accounts describe how unsettling the news of Jesus' resurrection was in the lives of those who were close to him. Matthew reported that after the women saw the tomb where Jesus had been buried, "they hurried away from the tomb half-overjoyed, half-fearful, and ran to carry the good news to his disciples" *(Matthew 28:8)*. In Mark's account of the event, the women's confusion is emphasized, "They made their way out and fled from the tomb bewildered and trembling" *(Mark 16:8)*.

Stubbornness and amazement were also a part of the disciples' reactions. "On their return from the tomb, the women told all these things to the Eleven and the others, but the story seemed like nonsense and they refused to believe them. Peter, however, got up and ran to the tomb. He stooped down but could see nothing but the wrappings. So he went away full of amazement at what had occurred" *(Luke 24:9, 11–12)*.

1. How would you react to the news that someone you loved had come back to life? What suspicions would you have? What questions would you ask?

2. Jesus calls you to accept him as your risen Lord. What do you find hard to accept about the resurrection?

Direct the candidates to read this text and choose three or four Scripture passages they wish to read, study, and pray about. Work closely with the candidates at first to be sure that they can pick out both the obviously human qualities of Jesus and the signs of his transformation.

The following are examples of what the candidates should be looking for:

The Risen Jesus

The risen Christ is not pure spirit. In at least two of his appearances reported in the Gospels, he bore the marks of the crucifixion. He was the same warm human being he had always been, greeting his friends by name, teaching, forgiving, consoling, and caring for them.

As a candidate for Confirmation, you are asked to have a firm belief in the resurrection. That belief can be strengthened by serious prayer and study of the Scripture. Either alone or in small groups, choose three or four of the following resurrection stories and carefully read, study, and pray about them. Before you begin, ask the risen Lord to send the Holy Spirit to you to help you read and respond. With each passage, ask yourself the following questions: *(a)* What human qualities does the risen Jesus exhibit in the appearance? *(b)* What evidences of his transformation are there? Jot down notes if you wish.

1. Mary Magdalene *(John 20:11–18)*

2. The gathered Apostles *(Luke 24:36–43 and John 20:19)*

3. Thomas *(John 20:24–29)*

4. Two disciples *(Luke 24:13–35)*

5. The ambitious Apostles *(Acts 1:3–9)*

- *Mary Magdalene* (John 20:11–18): Jesus showed human qualities in his appearance (he resembled the gardener) and in the way he spoke to Mary in a familiar way. He showed signs of his transformation because Mary didn't recognize him. He also told her not to cling to him.
- *The Gathered Apostles* (Luke 24:36–43): Jesus showed the Apostles his hands and feet and ate fish with them—a very human gesture. Yet, he seemed to be transformed—they thought they were seeing a ghost. He appeared even though the doors were locked.

If time permits, they should complete their work in class. Otherwise, direct the group to finish their work during the week and discuss it during the next Group Reunion.

REFLECT

From the Holy Father

Passover means "passing over." In the Old Testament, it meant the Exodus from the "house of slavery" of Egypt and the passing over the Red Sea, under special protection of the Lord God, towards the Promised Land. The wandering lasted for forty years. In the New Testament, this historic Passover was accomplished in Christ during three days: from Thursday evening to Sunday morning. And it means the passing through death to the resurrection, and at the same time the exodus from the slavery of sin towards participation in God's life by means of grace. Christ says in the Gospel: "If anyone keeps my word, that person will never see death."

Who is Christ? He is the Son of God who assumed human life in its temporal orientation towards death. He accepted the necessity of death. Christ is he who accepted the whole reality of human dying. And for that very reason, he is the one who made a radical change in the way of understanding life. He showed that life is a passing over, not only to the limit of death, but to a new life (Pope John Paul II, Rome, April 5, 1979).

REFLECT

Note: These sections may be done in class or as "at home" assignments.

The Word of God: Ask a volunteer to read this account of the finding of the empty tomb. Spend a few moments talking about the feelings of the three characters in the scene: Mary Magdalene, Peter, and the other disciple (John). Note Mary's initial response, "The Lord has been taken from the tomb! We don't know where they have put him!"

From the Holy Father: Read this section aloud for the group and use question 2 for discussion.

Dear Candidate

The many accounts of the resurrection of Jesus have in common the facts that Jesus died for your sins, overcame death, rose from the dead, and saved you from everything that would threaten to destroy you. The Church asks you to see Jesus with the eyes of faith—to realize that you are not yet prepared to understand everything about the mystery of his resurrection.

Put yourself in the place of the Apostles, and experience the confusion which they must have felt when they could not find Jesus. Begin to realize that your knowledge of Jesus is far from complete. No one fully understands the complete story of any human being. Learning about Jesus takes time, patience, and desire. You need to search just like the Apostles did.

But now, you can rejoice in knowing that your search is underway. Look back on the coming-to-life moments in your past. Use them to build for yourself a great future of trust and love with your brothers and sisters in Jesus Christ the Lord.

Your Family in Christ

RESPOND

Assign question 3 (poem exercise) as homework and tell the candidates to be prepared to share their poems during the next Group Reunion. You may wish to discuss question 1 with Dear Candidate and question 2 with From the Holy Father.

RESPOND

1. Although the Apostles and the disciples at first struggled with their faith in the risen Jesus, they eventually came to the point at which they could proclaim the resurrection to anyone who would listen. How do you come to grips with the resurrection? How do you try to make faith in the resurrection part of your daily life?

2. During one of Jesus' last appearances to his friends, he asked them to proclaim the good news of the resurrection to all nations. List some ways in which you can spread that good news in the way you speak and act.

3. Compose a short poem in which you give witness to your own faith in the resurrection.

PRAYER

Resurrection Dialog

Lord, you have risen from the dead.
Yet, I go about my routine as if the resurrection never happened—
   as if nothing happened.
I love you, Lord, but I find believing so hard.
I do believe.
Please, help my lack of faith.

My child, look back on your life.
Why do you doubt my love for you when everything in your life
   speaks of my presence.
I want to change your life.
I want to remove from your days all the obstacles that you try to
   put between us.
My love for you goes beyond the grave and death itself.
I have helped you so far, and I will continue to be with you.
Trust me and let the warmth of my love for you surround you and
   protect you from anything that could hurt you.

REACH OUT

Ask the candidates to think of one person they know whose life reflects the power and joy of the resurrection of Jesus. Ask them to write a letter to that person in their journal-notebooks explaining how that person's "coming to life" has affected the candidate's own life. The letter need not actually be sent, but it may be.

PRAYER

Give the candidates a few moments to read and reflect on this prayer in silence. Then use the Act of Faith on page 187 as a group response.

Ascension

AIM

To help the candidates reflect on the special vocations within the Family of the Church and realize that all of the followers of Jesus are called to be his witnesses in the world.

The notion of being called or having a special vocation to do God's will goes back to the early Israelites. Israel herself was called out of Egypt to fulfill God's special purpose in bringing salvation to the world. Abraham, Moses, and the prophets, too, saw themselves called to do the work of the Lord. At times they hesitated and were tempted to resist the task they were asked to do.

The vocations to priesthood or religious life address special needs in the community of faith. In this step, the candidates will focus on what the Lord is asking of them right now and begin planning more fully for their calling in life. Most of the candidates know sisters, brothers, and priests, but few begin thinking of those vocations as possibilities for themselves until the question is raised by someone else. A consideration of these special vocations within the Church is an appropriate part of Confirmation preparation. The candidates have the opportunity to reflect on their own sense of call and to assess their attitudes toward religious life and the priesthood. They are also reminded that each member of the community is called to active participation in the Church.

As part of this lesson, you may wish to ask a sister, brother, or priest from the parish to describe their own experience of being called. The best time for this personal witness would be at the end of the discussion of the questions in the section, "Are You Called?"

Resource

You may wish to meet with others on the Confirmation preparation team as Level I draws to a close. See the material in Form 17, Prayer and Planning Session—Corpus Christi.

AIMS

This step will focus on special vocations within the Family of the Church.

- Every follower of Jesus has a calling.

- The basic calling of each member of the Body of Christ is to continue his presence in the world.

- It is important for every Christian to be open to the special callings of religious life and priesthood.

- At his ascension, Jesus asked *all* his followers to "Go, teach all nations."

The Word of God

In the time after his suffering he showed them in many convincing ways that he was alive, appearing to them over the course of forty days and speaking to them about the reign of God. On one occasion when he met with them, he told them not to leave Jerusalem: "Wait, rather, for the fulfillment of my Father's promise, of which you have heard me speak. John baptized with water, but within a few days you will be baptized with the Holy Spirit."

While they were with him, they asked, "Lord, are you going to restore the rule of Israel now?" His answer was: "The exact time it is not yours to know. The Father has reserved that to himself. You will receive power when the Holy Spirit comes down on you; then you are to be my witnesses in Jerusalem, throughout Judea and Samaria, yes, even to the ends of the earth." No sooner had he said this than he was lifted up before their eyes in a cloud which took him from their sight.

They were still gazing up into the heavens when two men dressed in white stood beside them. "Men of Galilee," they said, "why do you stand here looking up at the skies? This Jesus who has been taken from you will return, just as you saw him go up into the heavens" *(Acts 1:3–11)*.

Group Reunion

In the last session, you discussed the experiences of coming to life which have their source in the resurrection of Jesus Christ. Since then, have you had any such experiences? How has the resurrection become more a reality for you? In what ways have you tried to act in such a way as to proclaim your faith in the risen Lord? If you have had the chance to discuss the resurrection with anyone outside this group, what were the results of your conversations?

This Scripture passage may be used as an opening prayer, or later as part of the *Reflect* activities on pages 169–170.

GROUP REUNION

Direct the candidates to read the material and begin discussing the questions. As the candidates share their experiences of coming to life, they may read their poems from the homework assignment of last week. Spend some time on the second question (How has the resurrection become more of a reality for you?) and review the significance of the resurrection in their lives now.

PREPARE

After reading the passage from Romans, ask for volunteers to describe some examples of special personal gifts within their own families. Continue the reading. Give special attention to the meaning of the last two sentences. There is no one "best" way to make Christ present in the world. Each person must find what is best for him or her.

PREPARE

Callings

In the *Introduction to the Devout Life*, Saint Francis de Sales wrote that every Christian is called to a life of holiness, and that living a Christian way of life makes every job or occupation more meaningful.

Saint Paul put it another way: "Just as each of us has one body with many members, and not all the members have the same function, so too we, though many, are one body in Christ and individually members one of another. We have gifts that differ according to the favor bestowed on each of us" *(Romans 12:4–6).*

Some people are called to the special vocations of religious life or priesthood. For some, the call comes through a homily or a conversation with a priest, a sister, or a brother. For others, the call arises from reading and prayer. Some have experienced the call through a day of recollection or retreat. This call is basically a recognition that Jesus is inviting you to live the Christian way of life as a priest or as a member of a special community of faith.

As part of your preparation for Confirmation, it is a good idea to examine these special vocational opportunities in the Church. You can daydream about what it might be like to become a sister, a brother, or a priest. In these daydreams, you might discover a germ of calling to follow Jesus in one of these ways.

But even in your dreaming and imagining, remember the disciples when they experienced the ascension of Jesus. When Jesus left from their sight and returned to the Father, they began to see that they were to be the presence of Jesus in the world. Gradually, they came to know that each of them was to make Christ present in his or her own way. No one way was better or best.

One-on-one

Spend a few moments daydreaming about what it might be like to have a religious vocation. Then, answer the following questions. Share your answers if you wish.

1. What do you plan to do or be when you are an adult?

2. How will what you plan be a means of holiness for you?

3. How can what you plan be a source of sharing the Good News with others?

4. Have you ever felt the call to religious life or the priesthood? Describe the experience.

Direct the candidates to read the material and then to answer the questions. Discuss the first three questions with the group. For question 1, be sure that each person expresses some choice of a life career. Stress that, although they may change their minds several times before finally deciding on a life's career or vocation, they need to begin thinking about it now. Next, ask those who are willing, to share their answers to question 4.

Ask the candidates to read the material and to do the exercise as the text directs: (1) Rate each answer on a scale of one to ten to reflect how close the attitudes are to their own, and (2) write a reaction to the statement. If there is time, record the candidates' responses on the board, newsprint, or transparency to see overall group response. For example, for statement 1, ask how many responded to it with a rating of one, how many with a two rating, and so on. Do this for each of the statements. Ask volunteers to share their reasons why they might consider a religious or priestly vocation, and why they might not.

▌STUDY

Are You Called?

You may or may not be considering either religious life or the priesthood. It won't hurt, however, to assess your attitudes toward both the religious life and the priesthood. The following statements are real statements made by real young people about both religious life and the priesthood. Express how close the attitudes are to your own by rating each answer on a scale of one to ten. Ten would show perfect agreement. Then, write two or three words to describe your reaction to the statement.

1. I am not holy enough to be a religious or a priest.

2. Well, I think I should consider it, but I'm going to wait a while and see.

3. I'll give two years to the Peace Corps instead.

4. I want to get married.

5. Some people are just made that way. I'm not.

6. I'm sure everybody thinks of it sometime. That's no sign the Lord wants me to think seriously about it.

7. I'm not all that smart, and I don't like studying that much.

8. If the priesthood or the religious life is so great, why do so many leave it?

9. I have thought often about religious life. I really want to know more about it.

10. It is very difficult to make any kind of permanent commitment today.

11. I am inspired by anyone who has the courage to serve others.

Now, write down three reasons why you personally *might* consider a religious or a priestly vocation.

Write down three reasons why you personally *might not* consider a religious or a priestly vocation.

In whatever way a person shows witness to Jesus Christ, he or she does so through the power of the Holy Spirit. Begin this section by discussing Confirmation as a sign of full membership in the community of faith. Point out the connection between full membership and the call to be active members. Then ask volunteers to take turns reading the bishop's message from the Confirmation ceremony. Allow them a few moments to fill out the description of how they plan to follow Christ by being an active member of the Church. Have them form small groups and present their descriptions.

Many Are Called

When you are confirmed, the bishop will remind you that your initiation into the Christian community joins you with all who have followed Jesus. The words the bishop says to you should assure you that there are no second-class citizens in the kingdom of God. You may receive a further call to become a religious or a priest, but for the moment, concentrate on the bishop's message.

When Saint Paul placed his hands on those who had been baptized, the Holy Spirit came upon them, and they began to speak in other languages and in prophetic words.

Bishops are successors of the Apostles and have this power of giving the Holy Spirit to the baptized, either personally or through the priests they appoint.

In our day, the coming of the Holy Spirit in Confirmation is no longer marked by the gift of tongues, but we know his coming by faith. He fills our hearts with the love of God, brings us together in one faith but in different vocations, and works within us to make the Church one and holy.

The gift of the Holy Spirit which you are to receive will be a spiritual sign and seal to make you more like Christ and more perfect members of his Church. At his baptism by John, Christ himself was anointed by the Spirit and sent out on his public ministry to set the world on fire.

You have already been baptized into Christ and now you will receive the power of his Spirit and the sign of the cross on your forehead. You must be witnesses before all the world to his suffering, death, and resurrection; your way of life should at all times reflect the goodness of Christ. Christ gives varied gifts to his Church, and the Spirit distributes them among the members of Christ's Body to build up the holy People of God in unity and love.

Be active members of the Church, alive in Jesus Christ. Under the guidance of the Holy Spirit, give your lives completely in the service of all, as did Christ, who came not to be served, but to serve.

On the lines below, briefly describe how you plan to follow Jesus Christ by being an active member of the Church. Then, in small groups discuss your description.

_____

_____

_____

▌REFLECT

REFLECT

Note: These sections may be done in class or as "at home" assignments.

The Word of God: Ask one or two volunteers to read the passage from Acts on page 163. Allow a moment for reflection and then discuss question 1 on the next page.

From the Holy Father: Read this message from the Holy Father aloud to the group. Spend a little time on question 2.

From the Holy Father

In the Gospel which we have heard today, we reflect on the call of Jesus to the first disciples. The first thing that Andrew did after meeting Jesus was to seek out his brother Simon and tell him, "We have found the Messiah!" Then Philip, in a similar way, sought out Nathanael and told him: "We have found the one Moses spoke of in the law—the prophets too—Jesus, son of Joseph, from Nazareth" *(cf. John 1:35–51).*

After the initial discovery, a dialogue in prayer ensues, a dialogue between Jesus and the one called, a dialogue which goes beyond words and expresses itself in love.

Questions are an important part of this dialogue. For example, in the Gospel account of the call of the disciples, we are told that "when Jesus turned around and noticed them following him, he asked them, 'What are you looking for?' They said to him, 'Rabbi' (which means teacher), 'where do you stay?' 'Come and see,' he answered" *(John 1:38–39).*

What begins as a discovery of Jesus moves to a greater understanding and commitment through a prayerful process of questions and discernment. In this process, our motives are purified. We come face to face with pointed questions such as, "What are you looking for?" And we even find ourselves asking questions of Jesus, as Nathanael did: "How do you know me?" *(John 1:48)* It is only when we have reflected candidly and honestly in the silence of our hearts that we begin to be convinced that the Lord is truly calling us.

Yet, even then, the process of discernment is not over. Jesus says to us as he said to Nathanael: "You will see much greater things than that" *(John 1:50).* Throughout our lives, after we have made a sacred and permanent commitment and after our active service of the Lord has begun, we still need the dialogue of prayer that will continually deepen our knowledge and love of our Lord Jesus Christ (Pope John Paul II, San Antonio, Texas, September 13, 1987).

Dear Candidate: Ask the candidates to read this letter quietly. Refer them to question 3 and invite the candidates to share responses.

Dear Candidate

The call to active membership in the Body is a call to love and service. Love and service are the cornerstones upon which the People of God build their community. In a special way, religious life shows everybody about the possibilities for loving and serving. The priesthood is a sacrament for the whole world because everyone needs that ministry.

However, not everyone is called to religious life or priesthood. Even so, no follower of Jesus should exclude these special vocations. It is important for every member of the People of God to be open to the kind of loving, serving witness God is requesting. It is even an excellent idea for you to pray every day that you might have a clear idea of how you, as a full member of the Body, can best love and serve others.

Your Family in Christ

RESPOND

Remind the candidates to review these questions before the next session. If there is time, discuss question 1 with The Word of God, question 2 with From the Holy Father, and question 3 with Dear Candidate.

RESPOND

1. Preparing for Confirmation is a way of preparing for a more active role in the Body of Christ. How have you become a more active member over the past year?

2. What personal qualities do you think you can develop in order to make Christ truly present to the people you meet?

3. Recall a priest or religious who has influenced your life. How has that person contributed something special to your life of faith? How would your faith life be different without the person's influence?

Be My Witness

Lord, over 800 years ago, Saint Francis of Assisi was born.
This "little poor man" really knew how to be your witness.
There is a little prayer that everybody calls his.
Help me, Lord, to make those words my own.
Help me be your witness till you come again.

Lord,
Make me an instrument of your peace.
Where there is hatred, let me sow love;
Where there is injury, pardon;
Where there is darkness, light;
Where there is doubt, faith;
Where there is despair, hope;
Where there is sadness, joy.

O Divine Master,
Grant that I may not seek so much to be consoled as to console,
To be understood as to understand,
To be loved as to love.
For it is in giving that we receive.
It is in pardoning that we are pardoned.
It is in dying that we are born again to eternal life.

REACH OUT

Very often, "Vocation Days" occur in schools and parishes only once or twice a year when members of religious communities and priests are available to discuss these special callings. Yet, most directors of vocations for religious communities and diocesan schools of theology (seminaries) have information that they can make available to the parish. Have the candidates develop a vocation information center for the parish. There are also numerous lay service groups and organizations, such as Jesuit Lay Volunteers, who have information available about the work of their organizations. Provide names and addresses of lay organization and religious vocation directors for the candidates to use in requesting information on the history and ministries of religious communities and other ministries.

Divide the list and have the candidates request the information (brochures, booklets, schedules of retreat or service weekends and the like) to be made available in the parish. Some may wish to work on a rack or display for the materials. Since Level I is coming to a close and to assure follow-up on the project, be sure the candidates have the information addressed to someone at the parish who will be available to gather and display the materials.

PRAYER

Read the introductory reflection aloud for the group. Then have the candidates read the Prayer of Saint Francis together.

Come, Holy Spirit

AIM

To help the candidates find and celebrate the Spirit in their lives and assess their progress in moving toward Confirmation.

People constantly experience the working of the Spirit through the love, joy, peace, patience, endurance, kindness, generosity, faithfulness, gentleness, and modesty shown by others in all circumstances of life. These are all signs of the quiet presence of the Spirit in the world today.

The Spirit is also present in the change of heart that so many people experience. That power to take a life of hopelessness and turn it toward fullness of life is truly a power of God. Most people experience the work of the Spirit in their lives in a quiet way—one that brings peace and joy after years of loneliness or times of stress. This is the work of the Spirit.

In this step, the candidates will examine the role the Holy Spirit plays in providing encouragement and spiritual renewal during times of discouragement and despair. They will see that the Spirit is always present and will provide strength for the journey. They will reflect on the signs of the Holy Spirit and think about how Christians traditionally invite the Spirit into their hearts.

Resource

As part of this step, you might wish to celebrate the end of Level I of the Confirmation preparation process by using the prayer service in Form 30, Looking to the Future.

AIMS

This step will help you celebrate the presence of the Holy Spirit in your life. It will also help you summarize how far you have traveled on your journey toward Confirmation.

- The Holy Spirit helps people keep up their enthusiasm for living the Christian life.

- Jesus promised that the Holy Spirit would be with the Church as Counselor, Teacher, Advocate, and Friend.

- There are signs of the Spirit's presence in your life and in the life of the Church.

- Christians traditionally invite the Holy Spirit into their hearts.

The Word of God

On the evening of that first day of the week, even though the disciples had locked the doors of the place where they were for fear of the Jews, Jesus came and stood before them. "Peace be with you," he said. When he had said this, he showed them his hands and his side. At the sight of the Lord, the disciples rejoiced. "Peace be with you," he said again. "As the Father has sent me, so I send you." Then he breathed on them and said: "Receive the Holy Spirit. If you forgive sins, they are forgiven them; if you hold them bound, they are held bound" *(John 20:19–23)*.

Group Reunion

As a final Group Reunion, consider some of the ways you have grown together as a group. How did sharing your faith story with others help you understand yourself better? What did you learn from listening to others? How important is it for you to have a small friendly group with which to share? How can you continue to support one another during the summer break?

This Scripture passage may be used as an opening prayer, or later as part of the *Reflect* activities on pages 179–180.

GROUP REUNION

Although continued regular contact among the candidates during the summer months may not be possible, some interaction should be encouraged. Direct the candidates to read the text and share their responses with the group. If the candidates have specific ideas for continuing to support one another during the summer break, try to get some commitments from them during this session. Supplement their ideas with the Reach Out suggestions on page 181.

┌ PREPARE

Turning to the Spirit

Father George Chirovsky was discouraged. After thirteen years in the priesthood, he was beginning to feel ineffective. His homilies were dry, almost mechanical. As a high-school religion teacher, he lacked enthusiasm in the classroom. Routine had replaced the excitement he had felt when he first began teaching. Then, he was a new priest with fresh ideas and great dreams for challenging young people with the Gospel of Jesus Christ. Now he felt that no one really cared about what he had to say.

One night as he sat in his room watching television, he received a phone call. It was from Tom, a former student with whom he kept in touch. Tom sensed discouragement in Father George and invited him to join him at a special prayer service held in a neighboring parish. With some reluctance, Father George accepted the invitation.

While meeting the members of the prayer group before the service, he noticed that the priests present seemed filled with the energy and enthusiasm he lacked. What really impressed Father George was that the other priests seemed to speak with real joy about their ministries. Inwardly, he felt a little envious, and he decided that he wanted what they had. During the prayer service, Father George prayed, "Holy Spirit, fill me with your love. Give me the power to enjoy my priesthood and to serve others. Give me the courage to use the gifts you have given me at Baptism, Confirmation, and Holy Orders."

Some people in the group prayed for Father George to experience the signs of the Holy Spirit in his life. He enjoyed the loving support of the prayer group and opened his heart to receive whatever the Spirit had to give him. Father George left the meeting that night with the sense that his ministry had possibilities after all.

As he prayed more by himself and with the members of the prayer group, Father George found his ministry taking on a new energy and meaning. His enthusiasm soon became contagious. Students who at one time had been completely bored now seemed willing to listen and to participate in class. One day in the corridor, Father George overheard what he felt was one of the greatest compliments he ever received. One of his students remarked, "Father George loves God and he loves his priesthood. You can see it in his eyes."

One-on-one

Take a few moments of silence to review the story of Father George. Then, answer the following questions. Share your answers.

Direct the candidates to read the instructions and then work individually on the questions. After they have completed their writing, ask volunteers to share their responses. Be sure to elicit reactions to question 1. When the discussion is finished, involve the candidates in a moment of spontaneous prayer. Call on the Holy Spirit to help all the members of God's Family deal with problems in their lives.

1. Does it surprise you that Father George would have to turn to the Holy Spirit to enliven his faith? Why or why not?

2. Describe a time in your life when you felt bored or discouraged. What happened to change things around?

3. Describe three areas in your life where you feel the need for the strength of the Spirit.

Ask three volunteers to read the three main paragraphs of this section. After each paragraph, highlight the main point of each paragraph. (1) Jesus sent the Spirit to teach and counsel (strengthen) his followers. Recall that after Jesus' resurrection but before the coming of the Spirit at Pentecost, the followers of Jesus were confused and in need of instruction. (2) There is nothing magical about the presence of the Holy Spirit in someone's life. If that person is open to the Spirit, there are clear signs that the Holy Spirit is working—love, joy, peace, etc. Jesus used the example of the good tree bearing good fruit to illustrate this reality. (3) The Holy Spirit is God's presence with his people. He is not an idea or a hope. The Spirit is the Third Person of the Blessed Trinity sharing divine life with the People of God.

Direct the candidates to form small groups and begin work on the chart together. You may assign each group one or two of the signs to work on in order to save time. When the groups have completed their work, ask them to share their results.

STUDY

The Promise

Before his death, Jesus promised his friends that after he had returned to the Father, he would send them the Holy Spirit who would *teach* them to understand everything that Jesus had said or done. This Spirit would be a Friend and a Counselor for the followers of Jesus. The Spirit would be the Spirit of Truth. Pentecost was the fulfillment of that promise.

The Holy Spirit is a Gift to help you understand the Gospel of Jesus Christ. There are certain signs of the Holy Spirit to help you see whether or not he is working in you. These signs are love, joy, peace, patience, endurance, kindness, generosity, faithfulness, gentleness, and modesty. If a person is filled with anger, hatred, jealousy, strife, conflict, alienation, and sadness, you can be fairly sure that the Spirit is not active in that person.

The Holy Spirit is a real Person—the Third Person of the Blessed Trinity. The Holy Spirit is God present with his people giving life, strength, understanding, and love. Before the arrival of the Spirit, the Apostles were uncertain of their mission. They were praying in the same room where Jesus had celebrated his Last Supper with them. With the arrival of the Spirit, what had been a discouraged group of people became a Church—the New People of God. The Spirit showed that the bad news of Jesus' departure was the beginning of some very "Good News." And the Apostles could not keep the Good News to themselves.

Use the chart on the following page to discover the signs of the Holy Spirit. For each sign, briefly give its meaning. Then, describe how that sign shows the presence of the Holy Spirit.

SIGN	MEANING	PRESENCE OF THE SPIRIT
1. Love		
2. Joy		
3. Peace		
4. Patience		
5. Endurance		
6. Kindness		
7. Generosity		
8. Faithfulness		
9. Gentleness		
10. Modesty		

Read the opening paragraph aloud to the candidates. Then, direct the group to read the prayer of invitation aloud. Complete the reading and ask the candidates to use the first two questions for group discussion. If there is time, allow a few moments for the candidates to compose a simple prayer to the Holy Spirit as suggested by question 3.

Fill the Hearts of Your Faithful

Traditionally, Christians rarely pray directly to the Holy Spirit. Except for prayers at Pentecost or during the sacrament of Confirmation, there are few formal prayers to the Holy Spirit. Because of the role the Holy Spirit plays in the life of the Church, the most common prayer addressed to the Spirit is a prayer of invitation:

> Come, Holy Spirit, fill the hearts of your faithful. Enkindle in them the fire of your love. Send forth your Spirit and we shall be created, and you shall renew the face of the earth.

In the past few years, there has been a renewal of awareness of the activity of the Holy Spirit in the Church. One aspect of this renewal has been the rediscovery of an ancient form of prayer—prayer in the Spirit, or spontaneous prayer. This type of prayer usually takes place in groups where people come together to pray in their own words. This Spirit-filled prayer allows people the opportunity to use their emotions in their prayers more freely than can usually be done in a liturgical setting.

1. When you think of the Holy Spirit, what images or symbols come to mind?

2. If you have ever participated in a prayer group, describe how you felt during the experience.

3. Compose a simple prayer or poem to the Holy Spirit. Remember to make the prayer an invitation.

REFLECT

REFLECT

From the Holy Father

In his cross and resurrection are found the basis for his "authority both in heaven and on earth" *(Matthew 28:18)*. This is the authority of the Redeemer, who through the blood of his cross ransomed the nations. In them he has established the beginning of a new creation, a new life in the Holy Spirit; in them he has planted the seed of the Kingdom of God. In the power of his authority, as he is leaving the earth and going to the Father, Christ says to his apostles: "Go . . . and make disciples of all nations. Baptize them in the name of the Father, and of the Son, and of the Holy Spirit. Teach them to carry out everything I have commanded you. And know that I am with you always, until the end of time" *(Matthew 28:19–20)* (Pope John Paul II, San Francisco, California, September 18, 1987).

The Word of God: Ask a volunteer to read the passage before working on the chart exercise in the section "The Promise," pages 176–177 of the text.

From the Holy Father: Ask the candidates to read this message from the Holy Father and spend a few moments discussing ways of becoming more visible as Christians in the world. Use question 2 on the next page for further discussion.

Dear Candidate

Dear Candidate: Read or summarize this letter for the candidates and then open a discussion on the changes that the candidates have experienced over the past year by using question 1 below.

Your journey toward Confirmation is well under way. You have moved out from the safety of childhood into a real wandering—a search for Jesus Christ. You have been looking at your own story and have tried to relate that story to the story of Jesus and his Church. With your group of fellow candidates, you have experienced what it is like to form Christian community. You have invited Jesus into your heart to help, to heal, and to challenge you.

But the journey is not over. The months ahead hold further discoveries—further challenges. But when those discoveries are made and those challenges are met, you will know that you are ready to embrace full membership in the Body of Christ.

The Holy Spirit is with you. He will console you when the going is rough. He will teach you when your mind seems muddled. He will be your strength in weakness and your joy in sadness. He will bring you gradually to that moment when you will be sealed with his power as a Christian forever. Enjoy the process because it is a privilege!

Your Family in Christ

RESPOND

Encourage the candidates to spend time reflecting on the questions and sharing their responses with their sponsors. If there is time during the session, use question 2 with From the Holy Father and question 1 with Dear Candidate.

⌐ RESPOND

1. The Holy Spirit is a Gift to help you understand the Gospel of Jesus Christ. Briefly, describe how you have begun to understand the Gospel better during the past year.

2. In your own words, what does becoming a fully initiated member of the Church mean to you?

PRAYER

A Pentecost Hymn

Come, Holy Spirit, and let your light shine on us.
Come, Father of the poor.
Come, Giver of God's gifts.
Come, Light of our hearts.
O loving Advocate, you are a kind visitor to our souls.
You bring relief and consolation.
If we are weary with struggle, you bring us refreshment.
If we are sorrowing, your words console us.
Most blessed Light, fill the darkest corners of our hearts, because
    without your help, there is no good in us.
Cleanse our injured spirits.
Soften the hardness of our hearts.
Warm our coolness and direct us when we stray away.
Give us again your sevenfold gifts, for we trust in you.
Reward us for our virtue.
Give us a death that ensures salvation.
Give us, O Holy Spirit, eternal happiness.

REACH OUT

Although the candidates will have different plans and schedules set for the summer break, there may be some who would enjoy getting together with others in the group on a regular basis to work on a summer project. Find out if there is a priest, deacon, catechist, or youth minister willing to work with the group and give them direction. Encourage the candidates to continue to support each other during the summer break. Help those who are interested to get involved in a study group, a community action group, or a prayer group.

PRAYER

If you do not incorporate a short prayer service in this lesson, use this prayer to the Holy Spirit to close the session. Ask the candidates to gather in a circle and recite this prayer together.

A Catholic Treasury

Let us love one another
because love is of God;
everyone who loves is begotten of God
and has knowledge of God.
God's love was revealed in our midst in this way:
he sent his only Son to the world
that we might have life through him.
Love, then, consists in this:
not that we have loved God,
but that he has loved us
and has sent his Son
as an offering for our sins.
If God has loved us so,
we must have the same love
for one another.
No one has ever seen God.
Yet if we love one another,
God dwells in us,
and his love is brought
to perfection in us.
The way we know
we remain in him
and he in us
is that he has given us of his Spirit.
We have seen for ourselves,
and can testify,
that the Father has sent the Son as
Savior of the world.

(1 John 4:7, 9–14)

THE CHURCH YEAR

The following notes will help you recall some important information about the liturgical, or Church, year. They are taken from the General Norms section of the *Sacramentary*, the altar book used by the priest at the Mass.

- *The Church Year.* Throughout the year, the entire mystery of Christ is unfolded, and the birthdays (days of death) of the saints are commemorated *(#1)*. The whole mystery of Christ, from his Incarnation to the day of Pentecost and the expectation of his coming again, is recalled by the Church *(#17)*.

- *Sunday.* The Church celebrates the Paschal mystery on the first day of the week, known as the "Lord's Day," or Sunday. This follows a tradition handed down from the Apostles, which took its origin from the day of Christ's resurrection. Thus, Sunday should be considered the original feast day *(#4)*.

- *Advent.* The season of Advent has a twofold character. It is a time of preparation for Christmas when the first coming of God's Son is recalled. It is also a season when minds are directed by this memorial to Christ's second coming at the end of time. It is thus a season of joyful and spiritual expectation *(#39)*.

- *Christmas Season.* The Church considers the Christmas season, which celebrates the birth of Jesus and his early manifestations, second only to the annual celebration of the Easter mystery *(#32)*.

- *Season of Lent.* The season of Lent is a preparation for the celebration of Easter. The liturgy prepares the catechumens for the celebration of the Paschal mystery by the several stages of Christian initiation. It also prepares the faithful, who recall their baptism and do penance in preparation for Easter *(#27)*.

- *The Easter Triduum.* Christ redeemed all people and gave perfect glory to God principally through his Paschal mystery. By dying he destroyed death, and by rising he restored life. The Easter triduum of the passion and resurrection of Christ is thus the culmination of the entire liturgical year *(#18)*.

- *Easter Season.* The fifty days from Easter Sunday to Pentecost are celebrated as one feast day, sometimes called "the great Sunday" *(#22)*.

- *Ordinary Time.* Apart from the seasons of Easter, Lent, Christmas, and Advent, which have their own characteristics, there are thirty-three or thirty-four weeks in the course of the year which celebrate no particular aspect of the mystery of Christ. Instead, especially on the last Sundays, the mystery of Christ in all its fullness is celebrated. This period is known as Ordinary Time *(#43)*.

- *Rogation and Ember Days.* On rogation and ember days, the Church publicly thanks the Lord and prays to him for the needs of all, especially for the productivity of the earth and for people's labor *(#45)*.

SACRED TIME

The division of the Church Year into Ordinary Time and special seasons follows a pattern inherent in nature. The pattern is ebb and flow. Violent storms are preceded and followed by extreme quiet. Tides rise and recede. Warm seasons follow cold.

Every year, beginning with Advent, the Church celebrates the birth, death and resurrection of Jesus. These events are marked by special seasons of the Church Year. The People of God celebrate the seasons by making the liturgies of the season special, just as they would make any important celebration special.

Color is an important part of the liturgical seasons. During Lent and Advent, the liturgical color is purple, a color which represents the solemn and penitential way the faithful feel during these seasons.

Christmas, Jesus' birth; Easter, his resurrection; Epiphany, his manifestation to the Gentile world; and Pentecost, the birthday of the Church and the coming of the Holy Spirit are times of profound joy! The liturgical color is white or gold.

The special seasons of the Church Year are filled with intense emotions as the faithful recall and commemorate Jesus' saving acts. The special seasons help them affirm their beliefs and renew their faith as they learn again the wonder of Jesus' teaching and life. Each year, they celebrate the same events, but because they have grown over the year and experienced many new things, they discover new meaning for Jesus in their lives.

The special seasons of the Church Year are marked by differences in liturgical celebration; they are times of learning and emotion; they are the "flow" of the Church Year. But the Church Year has an "ebb" time as well. This is called *Ordinary Time* and is celebrated for thirty-three or thirty-four Sundays every year.

During Ordinary Time, the Church celebrates special days which don't always fall on Sundays like Corpus Christi (on Thursday in some places), the feast of the Sacred Heart, Mary's Immaculate Conception, and the feasts of many saints.

Jesus knew about the sacredness of the ordinary. His stories are filled with the most common, everyday items, familiar to everyone. Coins, sheep, lamps, mustard seeds, lilies, bushel baskets, fig trees, and fish nets—all ordinary—all helped Jesus teach about the kingdom of God.

When Jesus wanted to give his followers something with which to always remember his death, he chose two very common items, bread and wine. Jesus knew that as long as his followers ate, they would have a daily reminder of him.

The Church's ordinary Eucharistic Liturgies, in which the bread and wine become Jesus' sacrifice, show the faithful how they can set aside their lives for God. The symbols of bread and wine and the ritual of offering gifts tell them that as Jesus' life is offered for them, so theirs must be offered to God and one another. The sense of community during an ordinary liturgy strengthens Jesus' followers for their work as Christians. The final benediction blesses them as they leave the Eucharistic Celebration to live Christ's teachings.

The liturgical color for Ordinary Time is green, the symbol of hope. Each Eucharist recalls in faith Jesus' crucifixion and resurrection, experiences the love of his followers' present ministry and mission, and looks forward in hope to the final coming of Jesus, when time will end and the kingdom of God will be established.

PRAYERS AND ACTIONS OF THE PEOPLE OF GOD

THE LORD'S PRAYER

Our Father, who art in heaven,
  hallowed be thy name.
Thy kingdom come; thy will be done
  on earth as it is in heaven.
Give us this day our daily bread,
  and forgive us our trespasses
    as we forgive those who trespass
    against us.
And lead us not into temptation
  but deliver us from evil.
  Amen.

DOXOLOGY

Glory to the Father,
  and to the Son,
  and to the Holy Spirit:
As it was in the beginning,
  is now, and will be forever.
Amen.

HAIL MARY

Hail Mary, full of grace,
  the Lord is with you.
Blessed are you among women,
  and blessed is the fruit
  of your womb, Jesus.
Holy Mary, Mother of God,
  pray for us sinners,
  now and at the hour of our death.
Amen.

PROFESSION OF FAITH

We believe in one God, the Father, the Almighty,
  maker of heaven and earth, of all that is seen
  and unseen.
We believe in one Lord, Jesus Christ, the only
  Son of God, eternally begotten of the Father,
  God from God, Light from Light, true God
  from true God, begotten, not made, one in
  Being with the Father.
Through him all things were made.
For us men and for our salvation he came down
  from heaven: by the power of the Holy Spirit
  he was born of the Virgin Mary and became
  man.
For our sake he was crucified under Pontius
  Pilate: he suffered, died, and was buried.
On the third day he rose again in fulfillment of
  the Scriptures; he ascended into heaven and is
  seated at the right hand of the Father.
He will come again in glory to judge the living
  and the dead, and his kingdom will have no
  end.
We believe in the Holy Spirit, the Lord, the giver
  of life, who proceeds from the Father and the
  Son.
With the Father and the Son he is worshiped
  and glorified.
He has spoken through the Prophets.
We believe in one holy catholic and apostolic
  Church.
We acknowledge one baptism for the forgive-
  ness of sins.
We look for the resurrection of the dead and the
  life of the world to come.
Amen.

THE MEMORARE

Remember, O most gracious Virgin Mary, that
never was it known that anyone who fled to
your protection, implored your help, or sought
your intercession was left unaided. Inspired
with this confidence, we fly unto you, O Virgin
of Virgins, our Mother. To you we come, before
you we kneel, sinful and sorrowful. O Mother
of the Word made flesh, do not despise our petitions, but in your mercy hear and answer them.
Amen.

THE WAY OF THE CROSS

 1. Jesus is condemned to death.
 2. Jesus takes up his cross.
 3. Jesus falls the first time.
 4. Jesus meets his Mother.
 5. Simon helps Jesus carry his cross.
 6. Veronica wipes the face of Jesus.
 7. Jesus falls the second time.
 8. Jesus meets the women of Jerusalem.
 9. Jesus falls the third time.
10. Jesus is stripped of his garments.
11. Jesus is nailed to the cross.
12. Jesus dies on the cross.
13. Jesus is taken down from the cross.
14. Jesus is laid in the tomb.

THE BEATITUDES

Blest are the poor in spirit;
  the reign of God is theirs.
Blest are the sorrowing;
  they shall be consoled.
Blest are the lowly;
  they shall inherit the land.
Blest are they who hunger and thirst for holiness;
  they shall have their fill.
Blest are they who show mercy;
  mercy shall be theirs.
Blest are the single-hearted
  for they shall see God.
Blest are the peacemakers;
  they shall be called children of God.
Blest are those persecuted for holiness' sake;
  the reign of God is theirs.

THE TEN COMMANDMENTS

1. I, the Lord, am your God. You shall not have other gods besides me.
2. You shall not take the name of the Lord, your God, in vain.
3. Remember to keep holy the sabbath day.
4. Honor your father and your mother.
5. You shall not kill.
6. You shall not commit adultery.
7. You shall not steal.
8. You shall not bear false witness against your neighbor.
9. You shall not covet your neighbor's wife.
10. You shall not covet anything that belongs to your neighbor.

PRECEPTS OF THE CHURCH

1. Participate in the Eucharist and do not do unnecessary work on Sundays and holy days.
2. Receive Holy Communion during Easter time.
3. Confess serious sin at least once a year.
4. Follow the regulations of the Church concerning marriage and other sacraments.
5. Do penance according to the local rules.
6. Help with the support of the Church.
7. Join the missionary spirit and apostolate of the Church.

CORPORAL WORKS OF MERCY

1. Feed the hungry.
2. Give drink to the thirsty.
3. Clothe the naked.
4. Shelter the homeless.
5. Visit the sick.
6. Visit the imprisoned.
7. Bury the dead.

SPIRITUAL WORKS OF MERCY

1. Convert the sinner.
2. Instruct the ignorant.
3. Counsel the doubtful.
4. Comfort the sorrowful.
5. Bear wrongs patiently.
6. Forgive injuries.
7. Pray for the living and the dead.

GIFTS OF THE HOLY SPIRIT

1. Wisdom
2. Understanding
3. Right judgment
4. Courage
5. Knowledge
6. Reverence
7. Wonder and awe (Fear of the Lord)

FRUITS OF THE HOLY SPIRIT

1. Love
2. Joy
3. Patient endurance
4. Kindness
5. Generosity
6. Faith
7. Mildness
8. Chastity

ACT OF CONTRITION

Heavenly Father, I am truly sorry for all my sins.
I ask for your help and forgiveness.
I know that you love me, and I want to be your
loving *(son, daughter)*.
I promise to ask Jesus for his help to keep me
away from everything that might lead me to
sin again.
Amen.

ACT OF FAITH

O my God, I firmly believe that you are one
God in three Divine Persons: the Father, the
Son, and the Holy Spirit. I believe in Jesus
Christ, your Son, who became man and died for
our sins, and who will come to judge the living
and the dead. I believe these and all the truths
which the holy catholic Church teaches, because you who know all have revealed them.
Amen.

ACT OF HOPE

O my God, trusting in your goodness and
promises, I hope to obtain pardon of my sins,
the help of your grace, and life everlasting,
through the merits of Jesus Christ, my Lord
and Redeemer. Amen.

ACT OF CHARITY

O my God, I love you above all things, because
you are all-good and worthy of my love. I love
my neighbor as myself for love of you. I forgive
all who have injured me, and I ask pardon of all
who I have injured. Amen.

HOW TO SAY THE ROSARY

1. Make the Sign of the Cross and say the Apostles' Creed.
2. Say the Our Father.
3. Say three Hail Marys and the Glory to the Father.
4. Meditate on the 1st Mystery, saying the Our Father, the ten Hail Marys, and the Glory to the Father.
5. Meditate on the 2nd Mystery, saying the Our Father, the ten Hail Marys, and the Glory to the Father.
6. Meditate on the 3rd Mystery, saying the Our Father, the ten Hail Marys, and the Glory to the Father.
7. Meditate on the 4th Mystery, saying the Our Father, the ten Hail Marys, and the Glory to the Father.
8. Meditate on the 5th Mystery, saying the Our Father, the ten Hail Marys, and the Glory to the Father.
9. Concluding Prayers:

The Joyful Mysteries (Mondays and Thursdays, Sundays of Advent, and after Epiphany until Lent)

1. The Annunciation
2. The Visitation
3. The Nativity
4. The Presentation
5. The Finding in the Temple

The Sorrowful Mysteries (Tuesdays and Fridays, and Sundays in Lent)

1. Agony in the Garden
2. The Scourging
3. The Crowning with Thorns
4. The Carrying of the Cross
5. The Crucifixion

The Glorious Mysteries (Wednesdays and Saturdays, and Sundays after Easter until Advent)

1. The Resurrection
2. The Ascension
3. The Descent of the Holy Spirit
4. The Assumption
5. The Coronation

PROCEDURE FOR RECEIVING THE SACRAMENT OF RECONCILIATION

1. Prayer for enlightenment.
2. Examination of conscience.
3. The priest greets me, and may read a Scripture passage, if we have not had a general prayer service. I tell the priest my sins, and try to identify motives behind my actions. (For example, "I missed Mass several times because of laziness" or "because I didn't believe in God and didn't see the point" are two entirely different motives, and need different types of assistance.)
4. The priest offers advice, and suggests a penance, or asks me to think of an appropriate penance.
5. I offer a spontaneous prayer of sorrow (Act of Contrition) or a learned one such as the following;

   "Oh my God, I am truly sorry for having offended you. I detest all my sins, because I fear the loss of heaven and the pain of hell. But most of all, I am sorry because my sins offend you, my God, for you are completely good and deserving of all my love. I firmly resolve with the help of your grace, to sin no more, and to avoid the near occasions of sin."

6. The priest gives me absolution, and forgives me in the name of Jesus and the Christian Community, the Church.
7. I return to my seat, thank God for His mercy, and do the penance the priest has given me—perhaps saying particular prayers, or reading Scripture.

Be Born Again

TEACHER'S MANUAL

Dedication
For my parents, Francis W. Parnell and Dorothy Lalor Parnell

Nihil Obstat:
Rev. Robert J. McManus, M.A., S.T.D.
Censor Deputatus

Imprimatur:
†Louis E. Gelineau, D.D.
June 29, 1989

Send all inquiries to:
Benziger Publishing Company
15319 Chatsworth Street
Mission Hills, California 91395

Printed in the United States

ISBN 0-02-655921-8 (Student Edition)
ISBN 0-02-655922-6 (Teacher's Annotated Edition)

2 3 4 5 6 7 8 9   93 92 91 90

Contents

Introduction

Water and Spirit is a comprehensive and flexible process for Confirmation catechesis which grew up out of need. Since the promulgation of the *Rite of Christian Initiation of Adults* in 1972, there has not been a high school Confirmation preparation process that fully reflects the understanding of the sacrament in the RCIA. *Water and Spirit* was written to address that need.

The RCIA is a process of initiation into the Christian community. This new rite was developed out of the awareness that Christianity is a way of life and a commitment to Jesus. As part of the initiation process, preparing for Confirmation involves more than assimilating a body of truths. It is a spiritual journey that takes place in the context of the community of the faithful. "Together with the candidates, the faithful reflect upon the value of the paschal mystery, renew their own conversion, and by their example lead the candidates to obey the Holy Spirit more generously" (*RCIA* #4). It is a time to learn what it means to live a Christian life.

The RCIA prescribes a series of stages for the initiation process. These are based on the practice of the early Church in accepting new members into the community. The first stage is a time for evangelization. The Gospel is proclaimed to the candidates, and opportunity for inquiry is provided. During the second stage, the candidates go through an extended period of spiritual formation and catechesis. The third stage occurs during Lent and involves an intensive preparation of heart and spirit to receive the sacraments of initiation. The last stage occurs after the new member is received into the community. It is a time for reflection on the mysteries of faith and strengthening ties to the community.

Water and Spirit implements the process established by the RCIA. The candidates for Confirmation are taken through stages of preparation aimed at helping them become fully involved in the Christian community. The *Water and Spirit* process actively engages the young people in a practical preparation for full membership through discussion, activities, prayer, Scripture, reflection, and service in the context of the parish community. The use of liturgy, prayer services, witness speakers, research assignments, and group projects keep interaction strong between the candidates and the local community.

The rhythm of the liturgical year is integral to the *Water and Spirit* process. The incorporation of the cycles of the Church year reinforces the content of the lessons and activities for the candidates. Themes of Confirmation preparation are presented during the appropriate liturgical season. It also keeps the candidates involved with the public prayer and worship of the parish community. As they move from season to season, they become more aware of how the Christian community renews itself by celebrating the life, death, and resurrection of Christ.

Since the Confirmation preparation process is one of full conversion to Christ and his message, it is important to allow the candidates as much time as possible to prepare for full initiation into the Christian community. *Water and Spirit* can be used as either a one-year or two-year process. Level I, *Be Born Again,* covers the first year. Level II, *Of Water and the Spirit,* covers the second. In parishes with a one-year Confirmation program, *Of Water and the Spirit* may be used with special cycling-in lessons as a complete preparation.

According to the RCIA, Confirmation is a sacrament which ratifies and strengthens the commitment made at Baptism. Like Matrimony and Orders, it entails a significant change in the life of the person receiving the sacrament. He or she must be prepared to live as a full member of the Christian community. And so the initiation of new members into the community places demands on all who are involved in the process: candidates, catechists, parents, sponsors, priests and deacons, the parish community, and the bishop.

In particular, the candidates must be willing to undergo a full conversion to Christ and his message and to be grounded in the fundamentals of the spiritual life and Christian teaching (see *RCIA #15*). As the primary educators of their children, parents, along with sponsors, should be intimately involved in the catechesis for Confirmation by witnessing to the candidates' morals, faith, and intention, meeting with the program director and staff, and attending rites and liturgies of the Confirmation preparation process (see *RCIA #42*, *National Catechetical Directory* #119). With the help of sponsors, catechists, and deacons, it is the responsibility of the pastors to judge the dispositions of the candidates and their readiness to be Confirmed (see *RCIA #16*).

It is for the bishop, in person or through a delegate, to set up, regulate, and promote the pastoral formation of candidates and to admit the candidates to their election and to the sacrament of Confirmation. If possible, he himself will celebrate the rite of election and the sacraments of initiation (see *RCIA #44*). The catechists play an important role both in teaching and guiding the candidates and in helping the local parish community become involved in the preparation process. They must be prepared to share their faith and give personal witness to the candidates (see *RCIA #48*).

Finally, the parish community as a whole has responsibilities. The members of the community should share the spirit of the Gospel with the candidates by inviting them into their families and engaging them in private conversation. They should be present at the rites for entrance into the catechumenate and election, the scrutinies and presentations, and, of course, at the celebration of the sacrament of Confirmation (see *RCIA #41*).

Water and Spirit provides the means to involve all the members of the parish community in a thorough preparation of candidates for the sacrament of Confirmation. The materials for the candidates will ground them in the spiritual life and the fundamental teachings of the Church and help them make a full commitment to Jesus and his message. With background material, sample rites and services, suggested days and evenings of reflection and planning, and notes for parents, sponsors, and pastors, the *Water and Spirit* process helps the parish community initiate the candidates into full membership in the Church in accordance with the Rite of Christian Initiation of Adults.

Water and Spirit was developed over several years in a parish setting. The process has been very successful in drawing the whole parish into Confirmation preparation and giving the participants a new understanding of the sacrament.

For the Program Director

The Catechist Guide and Resource Book

The Catechist Guide and Resource Book is a collection of materials designed to aid the program director and the teaching team in planning and implementing the *Water and Spirit* Confirmation preparation process. The materials may be used as suggested, or adapted to your specific parish needs. All pages may be removed and reproduced as needed.

For the Program Director provides background material to aid the director in administering the *Water and Spirit* process and adapting it to the needs of the parish.

For the Catechist offers suggestions for classroom procedure, background on adolescents and Confirmation, and ideas for adding creativity to the program.

Forms furnish material for parents, pastors, sponsors, and candidates as well as days of prayer and planning for the staff, sample rites for the Confirmation process, and prayer services.

Audiovisual Resources contains a guide for using media, names and addresses of sources, and suggestions for media to go with specific steps in Level I and Level II.

Cycling-in Lessons can be removed, duplicated, and used by the candidates as introductory lessons in parishes using only Level II in a one-year Confirmation program.

Lesson Plans contain introductions to each liturgical season and stage of the Confirmation process. Then they provide suggestions and strategies for using the material in the candidate text. Each plan offers the catechist an overview of the lesson, ideas for developing themes of the lesson, and options for extended class work or home assignments. Although the plans are designed to pace the catechist through the material, they are meant to be flexible. Each lesson plan contains the following components:

- *Aim:* objective of the lesson.
- *This Step:* background material and an overview of the theme of the lesson.
- *Resource Reference:* specific references to materials in the manual to be read or reviewed while preparing the lesson.
- *Group Reunion:* ideas for handling the opening group discussion.
- Suggestions for developing the material in each thematic section.
- *Reflect:* optional class or home procedure for using material in The Word of God, From the Holy Father, and Dear Candidate.
- *Respond:* suggestions for using the questions in this section for class discussion or home assignment.
- *Prayer:* ideas for using the final prayer in each step to close the session.
- *Summary:* a synopsis of the lesson at a glance.

Parish Policy on Confirmation

The following guidelines for setting policy for the parish are in accordance with *Sharing the Light of Faith: National Catechetical Directory (NCD)*. They reflect the guidelines proposed by a number of bishops throughout the United States.

Rationale. Candidates in both public and parochial schools are required to complete the one-year or the two-year Confirmation process in the parish.

Since the goal is to form Christian community among the candidates, it is believed that two years is the optimal time for candidates to pray, share, learn, worship, and serve together. The minimal time for the process would be one year. Perfect attendance in the Confirmation process is expected.

Adequate understanding. A diagnostic interview and diagnostic test can be administered at the beginning of the *Water and Spirit* process (Forms 2 and 3). A take-home test will be given at the end of the Process (Form 38), corrected by the catechist, and evaluated by the program director, as part of the evaluation process.

Attendance at liturgy. The Family of God gathers together as a parish community at the weekly liturgy. For this reason, candidates are expected to attend weekly liturgy at the parish. Frequent reception of Holy Eucharist and reception of the sacrament of Reconciliation are encouraged.

Stewardship. Confirmation candidates are asked to complete a service project which includes five hours as a class and ten hours of individual service. The service projects are accounted for by the candidates to aides appointed by the coordinator of the *Water and Spirit* process.

Participation in days of prayer and retreat. Candidates are to attend and participate in days of prayer and retreat. The purpose of these gatherings is to aid in the spiritual growth of the candidate, so that he or she will prayerfully approach the sacrament of Confirmation in full commitment to Jesus as Lord.

Christian living. The Confirmation candidate is expected to live a life consistent with his or her baptismal calling, which is sealed in the sacrament of Confirmation. Periodic interviews are held during which the staff can elicit from the candidate his or her growth and progress during the Confirmation process. Family members are encouraged to participate in the sacramental preparation process.

Administration. The pastor of the parish community is the individual who makes the final decision as to whether a candidate is ready to receive the sacrament of Confirmation. The staff of the Confirmation process may be involved to some degree in the evaluation of candidates, but the pastor, as chief educator of the parish, will make the decision.

Petition for Confirmation. As the final step, the candidates will write to the bishop requesting Confirmation and indicating readiness to make the commitment to live out the baptismal promises. (See Form 35 for a sample petition.)

The Water and Spirit Process

One of the purposes of the *Water and Spirit* process is to develop relationships. The relationship of the young person with Christ is fostered through prayer and study and expressed in apostolic action. Through apostolic action, the candidates will develop an awareness that the Lord is the source of all we have, or own, or do. We must be ready to give back to God all he has given us.

The approach of the process is personal. Time has proven that the most effective way of reaching a person for Christ is the way Jesus himself used: one-to-one. The process—one of preparation and initiation—is called the Confirmation catechumenate, and it involves four stages.

Getting Ready. The focus is on sharing experiences and faith and helping the candidates understand what it means to enter preparation for Confirmation. During this stage the candidates will explore their own lives and see the relationship of their faith stories to the story of Jesus and the Church.

The Journey. The emphasis in this stage is twofold: first, the candidates will explore what it means to be a Catholic Christian. Second, they will explore their own stories in relation to the stories of Jesus in the New Testament and the heroes and heroines in the Old Testament. They will also examine the relationship between the earliest Christian communities and the Church today.

Seeing the Light. The purpose of this stage is to help the candidates enter into the Lenten experience as a part of their journey. It is a time of personal purification and immediate preparation to receive the sacrament of Confirmation.

Alleluia! The final stage brings the newly confirmed members to growing faith through sharing, prayer, and a more active role in the community of the parish.

Where Do I Begin?

The Confirmation preparation process is one of conversion, and this conversion process must begin with the person who is directly responsible for the Confirmation—the program director. The more your life is centered on the Person and teachings of Jesus Christ, the more easily you will lead the group leaders and the young people through the process. You actually begin the process. As you grow in your prayer life and share your faith with the other leaders and the candidates, you will be able to build the kind of Christian community in which the Confirmation process can flourish.

Then what? You should begin to form a team of Christians to be leaders for the candidates entering the Confirmation process. Some questions you might consider about a possible leader are the following: Does this person have a strong faith life? Is the person familiar with the teachings of Christ and the Church? Is the person willing and able to share his or her life in Christ with the candidates?

At what age should Confirmation be administered? We should stop asking at what age Confirmation should be experienced. The important thing is the student's readiness for conversion. Most bishops seem to feel that the late teenage years are more suitable than the early teens; consequently, this process is geared for candidates in the middle-to-late teens.

Guidelines for Choosing Catechists

In discussing "Faith and the Adolescent," Reverend Alfonso Nebreda, S.J., suggests that our success as people serving the needs of youth depends on our spiritual situation in relation to our own faith. He maintains that if our own spiritual life is healthy there should not be problems in serving the spiritual needs of youth.

In choosing a team of adults to work with Confirmation candidates, you must search for leaders who are mature enough in their own faith walk that they will neither overwhelm nor underestimate the young people involved. Catechists of Confirmation candidates must indeed understand the needs of youth, but they must also have an understanding and acceptance of the truths of the Catholic Church.

It is important, therefore, to select those adults who have a clear grasp of such areas as the Creed, Catholic morality, the Church and parish community, prayer, and the sacraments. Catechists should have access to background and resource materials in the parish or school library.

The task of forming a Confirmation team may seem difficult, and it is a challenge, but in the last analysis, it is the Lord who will do the formation. The Lord is faithful and he is the one who will give to catechists the desire to teach and the eagerness to serve. He will literally "raise up" the individuals you need to form a team of leaders in the Confirmation process.

Testing and Evaluating Candidates

Some religious educators feel uncomfortable with any form of testing. They feel that the testing process, by placing too much emphasis on intellectual knowledge, can produce anxiety in the candidates. There must be a clear understanding of why and how to test. Program directors can share with their catechists the following guidelines for testing and evaluating.

- Evaluation should be a positive means for the candidate to realize how much he or she already understands about his or her own faith walk in relation to that of the other followers of Jesus. In other words, testing can be a way of affirming the candidate, and it should be just that—affirmation.

- Testing can be either written or oral. Often the candidate is able to share the presence of the Lord in his or her life better through the essay form than by responding to a test requiring objective answers.

- The testing process should actually be a means for the individual candidate to measure himself or herself against what the Lord is asking, not against the progress of other candidates. However, there are some very basic truths that must be assimilated, not merely learned, during the process of Confirmation preparation.

A sample diagnostic interview and sample diagnostic test are in Forms 2 and 3.

Policy on Parent Sessions

A candidate and parent session should be held at the beginning of the preparation process, preferably one or two weeks after class begins. Form 4 is a sample letter of invitation to this session. Your catechists should also attend this meeting and participate in the sharing session with the candidates and their parents.

The purpose of the meeting is to explain the Confirmation preparation process, review the covenant so the candidates and their parents can understand what is to occur during this process, and give the parents a chance to meet the catechists.

A sample plan for the session is Form 5. Use it as is or adapt it to your parish needs.

Policy on Sponsor Sessions

Approximately one month after the Confirmation process begins, the first sponsor session should be held. At this time the sponsors are given information about their roles and are given the opportunity to ask questions. Form 7 is a sample first sponsor session.

Sponsors meet monthly with their candidates throughout the rest of the process. At these classes, whether in homes or in a hall, discussion groups continue, with catechists as discussion leaders. Classes proceed as usual, with the sponsors and candidates meeting for individual sharing. For example, when the lesson specifies sharing with one other person, the candidates and their sponsors share insights and responses to the question or exercise.

Sponsors are also asked to keep in touch with their candidates between classes. They might wish to attend liturgical services together, or invite candidates into their homes for prayer and discussion.

The Right Sponsor Makes a Difference

Every year thousands of young people prepare for Confirmation. Although the young people come to Confirmation classes faithfully and are confirmed, the leaders of the Church still complain that "we are losing our young people." Why do some young people drop out and others stay involved? What can we do to keep our young people involved in the Church?

Young people who have a commitment to Jesus, and who try to keep that commitment, need the example of adult Christians. Sometimes the adults are parents, relatives, or friends. However, according to hundreds of young people questioned, the answer is sponsorship.

The *Rite of Christian Initiation of Adults* states that each candidate must have a sponsor "to show the catechumen (candidate) in a realistic and practical way the place of the Gospel in his or her own life and in society, to help with doubts or anxieties, to give public testimony for the candidate, and to watch over the progress of the baptismal life" (#43). These same norms can be useful in determining sponsors for the Confirmation process.

Reverend Ray Kemp, a priest in the city of Washington, D.C., has implemented the adult catechumenate in his parish for several years. He makes the point that the sponsor should be chosen, or at least validated, by the parish. The parish must make it clear that sponsorship carries more responsibility than merely appearing on the scene at Confirmation; sponsorship should be a lifelong commitment.

Qualifications of a Sponsor

Often, the people most willing to serve as sponsors are young people who have recently been confirmed. The idea of youth ministering to youth is a valuable one, and the enthusiasm of such recent candidates is invaluable. Perhaps one caution is to avoid asking people to sponsor more than one person since the commitment is lifelong and sponsorship of a different candidate each year or two minimizes the role. Directors and catechists of the process should avoid sponsorship. The following are qualifications of a sponsor:

- The sponsor must be a person of faith and a confirmed Catholic in good standing.
- The sponsor should reflect Christian values in word, worship, and service.
- The sponsor must be willing to attend at least one session a month with the candidate and weekly sessions during the Lent prior to Confirmation.

- The sponsor must be willing to meet personally with the candidate on a monthly basis, to discuss the candidate's prayer life, and to share faith and prayer.
- The sponsor must be willing to attend all liturgical rites of the Confirmation process.

In order to locate qualified sponsors, ask for volunteers from Marriage Encounter, Cursillo, and the Charismatic renewal of the parish. Then create a master list to be made available to young people who need help choosing their own sponsors. Each sponsor should be interviewed in advance to ensure his or her readiness for the role.

Candidate and Sponsor Sharing

The purpose of the candidate and sponsor relationship is to lead the candidate into a deeper relationship with Jesus. The faith sharing that occurs between candidate and sponsor builds their relationship and enables the candidate to accept the Holy Spirit more fully. As the candidate and sponsor share experiences of the past, explore the meaning of the present, and set goals for the future, they affirm one another in their journeys of faith.

Candidates and their sponsors should plan to meet at least once a month, but ideally, they should meet every two weeks to share with one another how the Lord has been leading them since their last meeting. A formal structured meeting is not necessary, but it one is desired, the following guidelines can serve as the structure for each candidate and sponsor meeting.

- Candidate and sponsor share an opening prayer, either spontaneous or formal.
- Sponsor discusses the questions found in Form 7.
- Sponsor and candidate pray together to close their session. They might want to mention special needs either of them has and pray for them.

Note: Program directors might want to reproduce Sponsor's Agreement and Sponsor's Questions for Candidates, Form 7, and distribute them as part of a special packet for sponsors.

Scheduling

The following is an overview of the *Water and Spirit* Confirmation preparation process. Whether done in a one-year or two-year program, all of these elements are important for the process to be an effective opportunity for conversion and reception of the sacrament.

Invitation

The parish should invite young people in the community who desire to prepare for the sacrament of Confirmation. The announcement should make it clear that the decision to enter the preparation process is a free choice. During this invitation, the parish community should be educated to the nature of Christian initiation and the importance of Confirmation in that process.

Diagnostic Interview

The diagnostic interview takes place before the young person is accepted into the process. It is an opportunity to explore his or her personal readiness for the sacrament. The interview should be a positive and supportive event to help the young person discern his or her relationship to Jesus Christ.

Stage One: Getting Ready	Initial classes provide the young people with an opportunity to explore further their readiness to prepare for the sacrament of Confirmation. This is a time for inquiry and clarification. During this period, the young people explore their own life stories, learn to share their stories with others, and reflect on the importance of commitment.
Parent Session	An explanatory meeting involving parents, young people, and catechists should be held toward the beginning of the preparation process— preferably during the second or third lesson of the process. (In a one-year process, this would occur during the cycling-in lessons.) The purpose of the meeting is to explain the policies and expectations of the Confirmation team.
Sponsor Session	Approximately one month after the Confirmation process begins, the first sponsor session should be held. At this time, the sponsors are given information about their roles and have the opportunity to ask questions.
Rite of Becoming a Candidate	The candidates' decision to prepare for and celebrate the sacrament of Confirmation should be celebrated by the parish community at Sunday Eucharist on or near the first Sunday of Advent. Form 8, The Rite of Becoming a Candidate, is based on the rite of enrollment in the RCIA.
Stage Two: The Journey	This is an intensive preparation period involving the candidates, sponsors, catechists, parents, and parish ministers. It extends from the beginning of Advent (year one) to the beginning of Lent (year two) in a two-year program, or from Advent to Lent in a one-year program. Catechesis during this period covers worship and spiritual development, the Christian message and tradition, and service—all done within the parish community. It is a time of discovering and affirming the gifts of the candidates, intro- ducing them to the joys and responsibilities of full Christian membership, and reinforcing them in their study of Jesus' message, the faith of the community, the sacraments, the Church's mission, and ministry.
The Presentations	The presentations of the Creed and the Lord's Prayer entrust the candidates with the documents which summarize the Church's faith and prayer. Either presentation may be made at the conclusion of an appro- priate lesson or at a separate ceremony during a day of recollection during the Journey stage.
Stage Three: Seeing the Light	This period covers the season of Lent prior to celebrating the sacrament of Confirmation. It is a time of purification and reflection for the candidates.
Rite of Election	The celebration of the Rite of Election, or enrollment of names, takes place during the first Sunday of Lent. It is an opportunity for the candidates to reaffirm their intention before the proximate preparation for the sacrament.
The Scrutinies	The scrutinies take place during the liturgies of the third, fourth, and fifth Sundays of Lent. They are intended to purify the candidates' minds and hearts, to strengthen them against temptation, and to make firm their decision to follow Christ.

Final Test/Concluding Interview

This is an opportunity to examine the readiness of the candidates to receive the sacrament of Confirmation. The interview is a time for the Confirmation team and the pastor to meet personally with each confirmand and discuss his or her growth during the preparation process. The final test should be given toward the end of Lent.

Preparation for the Sacrament of Confirmation

A practice session should be held before the celebration of the sacrament to prepare all involved.

Celebration of the Sacrament of Confirmation

If possible, the sacrament should be celebrated at the Easter Vigil or between Easter and Pentecost.

Stage Four: Alleluia

During this last stage, the newly confirmed members reflect on the mysteries of faith and prepare to take on active and responsible roles within the parish community. It is a time to prepare for mission and service as fully initiated members of the Body of Christ.

Planning Meetings

Planning meetings are a part of every successful parish program; it is necessary for team members to gather together to plan lessons and discuss various problems as they develop. However, if the meetings begin with praying and sharing, team relationships will grow, a sense of community will prevail, and much of the planning will flow more easily.

A preliminary day of recollection (see Form 9, Questions for the Confirmation Team) and then a monthly meeting for reflection and planning have proven to be substantial experiences which offer spiritual nourishment for all those involved. Forms 10 through 17 provide sample plans for these meetings.

For the Catechist

The standard teacher's guide is somewhat like a cookbook: follow the recipe to the letter, and you will produce definite results. Unfortunately, the process of conversion differs considerably from the process of cooking! Those who have been involved in religious education realize that no tightly structured program will necessarily produce the desired results.

Therefore, this Catechist Guide should serve as a resource center. Used as a base of operations, it can give you the impetus to pray, share, plan, and implement an individualized preparation process for your parish. For indeed, the key to the success of the entire process may be your parish community.

As you encourage people from your parish community to flow in and out of the process, as you invite speakers from different ministries of the parish, as you lead the young people into an awareness of where they can fit into the prayer-and-work life of the parish family, life will surge into your Confirmation process.

This catechist Guide and Resource Book contains all the necessary aids to guide you through a one-year or a two-year Confirmation preparation program. You may use these ideas and forms as they are or modify them according to your needs. They are organized as follows:

- *For the Program Director:* You may wish to read the material in this section for background.

- *For the Catechist:* These pages describe the candidate text, classroom procedures, the Forms that the catechist may wish to use, and the Lesson Plans.

- *Forms:* These are black line masters to use for student handouts, catechist handouts, letters to parents and sponsors, liturgies, or prayer services.

- *Audiovisual Resources:* The *Water and Spirit* process can easily accommodate the use of thematic slides, films, videotapes, and other resources. Included is a chapter-by-chapter list of suggested media and a list of media sources.

- *Lesson Plans:* These are divided into Level I and Level II.

- *Cycling-In Lessons:* These are black line masters of three chapters from Level I that can serve as an introduction if you are teaching only Level II in a one-year course.

Candidate Text

The *Water and Spirit* preparation process is divided into four stages, each reflecting a phase in the Rite of Christian Initiation of Adults. Level I of the text begins with the first stage, "Getting Ready," which parallels the precatechumenate stage and introduces the idea of story-telling and faith sharing. "The Journey" is the second stage, and it parallels the catechumenate stage. This phase has a twofold emphasis: an explanation of what it means to be a Catholic Christian and an exploration of the young people's own stories in relation to the stories of Jesus and other New Testament people.

Level II continues "The Journey," and then progresses to the third stage, "Seeing the Light." This stage is based on the illumination stage, or the election stage of Christian Initiation. This stage ends with the celebration of the sacrament. The fourth and final stage is "Alleluia," based on Mystagogy. It takes place after the sacrament and helps integrate the young people into the full life of the parish.

The process also follows the rhythms of the liturgical year. As the candidates celebrate Ordinary Time, Advent, Christmas, Lent, Easter, and Pentecost, each chapter (step) interweaves the lessons from the particular stage with themes from the liturgical season. This correlation encourages the young people to become increasingly connected to these celebrations and aware of how each season enriches the conversion process.

The basic units of instruction are called *steps*. The steps all follow the same pattern, and this pattern is repeated in the Lesson Plans found in this Catechist Guide. Each step is organized as follows:

This Step. This section explains the goals and objectives of the chapter.

Group Reunion. This is a significant element of the text. At the beginning of each session, the young people gather together to share faith and to experience an increasing development of the community dimension of their lives. A brief review of what has happened to them since the previous session serves two purposes. First, it links the *Water and Spirit* process to everyday experiences. Second, it helps the candidates settle into the next step.

The sharing should be based on the realization that the Christian life, in order to be lived fully, must involve prayer, study, and action. The Group Reunion can serve as a reminder that if any area of the Christian life is missing, changes need to be made.

Theme. This is a series of short sections developing the main ideas of the chapter. The sections vary in content and form, and include short stories, poems, charts, and other materials. There is a section called "Think" in which the young people respond in writing to questions on the thematic material.

Reflect. This three-part section contains the following components:

- *The Word of God.* This section further familiarizes the candidates with Scripture, both Old and New Testament, on the theme material.

- *From the Holy Father.* These passages from the writings of Pope John XXIII, Pope Paul VI, Pope John Paul I, and Pope John Paul II; reflect on or expand the theme of the chapter and under-score the need for young people to come into a personal relationship with Jesus and his Church.

   As the candidates reflect on each passage, you might ask: What does this passage say to you personally? How does the passage relate to the topic we are discussing? What is the relation-ship between what the pope, as head of the Church, is saying and what Jesus said? How would you apply the words to yourself?

   Encourage the young people to bring to class any of the writings by or about the pope from newspapers and magazines for discussion. Some of the candidates might want to form a papal study group to research the writings of different popes and periodically report to the class on their findings.

- *Dear Candidate.* These letters from "Your Family in Christ" personalize the chapter material and relate it to daily life.

Respond. These questions encourage candidates to think and write about their own experiences with the chapter material as a starting point.

Prayer. This is the final feature of each chapter.

A Catholic Treasury

At the end of each candidate text is a section entitled *A Catholic Treasury* containing certain prayers and formulas which are part of Catholic heritage. The National Catechetical Directory, *Sharing the Light of Faith,* emphasizes that "the great traditional prayers of the Church—such as the Apostles' Creed, the Sign of the Cross, the Lord's Prayer, the Hail Mary, and the Glory to the Father—should be known by all. Everyone should know some form of an act of contrition" (NCD, #143).

The other practices contained in this section are also significant. While the candidates should be familiar with them, they need not be memorized. The process of coming to know these practices should continue "gradually, flexibly, and never slavishly" (NCD, #176e). During the course of the year, it may be good to review the relevant items in this section such as the Creed, prayers to Mary, the commandments, the precepts of the Church, the corporal and spiritual works of mercy, and the gifts and fruits of the Holy Spirit.

This section also contains an explanation and summary of the Church year. Since the *Water and Spirit* process is planned around the liturgical year, make a point of going over this material with the candidates sometime toward the beginning of the year.

Lesson Plans

The lesson plans provide suggestions and strategies for using the material in the text. Each plan offers the catechist an overview of the step, ideas for developing the themes of the lesson, and options for extended class work or home assignments. Although the plans are designed to pace the catechist through the material, they are meant to be flexible. As the catechist continues working with the candidates, he or she will discover the approaches (individual/group work, class discussion/home assignment) that best serve the needs of the class.

The lesson plan for each step follows the same pattern as the step. It describes, explains, and offers teaching strategies for every section of the step. The lesson plan also contains the following additional aids:

Aim. This states the aim of the step.

Resource Reference. This is a listing of material within this Catechist Guide—teacher information and Forms—that apply to teaching methods, chapter theme, or liturgical celebrations.

Reach Out. This is an assignment presented near the end of each Lesson Plan. It offers suggestions on how you can encourage the candidates to carry out each particular step during the week.

Summary. This is a synopsis of the lesson plan for each step.

Cycling-In Lessons. These are special steps provided for those candidates who are using only Level II of *Water and Spirit* in a one-year program. These extra lessons are adapted from chapters appearing in the first stage of Level I, "Getting Ready," and are designed to lead candidates into the "Journey" stage, or catechumenate.

The lesson plans for each Cycling-in Lesson are found in the Level I Lesson Plans.

Suggestions for Teaching

Within one classroom you will have young people who have different styles of learning. Some learn best when given clear directions and activities in definite order. Others learn best with experiences that are not locked into logical order; they enjoy problem solving, role playing, and often conclude ideas through intuition. Some respond to words and symbols, and they like rational development and extensive reading; in contrast to these are the young people who enjoy multisensory experiences encompassing the unusual and creative. It is helpful to know that such differences in learning style exist in order to understand different levels of response to different types of activities.

Vary the Teaching Pace. No matter how carefully you may plan a lesson, the participants' moods and rhythms can disrupt your carefully executed plan. Pacing or timing is a delicate skill that is impossible to teach, but there are some signs that indicate when you need to speed up a lesson, slow it down, or change activities. If young people show signs of restlessness, or if there is no response to a discussion, it is time to speed up the lesson. If a discussion is going well, be flexible enough to forego your next activity and expand the discussion time. When you are giving directions or giving information to record, or if participants are deep in thought, slow down your delivery and your pace. If the young people show signs of distraction, or if the activity seems to be too difficult for them, change the activity. If they seem fatigued or have difficulty settling down after a school holiday, be prepared to change activities.

Give Note-taking Tips. Many students are unaware of how to take helpful notes in class, and you may need to encourage them to do the following:

- Put the date on your paper or notebook at the beginning of each class.
- Write the topic or theme of the class.
- Copy any material from the board that outlines or summarizes ideas.
- List any questions you need answered.
- At the end of class, summarize the lesson.

Planning a Prayer Service

There will be times you will want to plan a prayer service. Suggestions for planning, plus a sample prayer service, are found on Form 18.

Helpful Attitudes

Certain attitudes and actions of the catechist can make the difference between passive acceptance of the program and enthusiastic participation.

Willingness to share personal experiences. Students generally react positively to teachers who can share stories from their own experiences. Young people need to know how adults feel about the events of their lives.

Ability to listen critically. A catechist must be able to listen with respect, hear what is being said with an open mind to ideas, and then ask candidates the kinds of questions that will help them analyze and clarify their own values and beliefs.

Openness to spirituality. Although candidates are expected to learn specific information during the Confirmation preparation process, they also need to develop an openness to the Divine Presence. Catechists should help young people look for and be open to the signs of spiritual growth.

Attitude of intellectual honesty. Young people respect teachers or catechists who can admit they don't know an answer, and who can accept the fact that sometimes candidates might not be able to answer a question. In such honesty candidates affirm that neither adults nor young people are perfect and that everyone needs to continue learning.

Forms of Questioning to Use with the Candidates

In the past, *recall* was the most important form of questioning used in religious education. However, psychological and religious studies have shown that such questioning is not really the best form of questioning to use at all stages of spiritual growth. *Comprehension, evaluation, probing,* and *redirection* are other forms of questioning that have value.

Consequently, specific questions are included in the text which will aid in the conversion process leading to Confirmation and continuing spiritual growth.

Recall answers the questions *who, what, when,* and *where.* It is useful for drawing out specific facts, principles, and generalization.

Comprehension answers *how* and *why* and is useful for eliciting understanding, interpretation, summarization, examples, and definitions.

Evaluation answers *should, could,* and *would* and is useful for obtaining judgments, opinions, personal reactions, and criticisms.

To answer *what* and *why* in terms of differences of opinion and clarification, the use of *probing* and *redirection* can be employed.

Assignments and Service Projects

The use of assignments is essential to the Confirmation preparation process. One reason for the use of assignments is that in the brief time we have the candidates in class, it isn't possible to give them as much understanding of their faith as they have in other areas. They need an awareness of why they believe what they do and what they have yet to learn.

One form of helpful assignment is the researching of topics. Another is looking up a passage of Scripture each day and writing a response to that passage. Other useful assignments are a film and television analysis, book and newspaper assignment, and oral reports on various doctrinal matters to be studied during the Confirmation process. All these assignments will help the candidates prepare themselves for Confirmation.

Obviously, service projects are very important and must be an essential part of the candidates' preparation. Young people should understand what that service means.

The service project is an answer to the Gospel challenge to love our neighbor as Jesus loves us. He gave many examples of loving service. The Christian message includes a call to respond, and true response will be evident as the needs of others are met through service projects.

If the parish has a youth minister, he or she should be involved in working with the candidates, helping them to reach out beyond themselves to help others.

Each project will involve the community. If the needs of the community are not known, a notice could be included in the parish bulletin asking for specific needs. Then compile a list of possible projects for the candidates to choose from.

Two things for the candidate to remember are that he or she should freely choose something specific to do; the project should be special and not something already being done as a part of his or her daily routine. Have the young people follow these guidelines:

- Plan in advance what you are going to do.

- Carry out the project within a specific time.

- Consider how the project is helping to build up the kingdom of God.
- Reflect on your feelings while doing the project.
- Determine the possibility of following up on what you have done.

Some parishes prefer to have group projects rather than individual. This increases the range of opportunities to serve the community. A service club can be organized by a group of candidates and a list of services available to the parish provided. This could include things like having a child-care service during parish activities; assisting in the hot meal program for people who are confined to their homes; baby-sitting or grocery shopping for families who need the help; cleaning house and running errands for someone who is disabled or sick. The results of these projects will be twofold; the parish will benefit, but more important, young people themselves become an active part of the life of the parish.

Adult involvement is necessary in service projects, but candidates should be allowed to make the plans and carry them out.

Form 19 should be filled out before and after the project.

Class Projects

There are suggestions for class projects throughout the text. However, the additional projects which follow are special and unique: film and television analysis, New Testament reporting, liturgical drama, Scripture sharing, dance workshop. These projects can be adapted, combined, or used in any way that is most beneficial.

Film and Television Analysis. Either present films and videotapes in class or have the candidates report on movies or television programs they have seen that relate well to a topic being studied. Have the students use Form 20 to assist in their analysis of films and television programs. Another way of using the questions is to have various groups of candidates watch television for specified periods of time—such as an hour every night for a week—and then report on the experience.

Television, Book, and Newspaper Projects. Give the candidates a year-long assignment in which they jot down the various television programs they watch and note the following:

- emotions evoked—positive and negative
- scenes or techniques used most effectively
- message received
- influence—temporary or long lasting

Workers in the television industry who deal with ratings have stated that when people begin noting what they are watching, and for how long, they often become more selective, more critical, and more inclined to seek value in what they are watching.

Similar year-long projects involving books can also be valuable. When candidates keep track of the books they read and begin analyzing them, they might become aware of the fact that they are not reading enough quality material.

Another suggested project for the year is to have the candidates find articles in newspapers or magazines each week which in some way relate to the theme of that week. For example, articles demonstrating the plight of the suffering may be graphic illustration of the suffering Christ in the world today. Have the candidates date each article.

New Testament Report. The report form (Form 21) can be used for any book of the New Testament, or for the biography of a saint.

This report might be assigned toward the end of the first year of the Confirmation preparation process as a take-home exam to assess the candidates' progress throughout the year.

Liturgical Drama. Liturgical drama was used in the ninth through the thirteenth century when simple theatrical techniques were employed to present events of Scripture. Brief and simple theatrical interludes functioned as an integral part of the worship of Divine Office and the Roman Liturgy.

In 1210 Pope Urban IV instituted the Corpus Christi festival with miracle plays (lives of saints), mystery plays (plays from Scripture—from 1275 until the late sixteenth century), and morality plays (allegories).

The use of liturgical drama can be effective for you, either by having the candidates perform an adaptation of *Quem Queritis,* "Whom Are You Seeking?" which is provided in Form 22, or by having the candidates dramatize events from the Bible—the arrival of the shepherds and the coming of the Magi, the story of the good Samaritan, any of the miracles Jesus performed, or whatever you choose.

Young people can participate in writing the script, gathering props, making costumes, and assigning characters to each part. Keep it as simple as possible and at the same time, effective and meaningful.

The adaptation of "Whom Are You Seeking?" is very brief and can be performed during a class session. You might want to add traditional or contemporary hymns to the script. Make whatever changes you feel are needed for your group. Candidates might want to mime the play or utilize dance; this can result in an effective presentation completely in keeping with liturgical practice.

The play has only four characters. The materials required are a white alb, something to represent an altar, and an altar cloth. You can expand on these items by providing costumes and anything else that will convey the feeling and atmosphere of biblical times.

Scriptural Sharing. One of the most valuable forms of sharing is based on the Sunday readings of the week of class. Such sharing brings new meaning to the readings as the candidates begin to see the relevance of Scripture to their own lives.

Comparing their feelings and ideas will make the Liturgy and the Word of God come alive. The young people will realize that continual nourishment through the Word is a means for maturing in their faith. Form 23 contains a suggested method for Scripture sharing.

Liturgy

The time after Easter can be a joyful one and should involve the candidates in prayer, sharing, and making plans for a renewed Christian life. This is a time for song, rejoicing, and dance. A liturgical dance workshop for the mystagogical period is provided (Form 24) to help bring the candidates into new freedom.

Prayer plays a crucial role in preparing students for Confirmation. Young people should develop an active prayer life in order to become aware of and open to the Holy Spirit that dwells within each of them. Prayer services serve to underscore and illustrate the themes of Confirmation.

The *National Catechetical Directory* helps us understand the crucial nature of prayer in the Confirmation preparation process: "At the very heart of Christian life lies free self-surrender to the unutterable mystery of God. Prayer, for both individuals and communities, means a deepening awareness of covenanted relationships with God, coupled with an effort to live in total harmony with his will."

The Liturgy of the Hours has been a part of the Christian community since apostolic times. The revision of the Liturgy of the Hours has made prayer accessible to all of the People of God. As the *National Catechetical Directory* states, "Catechists need to experience the richness and beauty of this prayer in order to appreciate it and be able to introduce it to others," and suggests that "whenever possible . . . leaders in the parish community should provide opportunities for celebration of morning and/or evening prayer."

Pope John Paul II has stated that "the value of the Liturgy of the Hours is enormous." He sees the praying of the Liturgy of the Hours as a "school of sensitivity, making us aware of how much our destinies are linked together in the human family."

Therefore, the *Water and Spirit* process incorporates the Liturgy of the Hours, modified for high school students, as a viable means of introducing young people into the life of the Church. Praying the Liturgy of the Hours will help bring about one of the major aims of the process: to help the candidates realize how intimately they are united with the praying Church—the whole Body of Christ.

Even in parishes where the laity have not as yet become familiar with this form of prayer, young people can lead the way to an additional means of unity for the entire parish community.

The Liturgy of the Hours is presented in Form 25 in an adapted form which can serve as a pattern. The program director can tailor it to meet the needs of the individual parish.

Forms 26–32 are other sample rites and prayer services that can be used in their present form or adapted to suit your own parish.

It is important to have candidates participate in the preparations; for example, they might gather materials and prepare the classroom or church. This involvement will help the students realize that prayer and liturgy are the responsibility of all the People of God.

Characteristics of Adolescents

According to the *National Catechetical Directory*, "the awakening of a conscious spiritual life is normally an impetus to move to the next stage of development—adulthood." Catechists of adolescents should be aware of certain developmental characteristics in their students and note the ways in which the *Water and Spirit* process affects and interacts with the following characteristics.

Lack of self-confidence. This lack is typical of many maturing persons. The *Water and Spirit* process, calling the candidate to focus on his or her own life story and faith walk, enables the young person to realize the affirming love of God. By stressing the need for experiences of healing in all areas of life through prayer, sharing, and the sacraments of Eucharist and Reconciliation, the process creates an awareness of the Church's ministry. Opportunities for service through stewardship of time, talent, and treasure encourage the candidate to look beyond his or her own needs to the needs of the larger Christian community. As the candidate grows and matures in his or her faith life, self-confidence also increases.

Interior turmoil and difficulty in communication. Changes of mood can create problems for the adolescent. This process, by stressing prayer as an active listening and genuine response process, allows the young person to experience God's love. The realization of God's love calms turmoil and fosters an even temperament. Also, the process, in stressing the necessity of committed relationships in the Christian community, emphasizes the individual's intellect and free will as well as his or her ability to communicate with the members of the Family of God.

A new sense of responsibility. The process recognizes the young person as an individual capable of choice. Although the parents are still considered the primary educators of youth, and are involved throughout the process, the candidates must make their commitments to the covenant agreement to the pastor, and must take responsibility in fulfilling it.

Diagnostic testing, individual interviews, completion of service opportunities, and evaluations are means of viewing the readiness of the candidate for living a committed Christian life; this will provide a means for the candidates to demonstrate their responsibility in learning what they must know in order to fully participate in the sacrament.

Idealism and need for role models. The *Water and Spirit* process recognizes that the young person needs to view the adult Christian community as worthy of imitation. And so the process provides exercises in which the candidate can evaluate media such as television, publications, and movies according to ethical norms.

Need for intellectual growth. Many young people who have developed intellectually in other areas, know little about their faith. This process helps candidates see that by relating their experiences to the experiences of others, both people of today and of the past, they can understand the rational basis of their religious beliefs. Doctrine is the specific formulation of the community's faith experience.

Vocational awareness. As the candidate makes choices in other areas of life—education, sports, social life—the *Water and Spirit* process calls the young person to serious consideration of the Christian way of life as a vacation. Ministry is presented in all its forms and the candidate is shown that the vocations of marriage, single life, religious life, and priesthood are ways of living out the Christian commitment to service.

Need for various styles of prayer. Growth in prayer is an essential goal of the process. Various ways of praying are presented, and the candidates are invited to experiment with these throughout the process. Spontaneity is encouraged. However, liturgical piety is seen as central to the spirit and force of the process, since the Rite of Christian Initiation serves as the model for the process.

Respecting Individual Differences

In religious education as well as in secular education, we notice in young people a broad range of abilities and a wide diversion in cultural backgrounds and levels of faith. One way of dealing with these variations is to ignore them, to treat the class as a group, rather than as a collection of individuals. However, when we react this way, we deny the students their individuality.

Jesus recognized the differences in people and treated each of them as special and unique individuals. In the parable of the talents, Jesus pointed out that everyone is not granted the same gifts, but he also emphasized the obligation each person has to use his or her gifts as effectively as possible.

How do we deal with individual differences? We recognize that some young people may come from homes where the Catholic faith is obviously strong, where the family shares, prays together, and is open to the needs of others. Others, however, may come from families where faith barely exists or is nonexistent.

Consider, too, the motivational differences among the candidates. Various forces in students' lives affect levels of motivation in religious education. Our job as religious educators is to be aware of differences and learn to respond to all candidates in a way that will meet individual need.

Some religious educators believe that awareness of individual differences can lead to unequal treatment of the candiates, and this can be a real danger. After all, Jesus warns us against treating the well-dressed person in our midst better than the underprivileged. Jesus treated Nicodemus differently from the way he treated the Samaritan woman, and he expected a great deal of the rich young man.

Some catechists may tend to favor the more intelligent candidates. The key to avoiding this problem of unequal treatment is to be present to each individual and to realize that just as the Lord calls each of us as individuals, we must treat and teach each young person as an individual.

Program Versus Process

Bishop A. Ottenweller has made the statement that "our instincts are toward institutions, toward programs and projects and services; they are not toward community." He gives an example from his own life: "In the parish were I was, we were having some problems with our religious education program. The students were pretty well turned off, so we got our staff together and asked what we were going to do about that. We decided we needed to put out a better product. So we retooled, got some better textbooks, some audio-visual equipment and filmstrips, and gave our teachers better training. We worked at it. The trouble was that the next year, when we evaluated, there were fewer coming to CCD than the year before."

What's the solution? Bishop Ottenweller says "Our mistake was that we were pushing institution on them when they really wanted and needed community." All the new textbooks, sophisticated equipment, and well-trained teachers in the world will not work if we cannot create a sense of Christian community in our young people. Unless the candidates can develop the ability to pray and share their lives in a body of committed brothers and sisters, all our efforts may be useless.

The purpose of forming small groups of committed young Catholic Christians is to build up the Body of Christ in the local parish as it relates to the diocese and universal Church. But the younger, as well as the older, members of the parish community must experience trust, love, and community within the smaller group if they are ever to be able to relate to the larger group.

Consequently the preparation for Confirmation is actually a simple process in that the whole purpose is to develop *relationships.* The relationship of the young person with Christ is fostered through prayer and study, and expressed in Christlike action. But the relationship also develops through the rapport between director and group leaders, group leaders and youth, youth and sponsors, youth with one another, and members of the parish community with one another.

The most important element of each class, then, is the prayer and sharing at the beginning of each class. As young people begin to grow together, the presentation of ideas and doctrine is acceptable because the doctrine is seen in the context of their daily lives. If the sharing is superficial in group-building exercises, without ever getting to the depths, the youth who have complained of never learning to pray or share ideas and beliefs might not be adequately prepared for future struggles of faith.

Literature and the Arts

Some might feel that literature is out of place in preparation for Confirmation. They argue that literature is not doctrine. However, it is a way into the abstract ideas we are trying to teach the young people in this process.

The example of Biff in *Death of a Salesman*—a young man who learns the hard way that being well-liked may not be enough to produce happiness—can sometimes be more helpful in teaching moral theology than all the doctrine we have available. It deals with a reality the young people understand and experience.

Therefore, referring to poems and short stories, plays and music, and dance and art may be one of the most effective ways of reaching young people for Christ. Jesus used parables and poetic images to teach, and we can surely learn from his method of teaching.

Throughout this Confirmation process, reference is made to various novels, plays, poems, and art forms. The use of liturgical drama and liturgical dance is suggested because young people are open to all forms of art if they are presented in the right way. The more we present life in all its aspects, the more receptive candidates seem to be.

Playing the recording of a poem or an act from a play can lead into a discussion and sharing that no amount of talking about the art piece can equal. Many catechists are comfortable using popular music in class, but we should not be limited to any one use of the art forms. The creative Spirit of the universe knows no boundaries, and the more we utilize all forms of art to teach and inspire youth, the more they can learn to use all forms of art to praise God.

Witness Speakers

Many young people who are filled with the Spirit of God are those who have been on a spiritual retreat, have become part of a vital prayer group, or have become part of a Christian Life Community. In each situation they were brought to an awareness of the presence of Jesus in their lives through the witness of other young people and older people from the larger community of Catholic Christians who were willing to share their faith.

People who are fully alive in Christ, living out their faith with joy, and willing to be ministers of the Word, can be very effective as speakers to your group of candidates. Find people like these in your parish and community and allow them to minister to your students.

Spiritual fervor is contagious, and as young people listen to the witness of active and happy Christians, the Christian walk becomes an absolute, not an abstract idea.

Completing the Process

A sample program for Presentation of the Creed and Presentation of the Lord's Prayer are found on Forms 33 and 34. Form 35 is a sample Petition for the Sacrament of Confirmation.

A sample Rite of Election is Form 36. This rite, adapted from the Rite of Election for Adult Catechumens, takes into consideration the age of the candidates and may be used merely as a ceremony of recommitment, if the pastor or director prefers not to include inscription in the parish book.

This ceremony has been used successfully; the Rite is a viable means of allowing parish members to involve themselves more fully in the Confirmation process. However, this is only an example, and each parish is encouraged to create its own rites based on the RCIA.

Form 37 is a Confirmation Liturgy Form that can assist you in planning. You might also send a copy of the completed form to the confirming bishop.

Final Test

This test should be given during Lent, near the end of the process so that the catechist, director, and pastor might have some basis for beginning to determine readiness for the sacrament. Other signs of conversion may be more significant, but this test might serve as a jumping-off point for interviews prior to the Rite of Election. Whether written at home or during a session, the test is actually more of a review of the subject matter of the catechumenate than a show of knowledge. It is obvious that the answers to some of the questions will have neither a right nor wrong answer, simply a personal response.

The Final Test is based on the *National Catechetical Directory* and the Basic Teachings of the Catholic Faith. See Form 38 for the test.

Evaluation

Form 39 will give direction to the Confirmation and liturgical planning teams. Keep in mind why things occurred the way they did. Then plan any improvements needed in the celebration of the liturgy.

Forms

List of Candidates

Parish: _____ Town: _____

Pastor: _____

Additional contact person (religious education coordinator): _____

Time(s) and date(s) of confirmation: _____

Confirming (arch) bishop: _____

Master of Ceremonies: _____

Number of candidates: Total: _____ 1st Liturgy: _____ 2nd Liturgy: _____

Average age of candidates: _____ Number of adults: _____

Indicate the particular aspects/emphasis of your parish preparation program: theme(s), goals/objectives, symbols (banners, etc.), catechetical activities, projects, liturgies, retreats, community experience days, involvement of parish/sponsors/parents, others:

_____

_____

_____

_____

_____

_____

_____

_____

_____

_____

_____

_____

_____

_____

_____

_____

_____

_____

_____

_____

Sample Diagnostic Interview

Perhaps the most important interview is the one prior to the time the candidate is accepted into the process. Some parishes require candidates to come to the interview with their sponsors. Other parishes suggest that the candiate choose his or her sponsor after this interview. Individual parishes make their own decisions.

Another decision left to the individual parish is who will do the interviewing. In some parishes, the pastor, associate pastor, or director of religious education may be the ones to conduct the interviews. Or, the secondary coordinator might be the one chosen to do the interviews, assisted in some instances by the teachers.

The purpose of the interview is to determine if the young person is ready to make a commitment to living the life of a Catholic Christian. Individual contact, through the interview, contributes to a smooth introduction to the process.

Sample Questions

1. Why do you want to enter the Confirmation process?

2. What questions do you have about the Confirmation process?

Note: At this point you might want to explain to the prospective candidate what is involved in the preparation program.

3. Are you ready to deepen your prayer life, your understanding of Scripture, and your service to God and to others? How?

Sample Diagnostic Test

Some parish communities want to give the prospective Confirmation candidates a written diagnostic test, either before the interview or during the interview. The test questions may also be used as discussion questions between the interviewer and the candidate. Individual parishes might wish to modify the questions to suit their needs.

Sample Questions

1. Why do we call God "Father"?

2. What role do you think the Holy Spirit should play in your life?

3. What is the role of the Catholic Church in your life?

4. What is meant by the term "the communion of saints"?

5. Why do we receive the sacrament of Reconciliation?

6. What is the meaning of "resurrection"?

7. What is your favorite story about Jesus?

8. How would you defend Jesus if someone were to call him just another guy?

9. How would you defend the Catholic Church if someone were to say that all churches are alike?

Sample Candidate and Parent Letter

PARISH

CITY, STATE, ZIP

DATE

Dear Confirmation Candidate and Parents:

On _____ , at _____ ,

in _____ , a meeting will be held for all
candidates and parents of candidates. The purposes of the meeting
are to explain the Confirmation process, discuss the role of the
parents throughout the process, and give the parents an opportunity
to meet the catechists. The theme of the evening is "Commitment,"
and will include discussion and sharing, a brief explanation of the
Process, and a prayer service.

Your presence is absolutely necessary because we believe
strongly that the support of parents is essential to the success of
the candidates as they progress through the Confirmation process.

We are anticipating your presence and look forward to meeting
you and your children, the Confirmation candidates.

Sincerely in Christ,

Director of Religious Education

Parent Session

Introduction: Opening prayer and welcome. The opening prayer should be a spontaneous one by the director of religious education or director of the Confirmation program. A suitable Scripture passage and song can be included; for example, Acts 2:1–4 and the song "Spirit of God" from the *Spirit Alive* album (Weston Priory Productions, 1977).

Storytelling: Explain briefly the meaning and importance of group sharing in the *Water and Spirit* process. Then ask parents to share some of their thoughts and memories of someone who has been an inspiration in their lives.

The catechist's goals: Explain why you have chosen to journey with the young people preparing for Confirmation. You might begin by sharing a part of your story with the parents.

The process: Use an overhead projector, handouts, or the chalkboard to outline the elements of the *Water and Spirit* process with the candidates and their parents.

Sponsorship: Ask a Confirmation candidate and sponsor from last year's class to explain the role of sponsors and discuss the relationship between candidate and sponsor.

Questions: Allow time for questions. If possible, have these written and collected so that everyone will feel free to ask questions.

Plans: Decide on a time for the first meeting of sponsors and candidates. See Form 6 for a sample letter of invitation for this meeting.

Closing Song: Close the evening with a song, accompanied by slides which convey the spirit and substance of Confirmation. (If there are slides from last year's Confirmation, they would be appropriate at this time.)

Pledge forms: Before the parents leave, give each of them a Parent Pledge and ask them to prayerfully read it before signing. The form is for them to keep.

Parent Pledge

1. I believe that _____ is ready for Confirmation.

2. I fully understand the preparation process and the covenant.

3. The director and teacher of this process will have my complete cooperation and support.

4. I will help my child with Scripture reading, assigned lessons, or activities.

5. I will be supportive in service projects without taking over.

6. I will assist my child in choosing a sponsor and will encourage and support that sponsor.

7. I recognize this as a time of recommitment within our family and in my own life.

Personal Comments: _____

_____

_____

_____

Signed: _____

Sample Candidate and Sponsor Letter

_____

PARISH

_____

CITY, STATE, ZIP

_____

DATE

Dear Confirmation Candidate and Sponsor:

On _____ , at _____ ,

in _____ , a meeting will be held for all
candidates and their sponsors. The purpose of this meeting is to
explain the role of the sponsor throughout the Confirmation
process. The evening will include a brief explanation of the process,
a review of the covenant the candidates have agreed to and the
sponsor's responsibilities in helping the candidates fulfill their
covenants, and a prayer service.

Your presence is absolutely necessary, since we believe strongly
that sponsor support is essential to the success of the candidates as
they progress through the Confirmation process. We are anticipating
your presence and look forward to meeting you.

Sincerely in Christ,

_____

Director of Religious Education

First Sponsor Session

Introduction: Opening prayer and welcome. "Lord Jesus Christ, you accompanied your Apostles in the first three years of their lives with you. You guided them in their growth, and the knowledge you gave them of you sustained them throughout their lives.

"As we begin to journey with the Confirmation candidates, help us to be good tour guides and valid witnesses to your life. Help us to share our lives with these candidates as we grow with them into a new awareness of your great love for us. Amen." Then welcome the sponsors.

Sponsorship: It would be appropriate at this point for the director to introduce the concept of sponsorship by quoting the Rite of Christian Initiation of Adults. You may wish to distribute copies of these paragraphs to the sponsors and candidates.

> The candidate should be accompanied by a sponsor when he or she asks to be admitted as a catechumen. The sponsor should be someone who knows the candidate, helps the candidate, and witnesses to the candidates' morals, faith, and intention (#42).
>
> The godparent . . . is delegated by the local Christian community and approved by the priest. He or she accompanies the candidate on the day of election, in the celebration of the sacraments, and during the period of postbaptismal catechesis. It is his or her responsibility to show the catechumen in a friendly way the place of the Gospel in the candidate's life and in society. The godparent should also help the candidate in doubts and anxieties, give public testimony for the candidate, and watch over his or her progress in the baptismal life. Already a friend before the election . . . the sponsor's responsibility remains important when the neophyte has received the sacraments and needs to be helped to remain faithful to his or her baptismal promises (#43).

Then, as an effective technique for introducing the program and its objectives without launching into a formal lecture, have a sponsor and candidate from last year's class or the Level Two class role-play a typical meeting on their part, using the Group Reunion form of sharing which the candidates have been using in class.

An alternative plan is to have a candidate and sponsor from last year's class share with the new sponsors the ways in which the sponsor and candidate relationship has helped both of them. They can explain how their sharing and what they did together during the two years of the process caused the relationship to change and grow.

Covenant: Arrange for a pastor, priest director, or director of the process to attend the session, and at this point stress what the young people have agreed to in their covenant and what the sponsors' responsibilities are in helping the candidates fulfill this covenant.

Sponsor's agreement: Hand a copy of the Sponsor's Pledge (next page) to each sponsor and ask that he or she prayerfully read it before signing. Reading and signing the pledge can be an experience of commitment and can give the sponsor a sense of commencement into the process of Confirmation preparation. The form may be kept by the sponsor.

Closing: Close with prayer and a song.

(continued)

Candidate's Invitation

As I begin my journey in the preparation for Confirmation, I invite you to become my Sponsor, knowing that as such you'll be my special friend and spiritual guide.

Signed _____
CANDIDATE

Sponsor's Pledge

After prayerful consideration, I am willing and eager to guide this candidate in learning:

how to pray

how to witness

how to recognize the working of the Holy Spirit

more about the Catholic faith

more about the parish

how to participate in parish life

how to overcome bad habits and attitudes

I will cooperate in the service project, if invited. I realize my life must be a testimony of my commitment to the Lord and to the Church.

Signed _____
SPONSOR

Sponsor's Questions for the Candidate

1. Are you praying? How often?

2. Have you experienced Christ in your life since our last meeting?

3. Have you witnessed Christ's presence in someone else's life recently? Explain.

4. What Scripture have you heard or read that had special meaning for you?

5. Have you felt the presence of Christ in your home, your school, your neighborhood, your job, and your social life?

6. Do you have any questions about something you've read in the Scripture or something you've experienced since our last meeting?

7. Is there any specific problem or situation that I can help you pray about?

(After the Creed)

Celebrant: As we prepare for the coming of Jesus, we recognize the need to turn our lives over to Christ completely. We have among us today young people of the Confirmation program who are presenting themselves to enter fully into the process of preparation for this sacrament. They have been made one in Jesus through the sacrament of Baptism, and have been united more fully through the Eucharist. Now they are preparing for the third sacrament of initiation—Confirmation. Let us join with these young people and promise our support as we welcome them officially into the process of Confirmation preparation.

Now I'd like for all the members of our parish who have been confirmed to stand and to respond "We do," as we officially welcome the candidates. (Confirmed parishioners stand.)

Celebrant: Do you accept these members of our parish as candidates for the sacrament of Confirmation?

Respondents: We do.

Celebrant: Do you promise them your support in their process of preparation?

Respondents: We do.

Celebrant: Do you promise to share in their preparation for this sacrament through your prayer, your encouragement, and your example?

Respondents: We do.

Celebrant: Thank you. You may be seated.

Celebrant: Dear candidates, for the sacrament of Confirmation, *(name of Church)* Parish Community, a small part of the large family called the Catholic Church, invites you now to present yourselves as candidates for the sacrament of Confirmation so that you can dedicate yourselves to a life lived for, in, and through Jesus. Do you accept our invitation? Only you can decide to present yourself and enter a period of learning more about Christ, his teachings, and the Church. Today you will present a covenant, signed by you, in which you agree to fully participate in the prayer life and religious education program of our parish community. A covenant of sacred agreement, such as the one initiated by God and with the people of Israel, frees you to commit your lives fully to Jesus Christ, and to accept him as your Lord.

As your brothers and sisters, we thank God for your desire to live the Christian life, and we offer our prayerful assistance in supporting you.

Will you please stand and respond "We do," to the questions I am about to ask you.

(Candidates stand)

Celebrant: Candidates for the sacrament of Confirmation, do you understand that you are agreeing to a period of serious preparation for becoming a follower of Jesus Christ?

Candidates: We do.

Celebrant: Do you realize that we, the Church, require you to participate in a process of preparation?

Candidates: We do.

Celebrant: Do you enter this agreement with the parish of your own free will, eager to cooperate in and participate in this process of preparation for the sacrament of Confirmation?

Candidates: We do.

(continued)

35

Celebrant: Will the catechists please stand.
  (Catechists stand)

Celebrant: In your judgment, do you believe these young people are ready to embark on this next stage of their journey of the Christian life?

Catechists: We do.

Celebrant: Are you ready to share your own faith with these candidates, to pray with them, and to teach them the truths of their Catholic belief?

Catechists: We are.

Celebrant: Then I accept these covenants and place them on the altar of sacrifice. I recognize each of you as a candidate for the sacrament of Confirmation. Come forward and present your covenant, and receive a copy of the Bible, the Word of God. As you prepare for the acceptance of Jesus through Confirmation, let the Word become a joyful part of your life. Learn to read the Word, live the Word, and spread the Word in your families, in school, and with your friends. Share the message of Jesus everywhere you go.

  Would you please come forward, hand me your covenants, and receive the Good News.

  (Candidates come forward)

Candidate's Covenant

I _____ ,

a member of _____ Parish

in _____ , make the following agreement:

1. I will participate regularly in the sacraments of Reconciliation and the Eucharist.
2. I will attend the preparation classes and participate in them to the best of my ability.
3. I will use my skills in some form of Christian service.
4. I will pray regularly and attempt to show love for others.
5. I will attend the rites connected with the Confirmation preparation process.
6. I will assume more responsibility in my family, my parish, and my community.

I ask to become a candidate for the sacrament of Confirmation and to continue the Confirmation preparation process in my parish. I accept the responsibility to open my mind and heart to the activities of the Holy Spirit during this time.

Signature: _____

Date: _____

Witnessed by Parents: _____

Witnessed by Sponsor: _____

Approved by Director: _____

Signature of Pastor: _____

Date: _____

Questions for the Confirmation Team

To the Program Director

Before meeting with the team, plan a private time of prayer and reflection using the following questions.

- What basic core of Catholic doctrine is essential to ensure the consistent and continuing progress of living the Christian life?

- How can I recognize, accept, and accommodate individual differences in setting up the Confirmation process? How can I meet each candidate as an individual? How can I train my catechists to be aware of the individual needs of the candidates?

- To what degree am I threatened by teachers who seem to be more spiritually mature than I am?

- Who are the people in my life who threaten or frighten me in some way? How do I deal with this problem?

- Are there people in my life who I find difficult to accept? Why? Will this harm my effectiveness as a program director?

- Are there parts of myself that I find difficult to acknowledge and accept? What can I do about it?

To the Program Director and the Catechists

The following are some preliminary questions you may use for prayer, reflection, and discussion the first time you meet as the Confirmation team. These questions, which are based on the four stages of the *Water and Spirit* process, will help you become aware of your own understanding of the Apostles' Creed.

Getting Ready

- Where are you in your faith-walk?

- What experience of Christ in your life has brought you to this point of commitment in your life?

- Share the high point of your development in the past two years.

- Where do you want to go from here?

- What are some of the questions you have about your Church? What solutions have you begun to find?

The Journey

- Allow the Lord to show you what the word *Father* means to you. Go back in time and let him show you times when authority has been a problem to you. Let the Lord heal the part of you that was hurt because of the way you experienced authority.

- Who is *Jesus* to you? Who are the people in your life who have been brother? sister? friend? How have you been helped or hurt in your perception of these roles in your life? How have you experienced Jesus in your life recently?

- Who is the *Spirit* in your life? Who are the people who have served as counselor? helper? guide? How have you been helped or hurt in your perception of those roles? What are some of the ways you have experienced the work of the Spirit in your life? Share these times.

(continued)

- How do you see the *Church* in your life? How have you experienced Christian community in your life? in this parish? What do you expect from community? Share your perceptions of how your hopes can be fulfilled in this parish.

- What is your understanding of *sainthood?* What people in your life have you seen as helping you understand the meaning of sainthood? How do you see yourself growing in spirituality? How do we help one another in growth?

- Share times when you have given and received *forgiveness* in your life. How should we go about repairing wrongdoing in our lives? Share a time when you repaired wrongdoing in some way.

- What experiences of *life after life* have you had? How would you describe the perfect day? How do you see heaven as being an infinite extension of your perfect day?

Seeing the Light

- How have you experienced *conversion* in your life? What are some of the ways the Lord has called you to change? What are some of the areas in which the Lord is still calling you to change?

- See yourself on a hillside listening to Jesus speaking. Then picture yourself going apart from the crowd with him, letting him teach you about the Word.

- He asks you to go down to be crucified with him. Will you go? Why or why not? Under what conditions?

Alleluia

- How have you experienced *resurrection* in your life? Where have you met the Risen Lord in your life? Share one of those times.

- What are the fears you still have about giving your life totally to the Lord? How can you be freed from those fears?

- What is the Lord saying to you about your life right now? What are the ways you can bring him more effectively to all your environments: home, neighborhood, friendships, work?

Prayer and Planning Session—September

As members of the Confirmation preparation team, it is good for us to realize at the beginning of the year that we are not simply left to our own resources in leading the candidates through the Confirmation preparation process. All of the catechists in the process are here to help and support us in whatever ways we need them. As we gather for the first Prayer and Planning Session of the year, we should try to grow in trust with one another and learn to share our successes and hopes, as well as our questions and fears, with the other catechists.

Prayer

Read Mark 6:7–13.

Reflection

This short account from Mark's Gospel describes the sending of the Apostles on their first mission. Ask the group members to read this passage and reflect on the following:

- Jesus sent his Apostles off in pairs to support each other.
- The Apostles had few resources to work with. They were to rely on those to whom they preached for sustenance.
- Because of the authority given to them by Jesus, the Apostles were able to do great things—expel demons and cure the sick.

When they have finished reflecting, ask the members to write a short response to the following question: How do you feel about relying on others for help? Describe an experience when you really had to trust someone for something. How did you feel? Allow a few moments for the group to discuss their responses.

Discussion and Sharing

Ask the group to complete in writing each of the following statements.

My biggest problem right now is _____

_____ .

I need help from others right now with _____

_____ .

What I would like to have happen from this session is _____

_____ .

I think I can give help to others with _____

_____ .

Now, spend some time brainstorming with one another, suggesting ways of helping each other with problems as they arise.

Prayer Service

The theme is trust and service. Suggested Scripture readings: Luke 11:5–13, 12:22–34; 1 Thessalonians 3:1–13.

Prayer and Planning Session—October

In our roles as teachers and workers with youth, we often judge ourselves too harshly and set goals for ourselves that are impossible to realize. Rather than judge our weaknesses, we need to assess our strengths. While we are working toward change, we should learn to accept ourselves.

Prayer

Read Luke 24:1–12, Mark 16:9–14.

Response

After the reading, ask each group member to write his or her first reaction to the Scripture, choose a portion that has special significance, and then write how the passage relates to his or her own experience.

Goal Setting—Group and Personal

Ask the group to discuss the following questions, and through discussion, establish some goals for the team.

- If our goal as educators is to create a "community of saints," what are our strong points as a group?
- What are our weak points?
- How can we improve our efforts?

Next ask the group members to reflect silently, identify, and then share the weaknesses and strong points in their roles as educators. Lead the group in suggesting some effective ways of overcoming weaknesses and developing strengths.

Discussion of Needs for the Program

Involve the team in a discussion to identify any immediate needs that exist in the program, and then have a brainstorming session to generate practical ideas for meeting these needs.

Closing Prayer

Prayer and Planning Session—November

In working with youth, there is a skill that needs continual development—both in ourselves and in the young people with whom we work; that skill is listening. Often we listen but we do not hear. Therefore, as we strengthen our relationships with others and with God, we need to improve our skill of listening, and hearing.

Prayer

Read Isaiah 63:16–17, 64:2–7; 1 Corinthians 1:3–9; Mark 9:33–37

Reflection

Ask the group to reflect on the readings and then discuss the following questions.

- What do I hear the Scripture saying to me?
- What is God saying to me in my prayer life?
- What do I hear God saying to me through other people? Through my area of mission?

Listening Exercise

Have the group break into smaller groups to discuss and share with one another their responses to the following questions.

- Who are the people who listened to us during our childhood? Did they always hear us?
- Who did we listen to during our adolescence? Why did we listen?
- Did we always hear?
- Do we listen to God as he speaks to us? Do we hear? Why or why not?

Immediate Planning

Discuss and plan the immediate calendar.

Future Planning

Discuss and begin to formulate plans for Lent and beyond.

Closing Prayer

Prayer and Planning Session—Advent

Advent begins the time of waiting—for Jesus, for the celebration of his birth, for the celebration of Christmas. One of the hardest lessons to learn is to be patient—with ourselves and with others. Therefore, one of the most important tasks of those who work with youth is to teach young people to realize that instant gratification is a sign of immaturity, and the ability to wait is a sign of maturity and growth.

Prayer

Read Psalm 124, "The Lord, unfailing hope of his people."

Reflection

Ask a group member to read the psalm aloud. Then suggest that the group spend a few moments in silent reflection on the words that speak most directly to them.

Discussion and Sharing

Ask group members to discuss and share their responses to the following questions about waiting.

- When was waiting especially difficult for me?
- When have I failed to wait for the Lord to speak or act in my life?
- What were the results?

Prayer Service

You may use the following suggestions for planning a prayer service.

- Song—"Prepare Ye the Way of the Lord"
- Opening prayer
- Scripture reading: Luke 1:39–56
- Meditation of the theme of "Waiting for the Lord."
- Intention of the group
- Closing prayer

Prayer and Planning Session—February

In order to plan the future, we need to assimilate the lessons of the past and live in the present. Rabbi Abraham Heschel in *Who Is Man* says: "The authentic individual is neither an end nor a beginning but a link between ages. . . ." As we proceed through the Confirmation preparation process, let us take advantage of every moment, treating it as a link between the past and the future.

Prayer

Read Luke 12:22–31.

Reflection

Ask the group members to read and reflect on the following:

> It is by reflecting on God's mercies and blessings in the past
> that we appreciate his love today and look forward with hope
> to tomorrow.

When they have finished reflecting, ask them to write their feelings about the following:

> Tell about an experience when you really had to trust God and
> his providence. How did you react? What did God do?

Then discuss these experiences.

Discussion and Sharing

You might want to use a small-group format and use the following questions to generate discussion.

- Can I accept the past and release it?
- Am I able to live in, take advantage of, and really enjoy the present?
- To what extent do I reach toward the future with hope?
- Am I getting it all together—past, present, and future?

Planning the Future

Present objectives and discuss immediate and future plans. Discuss and plan the calendar.

Closing Prayer Service

Prayer and Planning Session—Lent

One method of drawing the Confirmation preparation team together is to take some time during Lent to pray, reflect, and plan. The following sample program can be adapted to the needs of your particular parish. It is written to encompass a time of approximately six hours. A Sunday afternoon or a weekday between 10:00 A.M. and 4:00 P.M. has been found to be a successful time for this type of meeting.

Prayer and Sharing

Sing a hymn to the Holy Spirit. Then pray: Father, we are joined with you today to pray and share, listen and speak, plan and reflect. Fill our hearts with love and grant us the wisdom to lead your young people. Give us the courage to carry out your will and give us the ability to do it well. We ask these things in the name of your Son and our Savior, Jesus the Lord. Amen.

As the leader of the group, you read Isaiah 40:9–11 and allow time for quiet reflection. Then have someone else read Mark 9:2–10 (the Transfiguration). Ask each person to write his or her personal response to the second reading, beginning with "The Transfiguration makes me feel . . ." Ask the group to share responses. Then have someone else read the same passage and ask anyone who wishes, to offer a special prayer based on the passage.

Discussion

Ask the group members to complete the statements below and then discuss their responses.

I believe the Lord is calling me to _____

_____

One problem I see in the Confirmation process is _____

_____

If I could do one thing to improve the Confirmation process next year I

would _____

_____

Collaborative Management Exercise

Divide the team into groups of three or four and have them work through the following steps, using the sample hypothetical situation or an actual problem that your parish is experiencing.

Situation

Your parish is having financial pressures, problems with declining enrollment, and dissension in the membership. However, you have definite ideas of gearing the parish more and more toward the goal of being a full Christian community. What can you do?

Discussion Guidelines

• State the problem in a way that all can agree on.

• List the needs of people involved, such as staff, leaders, parishioners.

(continued)

- Suggest alternative plans.
- Choose one plan of action acceptable to all parties.
- Determine how the staff, acting together, can implement or help others implement solutions to the problems.

Note: The break for refreshments may be before or after this management exercise.

Quiet Time

The team should reflect on the exercise above and then spend time praying and meditating.

Regrouping

The group should reflect briefly on the following statement and then share their answers with one another.

What I hear the Lord saying about my ministry is _____

_____ .

Then read Acts 2. The team should share its response to the reading and then discuss ways to be supportive to one another.

Play the gift game in which one person stays out of the group while the remaining members identify and list the good qualities of that person not in the group. As each person returns to the group, present him or her with the list of qualities the others see in him or her. Each person should sign each list.

Closing Prayer

Lord, we who have joined together today to do your work praise you and thank you. We have shared and planned in your name. Thank you for all your people, Lord, and help us who are your ministers to youth in this parish learn to listen, to hear, and to understand your plan for this parish, and to fulfill it with your guidance and love. Amen.

Prayer and Planning Session—April

The commemoration of Easter and thoughts of Jesus' resurrection remind us that we all experience times of rebirth in our lives. In order to experience rebirth we must recognize the need to change and be willing to make a commitment to change. This is one area in which we can learn from the young people in the Confirmation process. Young people generally welcome change and see it as a challenge and a new opportunity rather than a frightening unknown. We should celebrate the openness and vulnerability of youth and try to bring those qualities into our own lives.

Spontaneous Prayer and Song

There are many Easter songs from which to choose.

Reflection

"Go quickly and tell his disciples: The Lord is risen, alleluia." Have the group members write for ten minutes about a resurrection experience in their lives and then share what they have written with one another.

Discussion

Have the group members discuss the following questions:

- Do you feel the need for a greater sense of resurrection in your life? In what area?
- What aspect of the parish do you see as a resurrection or rebirth potential?
- What area in religious education do you think needs renewal?
- How can you help to implement this change?

Commitment Exercise

Have group members answer the following questions in writing. When they are finished, have them silently read their answers, evaluate their attitudes toward commitment, and then plan any changes they feel they want to make.

- When I am on the brink of commitment, I feel . . .
- When things start to get difficult in a commitment I have made I . . .
- When I think of giving my whole life to Jesus, I feel . . .

Planning

Involve the group in generating some goals for the next three years. You may use the following questions:

- What is already happening?
- What needs to be done to change or improve existing programs?
- What are the objectives for the coming year?
- How do these objectives fit into the concept of Christian community?
- What can we do to help?

Closing Prayer

This prayer can be a brief expression of praise or petition from each of the group members or from a few, with you closing the prayer.

Prayer and Planning Session—Corpus Christi

The order of the Liturgy gives a pattern which can be followed throughout our day, week, and year. We "spirit fast" and "spirit feast" as we follow a drama of death and resurrection.

Prayer

Read Deuteronomy 8:2–3, 10–16; John 6:51–58.

Reflection

Have the group reflect on the reading from Deuteronomy and then write a response to the following: How has the Lord "let you be afflicted" this year, and how has he "fed you manna"?

Then ask the group to reflect on the reading from John and write about a time when receiving the Eucharist held special meaning.

Prayer of the Faithful

Have the group join in prayer for one another.

Preparation of the Gifts

As the group works on scheduling the calendar, ask them to think of it in this way: As we present the calendar of activity and what it represents to the Lord, we offer him the simple gifts of our lives and ask that they become an exemplification of his life among us.

Closing Paraliturgy

"One Bread, One Body." Serve bread and wine or grape juice.

Preparing for a Prayer Service

Getting ready for prayer and celebration is an important part of the process of praying. We plan and prepare for a family party—decorating tables, cooking, and cleaning. It is also important to spend time preparing for a prayer service. As much care as possible should be taken to ensure that everything is ready. However, the catechist should never do all the preparation alone. Invite the candidates' participation at this preparation stage. Remember, prayer is the responsibility of all the People of God.

In planning a prayer service or paraliturgy, you first select a theme, with two or three options, and have the candidates vote for their choice. Then divide the young people into four committees. Their duties can be distributed as follows:

- *Readings committee.* Give this committee Bibles or books, and a piece of paper which tells how many readings to choose, with possible options. The candidates on this committee should look up each reading and reach a consensus on which to use. The committee should also choose the readers.

- *Prayer committee.* This committee should compose an opening prayer and petitions, and then decide how to pray the Our Father—spoken, sung, with or without movement.

- *Music committee.* This committee should select an opening song, a response to the reading, and a closing song. If possible, members of this committee should help lead the music or help with a tape recorder, record player, etc.

- *Environment committee.* This committee is responsible for making a banner or poster, or bringing flowers, or whatever else will be needed for the prayer service.

You may find the outline on the next page helpful as a checklist.

(continued)

Preparing for a Prayer Service (continued)

Date: _____ Time: _____

Place: _____

Props needed: (table, flowers, Bible, chairs, carpet squares, cross, candles)

_____

_____

_____

Artwork from the students: _____

    How it will be displayed: _____

    When it will be used: _____

Theme: _____

Opening Song: _____ Gestures: Yes   No

Prayer: _____

    Led by: _____

First Reading: _____ (Scripture or non-Scripture)

    Read by: _____

Response to the Reading: (song, psalm, poem, silence, dance, AV presentation)

_____

Optional Second Reading: _____ (Scripture)

    Read by: _____

Dialogue discussion: _____

Petitions: (Spontaneous, or read by: _____)

Our Father: spoken?   sung?   Gestures: Yes   No

Closing Song: _____ Gestures: Yes   No

Special Notes: _____

_____

_____

_____

_____

_____

Service Project

Before the Service Project

Description of the project _____

_____

_____

_____

Date the project is to begin _____

Date the project is to be completed _____

People who will be served by the project _____

_____

_____

I promise to complete this service project as part of my personal preparation for the coming of the Holy Spirit in the sacrament of Confirmation.

Signed _____

After the Service Project

The number of hours spent on the project _____

Tell how this project helped to build the kingdom of God. _____

_____

_____

_____

Describe your feelings while you were involved in the project. _____

_____

_____

_____

What kind of follow-up, if any, can you do on this project? _____

_____

_____

_____

Signed _____

Film and Television Analysis

1. What feelings and emotions did the film or program evoke in you?

2. What scenes or techniques were used to bring out those feelings?

3. What do you think the writers of the film or program were trying to say?

4. Can you apply that film or program to the Gospel message of this week's class? How?

5. Can you apply this message to your life? How?

6. If the message of the film or program was negative, how can that negative message clarify your own values?

7. What change in your behavior or attitude is a direct result of the film or program you saw?

New Testament Report

The following questions are about Jesus. If you have chosen a different character from a New Testament story, substitute the name of that person in each question.

1. What contribution did Jesus make to each of the following:
   a. the good of people around him?
   b. the growth of humanity or the progress of civilization?
   c. your personal life?

2. During his life, Jesus had to face many problems. Discuss two specific difficulties or problems he faced, and how he dealt with them, that can be of value to you in facing similar problems.

3. Describe in approximately one hundred words an interesting event in the life of Jesus that revealed his personality and ability. Be specific and vivid in your description. List the book in the New Testament in which you found your information.

4. Tell in one sentence an ideal of character or service that Jesus' life has inspired in you.

Liturgical Drama—"Whom Are You Seeking?"

Setting: Liturgy of Easter Morning

The character playing the angel enters slowly, dressed in a white alb, and sits in front of the tabernacle.
The other three characters follow and appear to be looking for someone as they approach.

Angel: (either in speech or in chant) Whom are you seeking in the tomb, followers of Christ?

Other characters: Jesus of Nazareth who was crucified, heavenly one.

Angel: He is not here. He has risen as he said he would. Go, announce to everyone that he has risen from the dead.

Other characters: (turning to the altar) Alleluia! The Lord has risen today. The strong lion, Christ the Son of God! Give thanks to God.

Angel: Come, see the place where the Lord was laid, Alleluia! Alleluia!

(The angel points to the altar containing tabernacle, picks up altar cloth and gives to the other characters.)

Angel: Go quickly, and tell everyone that the Lord is risen: Alleluia! Alleluia!

(The altar cloth is held up to the congregation, and then laid on the altar. The cloth represents the cloths which had once wrapped Jesus but are now empty.)

Other characters: (chanting, if possible) The Lord has risen from the tomb. He allowed himself to be crucified. Alleluia! Alleluia!

Suggested Method for Scripture Sharing

1. Darken the room and light candles to provide an atmosphere conducive to reflection.

2. Select either the Gospel or one of the readings from either the preceding Sunday or the approaching Sunday. Read the passage aloud, slowly and reverently.

3. Have each candidate in turn share one line or one thought which brought personal meaning, and tell how it related to some happening in his or her life.

4. Have the same passage read again, and this time ask if anyone wishes to add another dimension of response. Then go around the circle once again, and ask young people to share spontaneous prayers evoked by the passage.

5. Another way of proceeding is to have young people come prepared by bringing a newspaper or magazine article to illustrate the passage of the week.

6. Conclude the activity with a few minutes of silent reflection on the shared material.

Dance Workshop

Read the following aloud to the young people, reading slowly with background music, if you wish.

Body Awareness

Before we can dance, we must move, but before we can move, we must breathe, and realize ourselves as *existing*. Close your eyes, let your hands hang loosely at your sides, sit comfortably, and relax. Become aware that you *are*. Pay close attention to your breathing. Do not try to change your breathing but simply notice the rhythm of it.

Feel all the warmth that your body contains. Sense that you are absorbing oxygen which is helping to create new energy in you.

Begin to breathe more deeply and more slowly. Try to imagine a long, hollow tube, in which a light rubber ball is rising and falling as you breathe. Breathe and listen, see the world from deep within you.

Pray from deep within you the Jesus Prayer: "Lord Jesus Christ, Son of God, have mercy on me, a sinner." Still breathing deeply, slowly begin to raise your arms. Slowly, with your eyes still closed, let your arms rise over your head. Sway slightly in your seat. With your arms still over your head; sway slowly from side to side. Now begin to lower your arms to your sides again and become very still.

Open your eyes and see.

Slow Motion

Find a spot in the room and occupy that space. Realize that just for this moment, you are the only person on earth occupying this particular space.

Now, pretend that the air around you has become water. Begin to take a single step as if you are moving underwater. Allow your arms to carve out space as you explore the bottom of the ocean.

In the center of the room is an imaginary spot. As you move in slow motion, take your turn occupying that imaginary place. Linger there a moment, so as to realize how very special you are in the eyes of God.

Be brave enough to be a true deep-sea diver, and really open your eyes to see and be seen. Still in slow motion, stoop, bend, even recline in the water. Now rise up from the depths of the ocean, stretch toward the sun, and leap up above the surface of the water. Say "yes"—to life, to God, Creator of life!

Mirror Motions

Once we have become aware of ourselves as existing, we can know ourselves as we are. We can begin to move, to find a place for ourselves as people. However, to know ourselves as People of God, we must reach out to other explorers.

Turn to the person near you. Since we often learn to move by imitating others, look at one another closely. During this exercise, take turns leading in motion. For example, one of you pretend you are looking in a mirror. Facing one another, one is an example for the other. Begin to move in slow motion, lifting your arms, letting them fall. Sway slightly, then more. Move your feet, creating a simple pattern on the floor. Continue to watch one another and learn by being sensitive to the mood of the other person. Try to catch the mood of the song, too, and interpret the song being played.

(continued)

Realize from this exercise how greatly we can influence one another and how simply we can lead one another to praise Jesus, the Lord.

Community

Many times, Christ touches us in such a way that we can learn to reach out to our friends, our relatives, our neighbors, to share our faith with them.

Begin this exercise by facing a wall, all in a straight line. The person on each end of the line will begin to respond to the music, in motion and dance. Then, those two people, as they begin to dance, will touch the person next in line. As you are touched, respond to the music as you wish—by moving in slow or regular motion, by swaying and dancing to the music, by interpreting the words of the song in movement.

Now begin to dance into a large circle. Hold hands for a few minutes, as you all sway and move in unison. Now dance alone, remaining in the circle. At the end of the song, join hands again, and raise them to the Father in praise and thanksgiving.

Individual Response

The relationship between each person and God is unique. God speaks to each individual differently, and no two people praise God in the same way.

When we are constantly giving of ourselves to others, we must still return to God so he can continue to fill us with his Spirit and renew us. So, as a group, let us celebrate God's presence among us by praising him as individuals. As the music begins, start to leave the tightly knit circle. Offer yourself to God in dance by allowing yourself to be free in Christ.

Reach out in dance and let the motion come from within. Use more space, become bolder. Forget how you look to others. You are not dancing for yourself but to worship the Lord. As the Spirit of God fills you with his joy, let all that is within you cry "Holy, Holy is the Lord!"

Leader: Lord, come to our assistance.

All: Lord, make haste to help us.

Leader: Glory to the Father, and the Son, and the Holy Spirit.

All: As it was in the beginning, is now, and will be forever. Amen. Alleluia!

Opening Hymn

"This Is the Day"

Antiphon 1

Leader: Do not let your hearts be troubled; have faith in me. Alleluia.

Psalm 110

Reader: The Lord said to my Lord: "Sit at my right hand till I make your enemies your footstool."

Second Reader: The scepter of your power the Lord will stretch forth from Zion: "Rule in the midst of your enemies. Yours is princely power in the day of your birth, in holy splendor; before the daystar, like the dew, I have begotten you."

All: The Lord has sworn, and he will not repent: "You are a priest forever according to the order of Melchizedek."

Reader: The Lord is at your right hand; he will crush kings on the day of his wrath. . . . From the brook by the wayside he will drink; therefore will he lift up his head. Glory be to the Father . . .

All: (Repeat Antiphon 1.)

Antiphon 2

Leader: Let the peoples praise you, Lord God; let them rejoice in your salvation, Alleluia.

Hymn

"Sing to the Mountain," by Bob Dufford. (Recorded on *Earthen Vessels*, by Saint Louis Jesuits.)

All: (Repeat Antiphon 2.)

Antiphon 3

Leader: Through him all things were made; he holds all creation together in himself. His glory covers the heavens and his praise fills the earth, Alleluia.

Canticle: Colossians 1:12–20

Men: Let us give thanks to the Father for having made you worthy to share the lot of the saints in light.

Women: He rescued us from the power of darkness and brought us into the kingdom of his beloved Son. Through him we have redemption, the forgiveness of our sins.

Men: He is the image of the Invisible God, firstborn of all creatures. In him everything was created, visible and invisible. . . .

Women: All were created through him and for him. He is before all else and in him everything continues in being.

(continued)

Men: He is head of the body, the Church: he who is the beginning, the first-born of the dead, so that primacy may be his in everything.

Women: It pleased God to make absolute fullness reside in him, and by means of him, to reconcile everything in him, on earth and in heaven, making peace through the blood of his cross.

All: (Repeat Antiphon 3.)

Reading

Hebrews 10:12–14 (Reflection)

Intercessions

Lord's Prayer

Closing Hymn

FORM 26
The Prayer of Contemplation

Reverend Alan J. Placa, in *Contemplative Prayer,* suggests a method of prayer and sharing which is applicable to the life of any Christian. This four-step method is a practical way of leading catechists, and eventually candidates, into a deeper appreciation of the Word of God in their lives.

Step 1. *Read aloud.* Choose a Scripture passage and read it aloud, in order to become more aware of God's presence through speaking and breathing.

Step 2. *Read silently.* Notice which phrases or lines in the passage evoked strong feelings and reread them silently, line by line, reflecting on the feelings they evoke.

Step 3. *Meditate.* Meditate peacefully on the passage; be open to what the passage tells you of God and of you.

Step 4. *Contemplate.* This final step is the most important one. Acknowledge that God is contemplating you as you contemplate him. Allow his love to pour over you, and let him speak to you of the meaning of the Scripture passage for your life. Finally, share or report to others what you have found in this passage.

Sharing the Work of the Lord

(September—for Level One or Two)

Opening Hymn

"Come Up to the Mountaintop" (Weston Priory)

Meditation

Leader: Place yourselves in the presence of the Lord. Relax and let all thoughts drift away. Feel the rhythm of the ocean; hear the sound of the waves; become still inside.

Now picture yourself as a small child, the youngest member of a large family. Your parents have a paper route, and every Sunday you get up early and help them deliver the newspapers. The route is important because the money earned helps to feed and clothe you. It is also important because it is through reading the papers that people find out the news of the day and learn the happenings in the world.

You get up early on a cold, dark, rainy morning and drive with your parents and older brothers and sisters in the family station wagon through slippery streets. See yourself climbing the stairs of apartment houses where poor people live crowded together, and other apartment houses where rich people live in spacious rooms.

Now imagine that you are older—twelve or thirteen—and you are getting the papers ready for delivery. This time you are covering the route with only one other person—your older brother. He has a driver's license now and is driving the station wagon. You set off down familiar streets and some new streets; you feel good about your increased responsibility, and you are having a good time.

Finally, imagine that you are now the one driving the car, but you are not alone; your family is with you. Your brothers and sisters and both your parents are there to help you in the event you feel anxious or insecure about covering the whole route by yourself.

As you drive down the dark streets, your feelings of anxiety melt away because you realize that you are not alone. Your family loves you and their support gives you the courage to do your best.

If this kind of positive feeling can come from the presence and support of your family, how much more can you draw from the love and presence of the Holy Spirit.

In John 14:25–27, Jesus said, "This much have I told you while I was still with you; the Paraclete, the Holy Spirit whom the Father will send in my name, will instruct you in everything, and remind you of all that I told you. 'Peace' is my farewell to you, my peace is my gift to you."

Jesus promised a Comforter—someone who would always be with you to support and guide and to provide light for the dark roads that lie ahead, and he assures you that you will never be alone.

(Observe a moment of silence)

(continued)

Rite of Reconciliation

Leader: For the times we have resisted sharing the work of the Lord, Lord have mercy.

Response: Lord have mercy.

Leader: For the times we have complained because of the hardships in sharing the work of the Lord, Christ have mercy.

Response: Christ have mercy.

Leader: And for the times we have forgotten that the work is the Lord's and must be done his way, Lord have mercy.

Response: Lord have mercy.

Leader: Thank you for calling us, Lord. Give us the courage to enter the darkness, knowing that it is you who leads the way. Forgive us for our doubts and anxieties, and renew us in your love, as we set about doing your work of spreading the Good News of your kingdom. Amen.

First Reading: Exodus 15:22–27

Response: "Sing to the Lord a New Song" *(Songs of Praise)*

Second Reading: Luke 10:1–20 (Divide among five readers.)

(Observe another moment of silence.)

Reflection

My brother was one of those chosen, and I went with him to prepare for the Lord's visit to the next town. Before we went, we shared dinner with him and the Twelve, and listened to the Master teach his Way.

We set out on our journey, excited to tell others of the Master's Way, but we were soon disappointed. Few people wanted to hear what we had to say, and in one town the people threw stones at us because they thought we lied about the miracles the Master worked.

We went to another place where we were received more kindly and there we prayed over people for healing, and we saw people healed through the Lord's power in us. And there were more wondrous things that happened.

But, none of it happened just because of us. The signs and wonders were Jesus' way of letting people experience his love for them. It has been an incredible journey thus far.

Prayer

As we begin our incredible journey once more, let us offer our own spontaneous prayers, and let us respond, "Lord, help us to share your work."

(Spontaneous prayer)

Final Prayer

Father, you have heard our stories and our prayers. As we continue down the road, may all our work be done in your name, with your guidance, and in your Spirit. We ask this in the name of Jesus, the Lord. Amen.

Celebrant: Now is the time for us to consider conversion—the change from the people we are to the people we are called to be. Let us pray that the Lord will reveal to us the areas of our lives in which we need the gift of his grace to help us repent.

Father, you remind us in darkness that there are dark areas in our lives, corners where we have hidden for so long that only the gift of your merciful light will search those corners and reveal the places where we have not yet allowed you to enter. Let tonight be the night you call us to change. Give us the love we need to accept your call. We pray this prayer in the name of your Son Jesus, our Lord. Amen.

Meditation

Leader: We are called now to meditate on sin and conversion—on change. Before we begin, let us acknowledge that sin exists and that we are sinners, and let us acknowledge the fact that Jesus can save us from our sin and lift us out of it.

When Jesus taught about change, and about death and resurrection, he used parables to illustrate his message. Many of his parables were stories about nature—about flowers and seeds. Listen to the story of "The Kingfisher"—a parable like those Jesus told—and begin to reflect on change.

(Leader should now read "The Kingfisher.")

The Kingfisher: A Parable

Once upon a time there was a beautiful kingfisher. He nested in a tunnel, dug near a clear stream. But the kingfisher was troubled, for he had many duties tending to his family, and he often wished that he could soar far into the sky, above the tunnel in the clay, above the clear stream. He wished that the duties of caring for his family did not keep him tied down so much. He felt trapped in his tunnel, and could not even see the sky. Sometimes, when all was quiet, he would lie awake and dream of being free from his family, free from his responsibilities.

But then, one day, he was flying around looking for food for his family when he saw a strange creature. It had no wings; instead it had long appendages that he later learned were *arms* and *legs*. It had a strange way of singing—soft, and kind of crooning. Later, he would know the strange creature was a *woman*.

He stopped flying around and lighted near the woman.

"Hello," she said. "You are a beautiful kingfisher."

The kingfisher stared. In the woman's lap was a *child*.

The child spoke. "Hello, bird."

Suddenly the kingfisher was able to speak. "Hello, child, he said."

"Why are you sad, bird?" said the child.

"Because", said the kingfisher, "I have to fly around seeing to the needs of my flock. I want to be free!"

The woman spoke. "My husband has to make chairs and tables for people. He has to get food for us, too."

The kingfisher thought about what the woman said. Then he said, "I hope your son never has to be tied down to responsibilities."

(continued)

The child spoke. "When I grow up, I'm going to be just like my father. I'm going to take care of people."

The mother laughed, and said, almost sadly, "Yes, you will."

The kingfisher flew away. But he was happy. Often, he would come back to see the mother and the child. Sometimes the father of the little family was in the sunshine, too, and the kingfisher learned much from the family. He watched the child grow; he listened to the mother and father.

And all the time, he was happy.

He no longer envied the hawk that flew overhead. He no longer wanted to soar away and not come back. The family had served him well, for he had found friends. And, he had learned that in the midst of caring for the needs of his little flock of birds, he had the knowledge that he was loved by the family. And it became less and less of a burden and more and more a joy to do the little tasks that had been so boring.

When the day came that the little child first told his parents that he must be about his father's business, the kingfisher realized that his own flock was growing up. They would always need him, but they were growing up. They were, little by little, freeing him from more and more of his duties so that he could fly higher and longer each day.

There is no end to the story. For the kingfisher did not die as most birds do. He lived on and on, and when the child had grown up and was ready to go to his Father, the bird was ready. He fell asleep at the foot of a cross where strange creatures nailed his child-friend, now grown to be a man. And when, much later, his friend came to life, the kingfisher awoke, and greeted him with glad laughter.

Finally, on the day his friend ascended to his Father, the kingfisher soared and soared, and left behind all the earth which had trapped him for so long. He flew straight to the Father's feet. And the Father reached down, cupped the kingfisher in his hands and said, "Well done, my good and faithful kingfisher. Because you have done well in being who you are, and because you have such love, and such joy, and such patience, you will be with me forever."

And the kingfisher was forever free, to soar to his heart's content, and to sing forever with the boy, his foster-father, and eventually, the boy's mother. The kingfisher lived happily ever after.

The Beginning

Response

Hymn such as "Seek Ye First the Kingdom of God."

Reading

Celebrant: (Read Matthew 18:1–14.)

Leader: (Ask the people to spend a few moments in reflection and then to write a short prayer, expressing their response to the reading. These prayers will be used during the exposition of the Blessed Sacrament.)

Celebrant: (During the exposition of the Blessed Sacrament, ask the people to kneel before the tabernacle and read the prayers they wrote.)

Closing hymn

"Amazing Grace"

Celebration of a Penitential Rite

The leader should initiate the celebration with a welcome and then lead the group in a hymn that has as its theme the mercy of God.

Opening Prayer

Leader: Father of mercy and love, you call us to conversion, you call us to change. Give us forgiveness and peace. May we serve you with joy and compassion. We ask this through your Son, Jesus the Lord. Amen.

Lord Have Mercy

Leader: For the times you have called us to change and we have not listened, Lord have mercy.
Response: Lord have mercy.
Leader: For the times we have not repented of the idols of our lives—the false gods of security, and pleasure, and self-satisfaction—Christ have mercy.
Response: Christ have mercy.
Leader: And for the times we have not responded to your love with joy or compassion, Lord have mercy.
Response: Lord have mercy.

Reading

Lector: Ezekiel 37:12–14. The Lord will put his Spirit within us, and we shall live.
All: (Join in a hymn.)

Sharing

Leader: Share with one another a time when darkness seemed to fill your life, and when the light of Christ brought you into Resurrection.

Sign

Leader: (Leader gives each person a lit candle.) You are the light of the world. Continue to burn brightly.

Looking to the Future

Opening Hymn

A hymn based on Isaiah 49, such as "Be Glad, O People," by the Monks of Weston Priory, "Go Up to the Mountain" or "Be Not Afraid," by the Saint Louis Jesuits (Earthen Vessels).

Meditation

Leader: Lord Jesus, we acknowledge your presence here among us. We experience your love as you move among us. We feel ourselves relax in the stillness of your peace. We acknowledge your quiet light glowing within us. Come Lord, help us know your love and mercy. Help us face the future and be unafraid. Give us the wisdom to know what changes we should make in our lives and in our parish with your help.

(To the group) Imagine with me now that we are walking with Jesus. He turns to us and asks, "What do you want from me?" We find the places in us that need healing and we tell him, each in our own way. Then Jesus touches each of us and says, "Be healed, your sins are forgiven." And we know that we are indeed healed, forgiven, loved.

Reflection

Leader: Now I want you to think about the future, and for the next ten minutes, write what you want the Lord to help you change in your life; then write what your role can be in helping to bring about changes needed in the parish. Ask for the guidance of the Holy Spirit in what you write.

Sharing

Leader: Share with one another any part of what you have written.

Closing Prayers

Ask each person in the group to pray in his or her own words. Complete the service by playing the hymn based on Isaiah 49 once again.

The Church as Community

Opening Prayer

Leader: Father, you have called us to be a body of believers. Help us to accept ourselves with all our gifts, and to accept other people and recognize their gifts. Above all, grant us the awareness that all of life is a gift from your hands. Amen.

First Reading

Lector: (1 Corinthians 12:4–11)

Responsorial Psalm

Lector: God is our help and our strength, an ever-present help in difficulty. Therefore, we are not afraid although the earth be shaken and mountains plunge into the depths of the sea.

Response: The mighty Lord is with us.

Lector: There is a stream whose runlets gladden the city of God, the holy dwelling of the Most High. God is in its midst: it shall not be disturbed; God will help it at daybreak.

Response: The mighty Lord is with us.

Gospel

Celebrant: (The parable of the talents—Matthew 25:14–30)

Spontaneous Prayers

Closing Hymn

The Scrutinies

The scrutinies take place during the liturgies of the third, fourth, and fifth Sundays of Lent. These rites mark the completion of the candidates' preparation for Confirmation. The readings from cycle A are used: the Samaritan woman, the man born blind, and Lazarus. The scrutinies are celebrated by a priest or deacon who invites the community to pray for the elect.

According to the *Rite of Christian Initiation of Adults:*

> The purpose of the scrutinies is mainly spiritual, and this is achieved by exorcisms. The scrutinies are intended to purify the catechumens' minds and hearts, to strengthen them against temptation, to purify their intentions, and to make firm their decision, so that they remain more closely united with Christ and make progress in their efforts to love God more deeply (#154).

LIVING WATER

Introductory Rite

Celebrant: (Welcomes assembly and explains that the scrutinies have as their purpose the cleansing of our hearts and preparation for Confirmation, as well as strengthening us against temptation.)

Liturgy of the Word

(John 4:5–15, 19b–26, 39a, 40–42. Gospel of the Samaritan woman and homily on Jesus as Living Water.)

Prayer for the Elect

Celebrant: (Invites candidates and sponsors forward, and invites teachers and sponsors to pray for candidates, asking for a spirit of repentance and for freedom of the Holy Spirit. Celebrant then asks candidates to kneel as a sign of their willingness to turn back to the Lord.) Lord, you called the Samaritan to change her life. Help us through the acceptance of our Baptism to change our lives and accept the Living Water of your love for our lives. We ask this in the name of the Lord Jesus. Amen.

Reader: (one of the candidates) That like the Samaritan woman, we might look back on our lives and allow the Lord to reveal our sinfulness to us, let us pray to the Lord.

Response: Lord, hear our prayer.

Reader: That we may be delivered from all the idols in our lives—the desire to be popular, the fear of rejection, the need to rebel—let us pray to the Lord.

Response: Lord, hear our prayer.

Reader: That as we prepare for Confirmation we may crave for the living water of eternal life, let us pray to the Lord.

Response: Lord, hear our prayer.

Reader: That we will, like the Samaritan, become messengers of the Word to all we meet, let us pray to the Lord.

Response: Lord, hear our prayer.

Celebrant: I sign you all with water now and ask that this sign free you from the slavery of sin, and free you for love and service. Amen.

(continued)

LIGHT

(Have large candle burning.)

Introductory Rite

Celebrant: The theme of today's scrutiny is light. We reflect on the man who was born blind, and we ask the Lord to show us, in our lives, where we are blind.

Liturgy of the Word

Gospel: (Read John 9:1–6, or if you have more time, different candidates may read 7–12, 18–23, and 24–34, with the Celebrant finishing the reading with 35–40.)

Homily: The story of the man who was blind from birth might be the story of each of us. The disciples of Jesus ask him the question that many of us might ask, "Was it his sin or that of his parents that caused him to be born blind?" *(John 9:2)*. And Jesus' response is that neither his sin nor that of his parents have caused the blindness. Rather, says Jesus, "It was to let God's works show forth in him" *(John 9:3)*.

The character of the man born blind is interesting. He obediently accepts the mud Jesus places on his eyes and goes, as Jesus tells him, to wash in the pool of Siloam. As the neighbors, and then the Pharisees, question the man who has now been healed, the man answers their questions honestly. He states that Jesus is a prophet, and persists in believing in Jesus. When he is summoned a second time by the Pharisees, the man is thrown out by them because he still insists that Jesus could not have healed him if he were not from God.

Finally, Jesus himself questions the man, who expresses his belief in Jesus. Jesus says that he has come to make those who are sightless see, and cause those who think they see to be blind.

Where in our lives are we blind? What do we want to see and understand? Come, Lord Jesus, and help us see.

Prayer: (Celebrant invites catechists, sponsors, and all present to pray silently for the candidates.)

Celebrant: Let us pray for these young men and women, that they may be able to recognize where they have been blind, and will begin to see.

Response: Lord, help us to see.

Celebrant: That they may see into all the corners of their lives where they have not yet let Jesus be Lord, let us pray to the Lord.

Response: Lord, help us to see.

Celebrant: That they may overcome all blindness in relation to others, that they may be aware of ways of caring for the people you bring into their lives, let us pray to the Lord.

Response: Lord help us to see.

Celebrant: That they may see more clearly into their relationship with you, Lord, so that they may do what is right in their journey to holiness, let us pray to the Lord.

Response: Lord help us to see.

Celebrant: Let us pray. Lord, you helped the man born blind to believe in your Son, and through that faith to reach the Light of your kingdom. Free these, your chosen ones, from all the falsehood that surrounds

(continued)

them in their world which blinds them to your light. Let truth be their foundation, Father, as they prepare to receive the Light of your truth. We ask all these things in the name of your Son, Jesus.

All: Amen.

Celebrant: I invite each one of you now to light your candle from this Christ candle. As you do, be aware that in receiving the Light of Christ into your life, you are allowing Jesus to replace the darkness. As you return to your seats, listen to a final hymn, and join in the singing when your candle is lighted. Hymn: "The Light of Christ" or similar hymn.

RESURRECTION

Introductory Rite

Celebrant: The theme of today's scrutiny is rising to new life in Jesus. We reflect on the raising of Lazarus and ask the Lord to show us the power of his resurrection.

Liturgy of the Word

John 11:1–45. After the Gospel, celebrant gives a homily on the way in which Jesus raises us to new life in him. Then, the candidates are called forward.

Director of Confirmation: Would those who are about to experience the third scrutiny in preparation for their reception of Confirmation please come forward (or stand).

Prayer for the Elect

Celebrant: (Invites all present to pray silently for the candidates.) Celebrant then invites just the candidates to kneel as a sign of their decision to die to sin in their lives.

Celebrant: For these young men and women, that they may claim the power of the risen Jesus in their lives, and die to all sin, let us pray to the Lord.

Response: Let us rise in your name.

Celebrant: That they may die to all forms of sin, and learn to serve the Lord more faithfully each day, let us pray to the Lord.

Response: Let us rise in your name.

Celebrant: That in the sacrament of Confirmation, they may renew the promises made for them by their godparents at Baptism, let us pray to the Lord.

Response: Let us rise in your name.

Celebrant: That all of us may rise daily from our sins, and live only for God, let us pray to the Lord.

Response: Let us rise in your name.

Celebrant: Father, you want only life for us, and yet so often we choose death. Rescue all your children from all forms of evil, and pour into their hearts the power of your Holy Spirit. We pray for these young people who seek to be fully initiated into your Church as they prepare for Confirmation. Never let sin keep them from the victory of the resurrection. We ask this in the name of your Son, Jesus. Amen.

Hymn: "I Am the Resurrection and the Life."

(You may wish to have the catechists give each candidate a symbol of new life, such as a flower, as they are seated.)

Presentation of the Creed

With the presentations of the Creed and the Lord's Prayer, the Church entrusts the candidates with the documents which are a summary of its faith and prayer from ancient time. Either may be presented at the conclusion of an appropriate lesson (for example, on faith or prayer) or at a separate ceremony during a day of recollection prior to Confirmation. When possible, the presentations should be celebrated in the presence of the community of the faithful after the Liturgy of the Word at a weekday Mass.

Introduction: Tonight we celebrate life in a special way; we rejoice in the very real gift of faith which the Lord has given us, and we decide that the only true response is to accept the gift. Let us pray: Lord, thank you for the gift of faith. Let us accept the gift with a thankful heart, and realize the price you paid in order for us to receive this gift. Father, forgive us for the times we have taken the gift of faith for granted, and renew in us a spirit of trust, and hope, and love. We ask this in the name of your Son Jesus, our Lord. Amen.

Gospel: Matthew 16:13–18.

Homily: (The Creed. This homily can be a preview of the questions you are asking candidates, to determine their understanding of the Creed. These questions, found in Form 9, are the ones used in guiding the confirmation team in their own understanding of the Creed.)

Presentation: (After the homily, the celebrant invites the candidates to come forward and profess their faith.)

Celebrant: My brothers and sisters, accept the words of mystery as a sign of the deeper reality contained within them. Do you believe in God, the Father Almighty, creator of heaven and earth? Please answer, "I do believe."

Response: I do believe.

Celebrant: Do you believe in Jesus Christ, his only Son, our Lord, who was conceived by the power of the Holy Spirit, and born of the Virgin Mary?

Response: I do believe.

Celebrant: And do you believe that he suffered under Pontius Pilate, was crucified, died, was buried, and on the third day rose again? Do you believe that he ascended into heaven, and is seated at the right hand of the Father, and will come again to judge the living and the dead?

Response: I do believe.

Celebrant: Finally, do you believe in the Holy Spirit, the holy Catholic Church, the communion of saints, the forgiveness of sins, the resurrection of the body, and life everlasting?

Response: I do believe.

Celebrant: Then I invite all of you who are supporting these candidates to pray for them, that they will live out their beliefs into eternity. Let us pray for our brothers and sisters, daughters and sons in Christ, that Christ who has led them through the waters of Baptism and fed them with his Body and Blood will pour his Spirit into them so they can accept their Creed with all their minds, and hearts, and wills. I ask you all to pray in silence for a few minutes.

(continued)

Presentation of the Creed (continued)

(Celebrant extends hands over elect and says:)
Father, Lord of life, you have gifted your children with your love and
mercy. Hear our prayers for all these candidates, that they will grow in
wisdom, knowledge, and understanding. We ask this through Christ our
Lord.

Response: Amen.

Celebrant: As a sign of our commitment to support one another, let us
exchange the sign of peace.

FORM 34
Presentation of the Lord's Prayer

Hymn: "The Lord's Prayer" by Joe Wise

Leader: Let those who wish to receive the Lord's Prayer come forward.
(Candidates step forward with their sponsors, if possible. Sponsors put
right hands on candidates' left shoulders.)

A. *Leader:* Jesus taught his friends how to pray. As we listen to the story
from the New Testament, let us put ourselves into the scene and let
Jesus teach us. (Reading from the Good News according to Matthew,
6:9–13.)

or

B. *Leader:* Jesus taught his friends that those who see him see the Father.
Let us listen to this scene between Jesus and Philip and imagine
ourselves in the scene. (Have two candidates act out the scene from
John 14:8–11 found in The Word of God, page 21, *Of Water and the
Spirit.*)

(In the homily, or reflection, the leader or celebrant may wish to explain the
meaning of the Lord's Prayer, or read the Dear Candidate section on
page 21, *Of Water and the Spirit.*)

Leader (closing prayer): Let us pray now for these sisters and brothers who
have expressed the desire to continue the journey to full initiation into
the Church through the sacrament of Confirmation. Let us pray that
God, the Creator, will continue to bless, renew, and heal the candidates
as they meditate on and pray the Lord's Prayer. We ask these things in
the name of Jesus, the Lord. Amen.

Leader: Let us conclude with the singing of the Lord's Prayer. (One variation
is to have each candidate receive a copy of the entire Lord's Prayer, or a
phrase from it, before the closing prayer. The candidates then spend
some time apart from one another, reflecting on the phrase of their
choice or the phrase received.)

Petition for the Sacrament of Confirmation

I _____ , a member of _____ Parish

in _____ , ask you, Bishop _____ ,

to confirm me as a member of the Roman Catholic Church.

I would like to receive the sacrament of Confirmation because

_____

_____

_____

_____ .

My preparation for the sacrament of Confirmation has been

_____

_____

_____

_____

I have chosen _____ to present me to you on the day of my

Confirmation and to witness to my commitment. I made that choice because

_____

_____

You will seal my commitment to Jesus and his Church by anointing me with oil and by calling me by

name. The name I wish to be called at my Confirmation is _____ .

I have chosen that name because

_____

_____ .

I understand that the gifts of the Holy Spirit will help me build up the Church, and I wish to share in

building up the Church by

_____

_____

_____

_____ .

Rite of Election

Director of Religious Education or Deacon: The candidates who expect to receive Confirmation soon are entering a new stage in the preparation process. Having been interviewed by their teachers and the parish staff, these candidates ask that they be allowed to continue in the formation of their minds and hearts according to the Way of Jesus Christ.

Celebrant: Those who are continuing on the journey to Confirmation will please come forward with their sponsors (or teachers).

(Candidates and sponsors come forward. Candidates line up in front of the bottom altar step with sponsors standing in back of them.)

Celebrant: My brothers and sisters, these Confirmation candidates have asked to continue the journey to full initiation into the Church. For a year and a half, they have gathered regularly to learn more about God, the Church, and themselves. They have entered more fully into the parish through stewardship and are now learning how to pray and share with their sponsors. Now we ask that as Lent begins, they enter a more intense personal preparation for Confirmation, through a commitment to daily prayer, study of Scripture, apostolic service, and sharing their life in Christ with their sponsors. (pause) Sponsors, do you consider these candidates ready to continue in their preparation for Confirmation?

Sponsors: We do.

Celebrant: Candidates, do you agree to a deeper personal commitment to prayer, Scripture, and service in your life?

Candidates: We do.

Celebrant: And will you continue to live out the terms of the Confirmation covenant you have made?

Candidates: We will.

Celebrant: Would all the confirmed members of the parish please stand? (pause) Will you who have been fully initiated into the Catholic Church, through reception of Baptism, Holy Eucharist, and Confirmation, agree to support these candidates with your prayer and with the example of a Christian way of life? Please respond "We will."

Parish members: We will.

Celebrant: (This is optional.) The Confirmation candidates will now sign this book as an indication of their readiness for this sacramental preparation, and as a sign that they have been chosen and elected by the Lord to become fully initiated Christians.

(Candidate and sponsor step forward and candidate signs a suitable book which may be utilized for the process each year.)

Celebrant: In the name of the Catholic Church, and in the name of our Most Reverend Bishop, Bishop _____ , I accept you as candidates for the next phase of preparation. As we meditate during this Lenten season on the cross of Jesus Christ, we pray that you candidates will resist temptation in the days and weeks to come. May you pick up your crosses daily to follow Jesus. I bless you now, with the sign of the cross, in the name of the Father, and of the Son, and of the Holy Spirit. Amen.

(Candidates and sponsors return to their seats.)

Confirmation Liturgy Form

Liturgical Ministers: Lector(s) _____

Deacon(s) _____ Eucharist

Ministers _____ Leader of Song

_____ Commentator _____

Entrance _____ Greeting _____

Penitential Rite _____

Gloria _____

First Reading _____ Responsorial Psalm _____

Second Reading _____ Alleluia Verse _____

Gospel _____

Presentation of Candidates _____

Homily _____

Renewal of Baptismal Promises _____ Asperges _____

General Intercessions _____

Preparation of the Gifts _____

Preface _____ Holy, Holy, Holy _____

Eucharistic Prayer _____ Number of Concelebrants _____

(Ordinarily Eucharistic Prayer II is used. However, on special feast days and during special times the appropriate Eucharistic Prayer is used.)

Memorial Acclamation _____ Great Amen _____

Lord's Prayer _____ Lamb of God _____

Communion _____ Announcements _____

Concluding Rite and (Solemn) Blessing _____

Recessional _____ Parish Reception _____

Other Additions _____

Comments _____

_____

_____

_____

Final Test

Throughout the Confirmation preparation process, you have explored the way in which God has acted down through history to convince us of his love for us. The community of faith expresses its belief in God's love through the Creed. The following questions present the various elements of the Creed and ask you to comment on them. Answer each one from your own personal experience and describe what you think the Church is saying in each element of the Creed.

Prayer

Every Christian has a duty to pray, but there are many different ways to pray and many different forms of prayer.

1. Describe some of the different ways to pray.

_____

_____

_____

2. How do you pray?

_____

_____

3. Why do you pray?

_____

_____

Liturgy

Our greatest form of prayer is the Eucharistic Liturgy. Often we find ourselves just *going* to Mass. Sometimes it is hard for us to *pray* the Mass.

1. How are we called to be a part of the Mass? (Use your own words.)

_____

_____

_____

2. What is your personal attitude toward the Mass at this time in your life?

_____

_____

3. Why do you attend Mass?

_____

_____

4. What does it mean to worship God?

_____

(continued)

Revelation: God the Father

God has revealed himself to his people as a loving God.

1. How do you learn about God and his love? (Give a variety of ways—especially those which are most important to you right now.)

_____

_____

_____

_____

2. What does God's love mean to you?

_____

_____

_____

3. What does the word _Covenant_ mean to you?

_____

_____

Jesus Christ

God our Father has given us his Son, Jesus. Jesus helps us to know the Father, to love him, and to understand what is expected of us in our lives.

1. Who is Jesus? (Use your own words.)

_____

_____

_____

2. What do we mean when we say Jesus is our Savior and Model?

_____

_____

_____

3. What part does Jesus play in your life?

_____

_____

_____

_____

(continued)

Final Test (continued)

The Holy Spirit

Before Jesus died, he promised us a Spirit, a Counselor, who would be with us.

1. Who is the Holy Spirit?

_____

_____

2. How does the Holy Spirit help us be full and active members of the
   Christian community?

_____

_____

3. What are some other special gifts we receive from the Holy Spirit?

_____

_____

4. What does the Holy Spirit mean to you?

_____

_____

_____

The Church

Jesus also left us the Church—which is so much more than a building—to help
us in our lives and in our faith.

1. Using words like *people, Jesus, ministry, community,* and *love,* give a
   definition of the Church.

_____

_____

_____

_____

2. What should the role of the Church be in today's world?

_____

_____

_____

3. What does the Church mean to you in your everyday life?

_____

_____

_____

(continued)

4. What do we mean when we talk about the teaching authority of the Church?

_____

_____

5. In a few words, tell how the Catholic Church is structured.

_____

_____

_____

6. What are some special characteristics of the Church?

_____

_____

Sacraments

The Church is a special sign of Christ's presence in the world. The members of the Church celebrate other special signs which have been given us by Christ— the sacraments.

1. In your own words, what is a sacrament?

_____

_____

_____

2. What do we do when we participate in the sacraments?

_____

_____

3. Can you list three of four things the sacrament of _Baptism_ has done for you?

_____

_____

_____

4. What does the fact that you have been baptized mean to you?

_____

_____

5. What does the sacrament of _Confirmation_ do for you?

_____

_____

_____

(continued)

6. How is Confirmation related to the sacraments of Baptism and Eucharist?

_____

_____

7. How do you feel about receiving the sacrament of Confirmation?

_____

_____

_____

8. Tell in your own words what the sacrament of *Reconciliation* is all about.

_____

_____

_____

9. What are the ways we celebrate the sacrament of Reconciliation?

_____

_____

_____

10. Why has Jesus given us the *Eucharist*—himself—under the forms of bread and wine?

_____

_____

_____

11. What does it mean for you that Christ is present in the Eucharist?

_____

_____

12. In your own words, tell what the sacrament of *Holy Orders* means to you.

_____

_____

13. What is the sacrament of *Matrimony?*

_____

_____

14. Why does the Church say that the marriage bond is sacred and lasting?

_____

_____

(continued)

15. In your own words, tell about the sacrament of the *Anointing of the Sick.*

_____

_____

_____

Christian Life

The Bible, the Creed, the sacraments—all find their applications in the daily lives of Christian people. Take some time to think about your own life.

1. What does a good Christian life mean to you? (Use words like *Bible, Creed, sacraments, growth, change, helps, community,* to tell about a Christian life.)

_____

_____

_____

_____

2. What does it mean when we say that we are always in need of salvation?

_____

_____

_____

3. What do we mean by *original sin?*

_____

_____

4. If someone where to describe your life, what would you want them to say about the way you act as a Christian?

_____

_____

God's Law and Ourselves

We believe that Christians are guided in their actions by their consciences. Many elements (Jesus' example, our parents, priests, the Commandments, law, human decency, etc.) give us the basis for *morality*. When we act against our consciences, we sin.

1. Give a definition of sin.

_____

_____

_____

(continued)

2. What is the difference between serious (mortal) sin and less serious (venial) sin?

_____

_____

_____

_____

3. What things do you take into consideration when you are trying to discover what is right and what is wrong?

_____

_____

_____

_____

4. What do the Commandments mean to you?

_____

_____

_____

_____

5. What is the greatest Christian commandment? What does it mean to you?

_____

_____

_____

Christian Witness and Service

Christians are also called to a life of *witness* and *service.* These are the things we can do to help others and to work for God's kingdom.

1. What does it mean to witness to our faith in Jesus Christ?

_____

_____

2. How can you, as a young person, help Christian unity among members of the Church?

_____

_____

_____

(continued)

3. What do you think our relationship should be to people who belong to other Christian churches? To non-Christian religions? To those who have no religion at all?

_____

_____

_____

4. What do you think you can learn from people who believe differently than you do?

_____

_____

5. What does the word *justice* mean to you?

_____

_____

_____

6. What does it mean to be a just person? How can you live a just life at your stage of growth in faith?

_____

_____

_____

7. What does it mean to you when you hear that a Christian is called to live a *life of service?*

_____

_____

_____

8. What does it mean that a Christian is called to be a *peacemaker?*

_____

_____

_____

9. What do you think of when you hear that a Christian should have *respect for life?*

_____

_____

_____

(continued)

Final Test (continued)

Mary and the Saints

We Christians are not alone in the living of our Christian lives. We have help and example from those people who have gone before us. First among these is Mary, the Mother of Jesus and our Mother.

1. Why is Mary called the Mother of God and the Mother and Model of the Church?

_____

_____

2. Why is Mary special in the lives of Christians?

_____

_____

3. How is Mary important in your life right now?

_____

_____

4. Why do we show special reverence and respect (veneration) for the saints?

_____

_____

The Final Reunion

As Christians we believe that death is more than just the end of things.

1. What does death mean for us as Christians?

_____

_____

2. What do you think when you hear the sentence, "We are all judged equally by our love and our deeds"?

_____

_____

3. Why do we pray for those who have died?

_____

_____

4. What does the *resurrection of the dead* mean to you?

_____

_____

The answers you have written about your attitudes, beliefs, and knowledge of the Christian faith are a record of where you are now in your growth and development as a Christian, and they can be a help to you in the future.

Evaluation of the Liturgical Celebration

1. Did those who attended the confirmation celebration experience a genuine sense of prayerful worship? In what ways? _____

   _____

   _____

   _____

2. What was the central message of the Confirmation liturgy, and what did it reveal about the parish community? _____

   _____

   _____

   _____

3. In what ways did the liturgy convey:

   a. the community support to the candidates? _____

   _____

   b. welcome to the candidates at the culmination of the process of initiation? _____

   _____

4. In what ways did the proclamation of the Word of God create a real awareness of his presence?

   _____

   _____

   _____

5. Was all that is sacred in the sacramental celebration made evident to those who attended? How was this done? _____

   _____

6. How did the candidates respond to this awareness of the sacred? _____

   _____

7. In what ways did the choice of music unify those present, give added meaning to the prayer, and express joy? _____

   _____

8. If you feel the choice of music was not the best, what would your choice have been for the celebration? _____

   _____

Audiovisual Resources

Audiovisual materials can lend flexibility and variety to the *Water and Spirit* Confirmation preparation process. The use of films and filmstrips provides a change of pace in catechesis and is one good way to start a group discussion. Such materials can be used to fill gaps in lesson schedules or enrich the topic in any given lesson.

As far as possible, no film or filmstrip should be used with the class unless the catechist has the opportunity to preview the material in advance. Such a preview helps familiarize the catechist with the purpose and content of the material and eliminates the possibility of being taken by surprise.

It is also a good idea to read the teacher guide that usually accompanies the material. The producers of audiovisual materials take great care to provide guides that help the catechist make the maximum impact with the media.

Do not overuse media. The *Water and Spirit* Confirmation preparation process is designed to help the candidates get in contact with their own experiences. Often a good film or a good recording can help the candidates do just that, but if too many are used, the effect is lessened. It is also important that the catechist never just show a film. The media used during the session should always be part of a process of some sort. The real value of such material is in relating the vicarious experiences of the stories and scenes in the film or filmstrip to the life situations of the candidates and to the content of the lesson.

There is a very simple outline for using AV material which can be of great help to the catechist:

- Preview the material.

- Set the stage (provide a context for the AV experience).

- Show the material.

- Unravel the experience (provide some way, by means of discussion or activity, for the candidates to react to the experience).

- Follow up (tie the loose ends together and relate the experience to the lesson).

The following list contains the names and addresses of suppliers of audiovisual materials. There are many audiovisual resources available that can be used with the *Water and Spirit* Confirmation preparation process. It is a good idea to keep a folder or scrapbook of AV material. Most of the companies listed here will supply catalogs without charge.

Many of the companies also provide a thematic index for their material. It is a good idea to note in the margin of this manual those films and filmstrips that fit the various themes in the text. Even though they might not be used in the current year, the notes may be a handy reference for the next time the catechist goes through the material.

Churchill Films
12210 Nebraska Avenue
Los Angeles, CA 90025

DLM, Inc.
P.O. Box 4000
Allen, TX 75002

Contemporary Films
(McGraw Hill)
1221 Avenue of the Americas
New York, NY 10020

National Film Board of Canada
Box 6100

Don Bosco Films
475 North Avenue
New Rochelle, NY 10802

Franciscan Communications
1229 South Santee Street
Los Angeles, CA 90015

Ikonographics
807 Gray Street
P.O. Box 4454
Louisville, KY 40204

Thomas S. Klise Company
203 N.E. Perry
P.O. Box 3418
Peoria, IL 61614

Peter Li, Inc.
Dayton, OH 45439

Mass Media Ministries
2116 North Charles Street
Baltimore, MD 21218

National Catholic Reporter
P.O. Box 419281
Kansas City, MO 64141

Sta. A
Montreal, PQ
H3C 3H5

Our Sunday Visitor
200 Noll Plaza
Huntington, IN 46750

Paulist Productions
P.O. Box 1057
Pacific Palisades, CA 90272

Pyramid Films
2801 Colorado Boulevard
P.O. Box 1048
Santa Monica, CA 90404

ROA Films/Wm. C. Brown
2460 Kerper Boulevard
Dubuque, IA 52001

Twenty-Third Publications
185 Willow Street
P.O. Box 180
Mystic, CT 06355

Word, Inc. (Creative Resources)
4800 W. Waco Drive
Waco, TX 76796

Suggestions for Level I

Audiovisual resources can be used to substitute material and exercises within the lesson or to supplement the topic presented in the text. Here are a few suggestions for specific lessons in Level I:

6. **Responsible Friendship**
The Velveteen Rabit, Mass Media Ministries (Billy Budd Films), 15 min. Theme: friendship and growth.

9. **Rejoice**
Missing Person's Bureau, Paulist Productions (Insight Film), 27 min. Theme: the presence of God and forgiveness.

10. **Christ with Us**
Ruby Duncan—A Moving Spirit, Franciscan Communications (Teleketics Film), 15 min. Theme: commitment/sacraments/social concerns.

11. **Stewards in the Kingdom**
The Eye of the Camel, Paulist Productions (Insight Film), 28 min. Theme: commitment.

15. **Living Water**
Everyone, Everywhere, Franciscan Communications (Teleketics Film), 11 min. Theme: commitment/ministry/social concern.

16. **New Life**
Water and Spirit, Franciscan Communications (Teleketics Film), 6 min. Theme: prayer/worship/sacraments.

17. **From Death to Life**
    That's Life, Mass Media Ministries (Faith and Fantasy, Inc.), 8 min. Theme: death and resurrection.
    Death Be Not Proud, Mass Media Ministries, 81 min. Theme: death and the meaning of life.

Suggestions for Level II

Audiovisual resources can be used to substitute material and exercises within the lesson or to supplement the topic presented in the text. Below are a few suggestions for specific lessons in Level II.

6. **Suffering Servant**
   God in the Dock, Paulist Productions (Insight Film), 27 min. Theme: the mystery of suffering.

7. **Risen Lord**
   I Heard the Owl Call My Name, Mass Media Ministries, 78 min. Theme: death and human dignity.

10. **The Gift of Peace**
    Ruby Duncan—A Moving Spirit, Franciscan Communications (Teleketics Film), 15 min. Theme: commitment/sacraments/social concerns.

13. **Justice**
    Gods of Metal, Maryknoll Films, 27 min. Theme: the nuclear arms race.

15. **Courage**
    The Prisoner, Paulist Productions (Insight Film), 27 min. Theme: the courage of Father Maximillian Kolbe.

17. **Celebrating Confirmation**
    And Then . . ., Mass Media Ministries, 16 min. Theme: Confirmation and commitment.

19. **The Eucharist**
    Living Eucharist, Franciscan Communications (Teleketics Film), 10 min. Theme: the human dimension of the Eucharist.

Special Uses

Some parishes hold Confirmation ceremonies several weeks after Easter and still wish to use the last stage of the Confirmation preparation process, Alleluia, as a post-Confirmation catechesis. In this case, there are audiovisual resources available to help make the time between the third and fourth stage of Confirmation preparation a meaningful time for review and reflection. Here are a few suggestions. Remember, each resource listed has a complete guide book for group discussion.

Jesus of Nazareth, Don Bosco Multimedia (Franco Zeffirelli, director), 14 parts of 26 minutes each.

Acts of the Apostles, Don Bosco Multimedia (Roberto Rossellini, director), 10 parts of 27 minutes each.

The Christ, Franciscan Communications (Teleketics Filmstrip), 4 filmstrips/ 68 minutes. Themes: the formation of the Gospels, Jesus' message, Jesus and the cross, the resurrection.

TEACHER'S NOTES

TEACHER'S NOTES

TEACHER'S NOTES

TEACHER'S NOTES

TEACHER'S NOTES

TEACHER'S NOTES